# Nuts & Bolts
## of Research Methodology

# Nuts & Bolts of Research Methodology
## From Conceptualization to Write-up

Nadini Persaud • Dwayne Devonish • Indeira Persaud

IAN RANDLE PUBLISHERS
*Kingston • Miami*

First published in Jamaica, 2019 by
Ian Randle Publishers
16 Herb McKenley Drive
Box 686
Kingston 6
www.ianrandlepublishers.com

© 2019 Nadini Persaud · Dwayne Devonish · Indeira Persaud
ISBN 978-976-637-973-5

**National Library of Jamaica Cataloguing-in-Publication Data**

Persaud, Nadini
    Nuts & bolts of research methodology : from conceptualization to write-up / Nadini Persaud, Dwayne Devonish, Indeira Persaud.

    p. ; cm
Bibliography: p.
ISBN 978-976-637-973-5 (pbk)

1. Research – Methodology
2. Academic writing – Handbooks, manuals, etc.
3. Report writing – Handbooks, manuals, etc,
I. Devonish, Dwayne    II. Persaud, Indeira
III. Title

001.4 dc 23

All rights reserved. No part of this publication may be reproduced, stored in a retrieval system or transmitted in any form or by any means electronic, photocopying, recording or otherwise, without the prior permission of the publisher and authors.

Cover and book design by Ian Randle Publishers

Printed in the United States of America

# CONTENTS

**LIST OF FIGURES** — viii
**LIST OF TABLES** — ix
**FOREWORD** — xi
**PREFACE** — xiii

## 1. RESEARCH QUESTIONS, HYPOTHESES, AND VARIABLES — 1
- The Research Process — 1
- The Research Topic — 3
- Quantitative Research — 5
- Variables in Quantitative Research — 7
- Research Questions in Quantitative Research — 9
- Research Hypotheses in Quantitative Research — 12
- Qualitative Research — 15
- Research Questions in Qualitative Research — 16
- Applied vs Basic Research — 19

## 2. LITERATURE REVIEW — 21
- The Literature Review or Review of Literature — 21
- Sources of Literature — 23
- The Literature Review Process — 26
- Citations and Quotations — 29
- References — 37
- Plagiarism — 41
- Searching for Sources — 46
- Links to Useful Resources — 49

## 3. METHODOLOGY AND STUDY DESIGNS — 50
- Research Methodology — 50
- Experiments — 54
- Observations — 58
- Surveys — 60
- Interviews — 63
- Focus Groups — 64
- Case Studies — 66
- Document Review and Analysis — 68
- Mixed Methods Approach — 69

## 4. INSTRUMENTATION AND MEASUREMENT — 72
- Conceptualization and Operationalization — 72
- Measurement — 74

- Questionnaire Design ... 77
- Close-ended Questions vs Open-ended Questions ... 79
- Reliability ... 84
- Validity ... 86
- Validated Instruments/Scales ... 89
- Scale Construction ... 91
- Interview Schedule Design ... 94

## 5. SAMPLING ... 98
- Sampling Frame ... 98
- Sample Size ... 100
- Probability Sampling ... 103
- Sampling Error ... 107
- Sampling Bias ... 108
- Non-probability Sampling ... 110
- Response Rate ... 112
- Pilot Study ... 113
- Incentives ... 115

## 6. ETHICS AND DATA COLLECTION ... 117
- International Research Protocol and Institutional Review Boards (IRB) ... 117
- Ethics in Data Collection ... 120
- Data Retention and Data Security ... 122
- Preparing for Interview Fieldwork ... 124
- Conduct in the Field ... 127
- Interviewing Skills ... 129
- Coding Quantitative Data ... 132
- Coding Qualitative Data ... 138

## 7. QUANTITATIVE DATA ANALYSIS ... 141
- Descriptive Statistics ... 141
- Measures of Central Tendency ... 143
- Measures of Dispersion ... 148
- Frequency Analysis and Crosstabulations ... 151
- Inferential Statistics ... 153
- Associational Inferential Statistics ... 155
- Comparative Inferential Statistics ... 163
- Effect Sizes ... 173

## 8. QUALITATIVE DATA ANALYSIS ... 178
- Qualitative Data ... 178
- Thematic Analysis ... 181
- Discourse Analysis ... 183
- Interpretive Phenomenological Analysis ... 187

- Narrative Analysis ... 189
- Conversation Analysis ... 191
- Grounded Theory Analysis ... 193

## 9. THE RESEARCH PAPER ... 197
- Planning Tips for the Research Paper ... 197
- Writing Tips for the Research Paper ... 203
- Structure of the Research Paper ... 205
- Presenting the Research Paper ... 210

## 10. PUTTING IT ALL TOGETHER: THE RESEARCH PROCESS CHECKLIST ... 214
- Topic Identification ... 215
- Determine Research Methodology ... 216
- Determine Research Design ... 217
- Determine Sample Design and Demographics ... 218
- Develop Data Collection Instrument ... 219
- Determine if IRB Approval is Required ... 220
- Data Collection and Security ... 221
- Data Sorting, Coding and Entry ... 222
- Data Analysis and Interpretation ... 223
- Data Reporting and Write-up ... 224

**BIBLIOGRAPHY** ... 227
**INDEX** ... 231

# List of Figures

| Figure 3.1: | Independent Measures Design | 56 |
| Figure 3.2: | Repeated Measures Design | 57 |
| Figure 4.1: | Common Threats to Internal Validity | 87 |
| Figure 7.1: | Normal Distribution | 147 |

# List of Tables

| | | |
|---|---|---|
| Table 2.1: | Examples of Primary, Secondary, and Tertiary Sources | 25 |
| Table 2.2: | Basic APA Citations | 29 |
| Table 2.3: | Illustration Showing How an In-text Citation and Reference would be done using APA, Chicago, and Harvard Styles | 35 |
| Table 2.4: | Discipline-specific Citation Styles | 36 |
| Table 2.5: | Types of Plagiarism | 42 |
| Table 2.6: | Databases by Discipline | 48 |
| Table 3.1: | Pros and Cons of Various Research Methods | 51 |
| Table 3.2: | Types of Survey Questions | 61 |
| Table 3.3: | Pros and Cons of Common Survey Types | 62 |
| Table 3.4: | Pros and Cons of Formal vs Informal Interviews | 63 |
| Table 3.5: | Illustration of a Mixed Methods Approach in Education | 71 |
| Table 4.1: | Basic Overview on Levels of Measurement | 75 |
| Table 5.1: | Sample Size Illustration | 102 |
| Table 7.1: | Univariate, Bivariate, and Multivariate Statistical Applications | 142 |
| Table 7.2: | Crosstabulation of Nationality and Return Visits to Barbados | 157 |
| Table 7.3: | Chi-Square Tests of Nationality and Return Visits to Barbados | 157 |
| Table 7.4: | Pearson Correlation Tests of Satisfaction with Prices and Shopping Expenditure | 159 |
| Table 7.5: | Assessment of Overall Effect of Independent Variables on the Dependent Variable | 161 |
| Table 7.6: | Overall Effect of Regression Model on Dependent Variable | 161 |
| Table 7.7: | Effects of Independent Variables on the Dependent Variable | 162 |
| Table 7.8: | Overall Satisfaction with Destination for European and US Tourists | 165 |
| Table 7.9: | Levene's Test for Overall Satisfaction for European and US Tourists with Destination | 165 |
| Table 7.10: | Pretest-Posttest Mean Scores on Employee Mental Health | 167 |
| Table 7.11: | Pretest-Posttest Results on Employee Mental Health | 168 |
| Table 7.12: | Descriptives on Overall Satisfaction with Destination by Age Group | 169 |
| Table 7.13: | Levene's Test of Homogeneity of Variances | 170 |
| Table 7.14: | ANOVA Results for Overall Satisfaction with Destination by Age Group | 170 |
| Table 7.15: | Post Hoc Tests for Overall Satisfaction with Destination by Age Group | 171 |
| Table 8.1: | Strengths and Limitations of Qualitative Research | 180 |
| Table 9.1: | Baseline Master Plan for a Typical Research Project | 201 |

# Foreword

Finally, a research methods book written directly to students instead of being aimed mostly towards those of us who research different ways of collecting and analysing data in today's specialized world. This book is problem focused, taking students through the complete research process from identifying a useful research project to writing a research paper that presents results in a coherent way.

A fundamental premise of this book is that useful social science research can be accomplished in many different ways. It may be quantitative or qualitative, applied or basic, and use different approaches to measurement. It describes both probability and non-probability methods for selecting respondents. These possibilities are systematically described, with illustrations, definition boxes, and examples appearing on nearly every page. In contrast to many books, this book is not an attempt to sell a particular method for doing social science research, but rather aims to help students and other users of social science research methods to understand alternative approaches to data collection and the potential that each has for contributing to knowledge and practice.

The writing is straightforward and clear, without being simplistic. The careful reader of this book will come away with sufficient detail to understand the various levels of measurement (nominal, ordinal, interval and ratio) and types of validity, and the manner in which those concepts are used by scholars throughout the world. The content and organization of this book provides the building blocks essential for understanding the nature of high quality research. Students who use the concepts methodically introduced here to carry-out research projects, should find themselves nicely prepared for understanding and mastering advanced treatments of specific research methods.

***Nuts and Bolts*** is organized so that it can be read in a linear fashion from first to last steps of conducting a research project with a research report as the final product. But, it can also be used as a reference source where the need is to find details on how to accomplish specific research tasks. Carefully captioned and illustrated sections define and describe detailed steps of planning and executing research projects which make it possible to search for and immediately find details on each step of a research undertaking, such as defining and developing hypotheses and formulating respondent questions, to developing measurement scales, and sampling methods. The book also conveys when and how to use inferential statistics and various analytical methods. Students who are closely attuned to how to ask questions on the world-wide web and quickly obtain answers, will find the book organized in a fashion that parallels that process.

Both graduate and undergraduate students who are learning how to undertake meaningful research will find this book useful. The book's 'Nuts and Bolts...' conveys the importance of selecting parts of the research process that are designed to fit together, rather than simply providing an assortment of possibilities. Doing that makes this book especially useful. Meaningful social science research is not a task that can be accomplished by haphazardly choosing an assortment of possibilities, a point made by both the content and organization of this carefully crafted book. Consequently, students from many different disciplines will find this book useful.

January 2019

Don A. Dillman
Regents Professor of Sociology
Washington State University, Pullman Washington

# Preface

*Nuts and Bolts of Research Methodology: From Conceptualization to Write-Up* is designed to make research accessible to everyone. It breaks down complex research processes into easily understood, user-friendly steps, and provides a hands-on approach that allows any academic (e.g., social scientists) or practitioner (e.g., evaluators), whether novice or experienced, the opportunity to translate research techniques and skills into real world applications with the end goal of a formal research paper or a credible professional evaluation.

Other research methodology books tend to focus on just one area of research methodology, cater mainly for experienced researchers through more complex presentations of material, and/or rely on other books to provide explanations and background knowledge of a research methodology area. Our book is different! From the united perspectives of veteran educators, *Nuts and Bolts* is written to allay the general fears of understanding, conducting, and presenting research, through creative and innovative narratives and examples, that enable the reader to move seamlessly from conceptualization to write-up. This approach makes the learning process easy, smooth, user friendly, and practical, while it simultaneously provides global appeal.

A number of considerations guided our vision for this book. First and foremost, we wanted to produce a book that could be used as a stand-alone resource since students frequently complain about the cost of textbooks and question why so many different books are required for one subject. Second, we needed to demystify the research process and make it sufficiently simple, so that students and practitioners will be motivated to conduct research. As such, our writing deliberately avoids abstract and theoretical narratives, since these often turn off the novice researcher. Third, we sought to ensure that our book provided a systematic progression to enable the researcher to successfully move from conceptualization of a research idea, to application in practice, and finally to write-up. Finally, we aimed to make our book user-friendly since research methodology can be intimidating for many persons.

In designing our book, we used several strategies to ensure user-friendliness. First, the list of the topics to be discussed in each chapter is provided at the start of the chapter, so that the reader can see exactly what will be discussed. Second, each new chapter topic is defined and highlighted via a specially designed call out box. Each topic also ends with an important tip. Third, topics are broken into different subheadings. Both students and practitioners complain that they have to read pages of text to find information pertaining to a specific issue that they are unclear about. In comparison, our subheadings allow readers to navigate immediately to information that they need to review. For example, one of the topics discussed in chapter 2 is *Plagiarism*. The discussion for this topic is presented under three subheadings: *What Constitutes Plagiarism?*, *Types of Plagiarism*, and *Strategies to Avoid Plagiarism*. By breaking up the discussion on plagiarism, we highlight and draw attention to critical issues that the reader may not be aware of and may probably miss if the narrative was continuous. We believe that these headings will encourage readers to cover the topic in its entirety because the reader may then think, '*I never knew that there are strategies for me to use to avoid plagiarism. I must read this section.*' Fourth, numerous examples are incorporated throughout the narrative to highlight best practices, which are clearly visible in uniform callout boxes. Fifth, tables, figures, and graphical images are embedded throughout the narrative. This use of artwork serves several purposes – to clarify the text, to highlight important information, and to provide another mode of learning for readers.

In closing, we hope that our book will inspire you to want to conduct research since it can be truly exciting. We believe that you will enjoy using this book and that you will actually be able to move from start to finish in the research process on your own and produce an impressive research paper or professional evaluation report.

Finally, we wish to take this opportunity to express our sincere thanks to Dr Don Dillman (Regents Professor, Washington State University) for his endorsement of our book, our families for their support, and most importantly our students and practitioners for causing us to recognize the vital need for a user-friendly, start-to-finish, research methodology book that caters to a broad-based audience of academics, practitioners and educators.

# 1 Research Questions, Hypotheses, and Variables

- The Research Process
- The Research Topic
- Quantitative Research
- Variables in Quantitative Research
- Research Questions in Quantitative Research
- Research Hypotheses in Quantitative Research
- Qualitative Research
- Research Questions in Qualitative Research
- Applied vs Basic Research

## THE RESEARCH PROCESS

**The Research Process comprises a set of interrelated, sequential steps through which a researcher typically travels, ranging from the identification of a key research topic to the generation of a completed research report.**

### Research Defined

Research is normally defined as *a scientific process of investigating a particular phenomenon, problem, or topic area*. Oftentimes, people confuse the act of collecting data with research. However, research is much more than simply gathering data. Research follows the scientific method which suggests that it adheres to strict investigative guidelines and procedures which ensure the data gathered is unbiased, reliable, and valid.

### Attributes of Good Research

It is important for researchers to understand that research embraces a number of key attributes, including *orderly*, *systematic*, *objective*, and *empirical* (or data-based). *Orderly* suggests that research involves a careful and methodical approach to data-gathering and analysis. *Systematic* suggests that research is not a single activity but rather comprises a cross section of robust, scientific activities and methods that are implemented in a particular sequence and for a particular purpose. *Objective* suggests that research is a value-free, unbiased, and rational investigative process. *Empirical* depicts that research is based on collection of data from various sources, including primary and secondary sources (see chapter 2) in order to achieve some objective or outcome.

## Navigating the Research Process

The research process typically begins with a topic and set of related aims, objectives, or questions that serve to guide the process from start to finish. Generally, the scientific research process represents a sequence of interrelated steps that a researcher normally takes when engaging in a scientific research study. The process involves the researcher performing the following activities:

- Identifying and refining a topic worthy of investigation.
- Developing a clear and guiding research purpose in the form of specific research questions or hypotheses.
- Conducting a thorough review of the literature and synthesizing the information of the various sources (see chapter 2).
- Designing the methods and strategies of the research study related to sampling, instrument design, data-collection, and analytical techniques (see chapters 3, 4, 5, 6, 7, 8 and 10).
- Gathering the necessary data to fulfil the overall research purpose using either primary or secondary data-collection methods.
- Analysing and interpreting the data gathered using a range of analytical techniques and procedures to address the overall research purpose (see chapters 7 and 8).
- Stating the key conclusions emanating from the analyses (see chapter 7).
- Generating and disseminating the research report comprising the activities conducted and key findings outlined in the prior steps (see chapter 9).

The research process can be daunting for many novice and beginning researchers. Although it seems to follow a linear path, challenges, barriers, and other obstacles at different stages can force a researcher to revisit earlier stages. Hence, the process often resembles an iterative process in which a researcher may travel back and forth throughout the various steps. However, it is important to appreciate that the steps are interrelated and interdependent, where certain actions at earlier steps will directly affect actions at the later ones.

### Summary of the Research Process

> *Identify and refine the topic*
> *Develop the research purpose (research questions/objectives)*
> *Conduct the review of the literature*
> *Design the research study*
> *Collect the data*
> *Analyse and interpret data (or present findings)*
> *Make key conclusions*
> *Prepare and disseminate report*

Given that the stages of the research process are interdependent and interconnected, it is possible that improper decisions or poorly implemented actions can adversely affect other stages within the process. In many cases, researchers have to go back to previous steps to make corrections or modifications to various decisions and actions before moving forward. Hence, the process can be viewed as iterative rather than linear.

# THE RESEARCH TOPIC

The Research Topic is the key area of interest that a researcher seeks to explore or investigate through the implementation of the research process. It represents the first step within the research process.

## Starting the Research Project

The starting point of any research project is the identification of the research topic. The identification of the research topic triggers the next steps of the research process. Choosing and refining a research topic is often a difficult exercise for many novice researchers. Every subject area or discipline represents an almost infinite pool of research ideas or topic areas. Good and useful topics normally fulfil a number of key criteria to be considered *research worthy*.

## Questions to Consider when Conceptualizing Your Research Topic

Researchers need to ask themselves a number of questions when choosing a research topic. These include:

*Attractiveness of the Topic:* Within a subject area of choice, field, or discipline (e.g., management, tourism, accounting, psychology) *what specific areas of interest are currently attractive?* Attractive suggests that the specific areas of interests are generating a significant amount of discussion and attention within the overall subject area. For example, in the area of human resource management, you may find that the topic of *employee performance* is gradually dominating the conversation within contemporary academic readings and research studies. You may also realize that the local media in your country are constantly highlighting the issues of employee performance and even practitioners in various organizations are having conversations about addressing problems with *employee performance* and *productivity*. Hence, the attractiveness of employee performance is indubitable, in light of its popularity in both academic and practitioner circles.

*Significance of the Topic:* Normally, there is a strong relationship between a topic's attractiveness and its significance. A topic's significance is a function of how impactful it is within the academic literature and practice. Generally, the more impactful a topic, the more attractive the topic. Two categories of significance are academic significance and practical significance. *Academic significance* concerns a topic's actual or potential positive contribution to a given subject area in terms of advancing theoretical thought or the body of evidence or knowledge. *Practical significance* concerns a topic's actual or potential contribution to practical settings and practitioners who operate within a field relevant to the topic area. Both academic and practical significance are established by a researcher seeking to identify the benefits a tentative topic area elicits for both academia and practice respectively.

*Realism of the Topic:* Not all topics are realistic. One topic area might be significant or attractive but prove illogical or unfeasible. Seeking to completely alleviate poverty or all human diseases – albeit noble – is a futile endeavour. When examining the realistic nature of topics prior to selection, it is critical that the researcher determines whether the topic is *feasible, manageable,* and *logical*. Considering access to certain resources such as time, money, and technical and human support helps the researcher to work out exactly how realistic a topic would be as a potential area worthy of investigation.

## Useful Strategies for Selecting Research Topics

There are a number of strategies used to arrive at topics that are worthy of research. Using a combination of these strategies can help to maximize one's success of choosing a worthy area for investigation:

*Brainstorming*: Brainstorming can help new researchers generate a useful list of possible topic areas for investigation within a wider subject area. This activity is best conducted within a team setting in which a team of researchers can collectively brainstorm to arrive at a wide range of possible topic areas. However, brainstorming should be accompanied by more rigorous strategies (to be discussed shortly) to ensure topics chosen are attractive, significant, realistic, and focused.

*Reviewing Resources on the Topic:* Researchers can identify very useful areas of investigation through their exploration and review of the literature, which represents the store of writings and sources of information that attends to a given subject area. By reviewing these materials, researchers can point to specific topic areas that are attractive, impactful, and realistic. The literature is normally filled with advice and guidance for new researchers by pointing to areas of interest that have been dominant as well as areas of interest that are still in need of further investigation (i.e., gaps in the body of knowledge).

*Having Conversations on the Topic of Interest:* Having discussions with colleagues, academics and practitioners can help researchers to improve their understanding of a given subject area to arrive at a more focused, specific topic area. Without understanding what currently exists in the *real* world (i.e., the world outside of reading), a researcher is bound to come up with topics that do not generate the necessary interest among those whom you expect to reach or target. Do not discount simple conversations with friends or colleagues who may work in an area close to a given topic area. For example, you might be interested in *Small Business Ownership* in your country and through a casual innocent conversation with an acquaintance (who happens to be a small business owner) you realize that a research study investigating 'Challenges of Small Business Owners' might be a more useful, focused area of investigation. You may decide to investigate this issue rather than your broad original issue.

## Focusing Your Research Topic

Overall, research topics, when conceptualized, are often broad and ambiguous. It is important to find ways to narrow or focus a topic. The goal is to move from a rough topic area, to a clearly defined and formulated topic, to a set of well-structured and specific research questions.

When focusing a topic, a number of considerations are worthy of mention:

- What specific areas of interest concerning my selected topic are particularly interesting or meaningful to me and others?
- Have these areas of interest already being thoroughly investigated or do they represent new or novel gaps in the literature on the topic?
- What kinds of research questions are pertinent (and perhaps not yet answered) to this selected topic?

**TIP:** Reading contemporary sources of literature in a particular subject area or discipline is an excellent starting point for arriving at a workable and worthwhile topic of study.

# QUANTITATIVE RESEARCH

Quantitative Research is a scientific research methodology which emphasizes the objective and quantifiable measurements of data.

## What is Quantitative Research?

Quantitative research is considered to be the most popular research methodology utilized by researchers across various disciplines. This approach embraces the notion that research should involve an objective capture of data in the form of numerical or mathematical measurements of observations. The use of statistical techniques and assessments is the hallmark of this approach. Quantitative researchers normally engage the research process by choosing theoretically-driven (or empirically-driven) topics, posing scientific hypotheses, and testing these hypotheses through the collection of data measured by pre-existing (validated) close-ended quantitative measures and/or tools.

## Common Categories for Quantitative Research

The purpose of quantitative research may fall into a number of general categories:

- To provide statistical description of phenomena
- To examine statistical correlations or relationships among various phenomena
- To examine statistical differences among various categories of respondents
- To examine cause and effect among various phenomena

## Nature of Quantitative Research

Quantitative research often follows a deterministic (predetermined) approach which requires researchers to often rely on prior or existing models and bodies of evidence to influence or shape the design and execution of a current or proposed quantitative design strategy.

Overall, quantitative research normally sets the standards that affect the ways in which research questions are framed, research measures or instruments are designed, samples and sampling procedures are employed, and data are gathered, collated and analysed.

## Attributes of Quantitative Research

There are a number of important attributes that make quantitative research distinct from other approaches of research:

- It is normally guided by clear, structured research questions or hypotheses.
- It is often driven by or rooted in existing theory or empirical work.
- It is normally deductive (top-down) and seeks to generalize key findings to larger populations.
- The data are normally gathered using structured, quantitative measures and indicators.
- This research normally depends on large random samples.
- The methods chosen are normally structured and designed based on pre-existing standards and norms.
- The data are normally in the form of numbers and statistics and are arranged with tables, graphs, figures, and other non-textual formats.

## Common Methods of Data Collection in Quantitative Research

Quantitative researchers tend to utilize the following methods of data collection:

- Standardized surveys, questionnaire scales, and pre-existing close-ended measures
- Experiments
- Standardized observations (with checklists and scales)
- Secondary data analysis

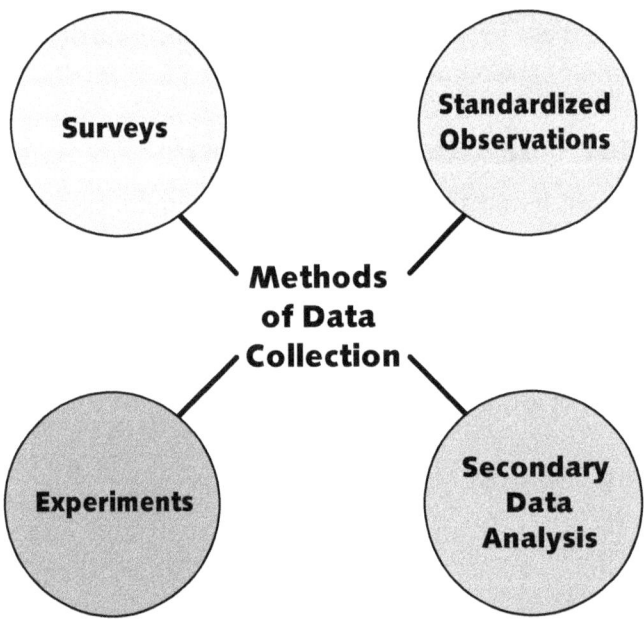

**TIP:** Always remember that quantitative research comes with its own established procedures, protocols, and guidelines for conducting research. It follows a pre-determined approach to its sampling, instrument design, and overall data-collection processes.

# VARIABLES IN QUANTITATIVE RESEARCH

Variables in Quantitative Research is a term used to describe a characteristic that is measured and observed within a given study design.

## Overview of Variables in Quantitative Research

Variables are at the heart of quantitative research. Variables represent the phenomena of interest for all quantitative studies and represent the key factors that are subject to numerical measurement and statistical analysis. For example, a researcher examining the impact of work-related stress on absenteeism among police officers is focused on collecting data on at least two key variables: (1) *work-related stress* (a subjective experience measured via a structured questionnaire) and (2) *absenteeism* (a behavioural outcome that can be measured using organizational records depicting the number of days or times an employee was absent within a given period).

Both work-related stress and absenteeism are core variables because the researcher considers them as key factors of interest within his or her topic space that require quantitative measurement. Work-stress can range from low to high work stress, and absenteeism can range from low to high absenteeism. Hence, variables have the potential to vary across some numerical scale or continuum. Without variables, quantitative researchers are unable to investigate their topics in ways that allow for scientific and mathematical observations and analyses. Hence, it is important for all quantitative researchers to identify, define, and operationalize (i.e., measure) all variables within a given study (see chapter 4).

## Types of Variables

In quantitative research, researchers need to be familiar with a number of different types of variables (which can appear under more than one classification) including nominal, ordinal, interval, or ratio (see discussion in chapter 4 under Measurement); dichotomous or binary (i.e., two categories such as yes/no which is a nominal level of measurement); multichotomous (i.e., more than two categories such as religion which is also a nominal level of measurement); continuous (e.g., age or time which are ratio levels of measurement); independent variables versus dependent variables (to be discussed shortly); and extraneous variables which are confounding variables that can potentially influence an experiment (see discussion in chapter 4 under Experiments).

## Independent vs Dependent Variables

In some quantitative studies, variables can play different roles. For example, two main roles are independent and dependent variables.

> ***Independent Variable:*** A variable that is assumed to influence or affect another variable (through some theoretical, logical, or empirical reasoning).
>
> ***Dependent Variable:*** A variable that is influenced or affected by the independent variable. It is also called the effect or outcome variable.

To illustrate, if we were interested in studying the effects of customer satisfaction with a particular brand on customers' loyalty (e.g., returning to a store to purchase a product or brand), our independent and dependent variables will be:

**Independent Variable** → **Customer Satisfaction**

**Dependent Variable** → **Customer Loyalty**

Because one's customer loyalty depends on whether one is satisfied (or not) with some particular brand or product

In different study designs, independent and dependent variables are defined and measured in different ways. For example, in an experimental design, an independent variable is the variable which an experimenter manipulates to observe its effect on a dependent variable. However, in a survey or an observational design, the independent variable is not manipulated but naturally observed through a recording device (e.g., a questionnaire). In experiments, causal relations are explored between independent and dependent variables. In contrast, in a survey research design, it is not possible to determine causality beween the independent and dependent variables. We can only say that the variables are correlated or related in some way.

**TIP** → Variables need to be carefully defined so that they can be properly measured.

# RESEARCH QUESTIONS IN QUANTITATIVE RESEARCH

Research Questions in Quantitative Research are more specific close-ended questions depicting the overall purpose of quantitative research studies.

## Overview of Quantitative Research Questions

Quantitative researchers guide their research investigations by clear and specific research questions on a particular topic area. The types of research questions asked or investigated by quantitative researchers reflect their strong, mathematical orientation towards data-gathering and analysis. In quantitative research, the research question outlines the overall purpose of a research study and allows the researcher to communicate the overall direction and scope of a given study. Within a given research question, there is at least one variable of interest under study.

Generally, research questions in quantitative research are naturally close-ended and specific in nature, comprising at least one variable of interest for a given study. Research questions can also be taken directly from prior studies to allow for direct comparisons between previous answers and current answers or findings.

## Quantitative Research Question Categories

There are generally three categories of quantitative research questions:

### Descriptive Research Questions

These quantitative questions seek to provide a statistical or mathematical account or description of a single variable under study. The goal is to examine the extent to which a particular phenomenon or variable exists or occurs within a given study space.

For instance, the research question in example 1.1 statistically describes a single variable (the utilization of modern, interactive teaching practices). The *quantitative descriptor* is a percentage.

### Example 1.1

What percentage of secondary school teachers utilize modern, interactive teaching practices within the classroom setting?

In example 1.2, the research question uses a mean or average as a *quantitative descriptor* for the variable *customer satisfaction*. Hence, the descriptive research question contains an element of quantification.

### Example 1.2

What is the average level of customers' satisfaction with their life insurance policy?

Finally, the research question in example 1.3 quantifies the extent to which managers motivate employees to apply their competencies. Here, the question elicits some feature of quantification by the use of the term *to what extent*. For example, *to what extent* may refer to the percentage of managers who actually motivate their staff or the average level of motivation.

**Example 1.3**

To what extent do managers motivate their employees to apply newly learnt competencies within the work environment?

## Associational Research Questions

Associational research questions seek to examine the relationship(s) or association(s) between two or more variables within a given study. Within its structure, it contains at least two variables under study: an independent variable and a dependent variable.

The research question in example 1.4 examines whether two variables (work stress and absenteeism) are related to each other in some way. A relationship depicts some correlation between two or more variables in which at least one variable (independent variable) is seen to impact or affect another variable (dependent variable). In this case, work stress is the independent variable and absenteeism is the dependent variable.

**Example 1.4**

Is there a relationship between work stress and absenteeism?

In example 1.5, the research question examines if an association exists between job satisfaction (independent variable) and job performance (dependent variable). The term *influence* (or *affect*) denotes that some correlation or relationship is being explored.

**Example 1.5**

Does a police officer's job satisfaction influence his or her job performance?

## Comparative Research Questions

A comparative research question seeks to examine a statistical difference between two or more groups of respondents. Similar to the associational research question, it contains at least two variables: an independent and a dependent variable.

The research question in example 1.6 is seeking to statistically compare male and female teachers on job satisfaction. The independent variable is teacher sex (male versus female) and the dependent variable is job satisfaction. If an empirical or statistical difference is revealed in the research, we can say that job satisfaction depends on a teacher's sex (i.e., whether a teacher is male or female).

### Example 1.6
**Is there a difference between male and female teachers in terms of job satisfaction?**

Similarly, in example 1.7 we again observe a direct comparison being made in the research question where we are assessing whether one group of respondents (senior officers) are experiencing work stress to a different degree compared with another group of respondents (junior officers). In this example, police rank is the independent variable, whereas work stress is the dependent variable.

### Example 1.7
**Do senior police officers report higher levels of work stress than do junior police officers?**

## Summary of Types of Research Questions in Quantitative Research
- *Descriptive Research Questions (statistical descriptions)*
- *Associational Research Questions (statistical relationships)*
- *Comparative Research Questions (statistical differences)*

Quantitative research questions are classified as descriptive, associational, or comparative.

Descriptive questions do not have independent and dependent variables; however, associational and comparative questions comprise at least two variables in a potential relationship.

# RESEARCH HYPOTHESES IN QUANTITATIVE RESEARCH

Research Hypotheses in Quantitative Research are predictive statements or propositions about how certain phenomena should relate to each other or operate within certain situations or conditions.

## Research Hypotheses in Quantitative Research

A research hypothesis is a specific, testable prediction. Quantitative researchers, instead of advancing research questions, may pose research hypotheses when they are interested in testing existing theories, models, or determining whether particular outcomes derived from the existing body of evidence are also likely for a given research study. Hypotheses should never be advanced in the absence of sound theory and/or empirical evidence.

## Important Characteristics of a Research Hypothesis

A research hypothesis should consist of the following characteristics:

- Explain what is expected to occur.
- Is clear and understandable.
- Is testable and measurable.
- Consists of at least one independent and one dependent variable.

## Types of Research Hypotheses

There are two main types of research hypotheses in quantitative research: an associational hypothesis and a comparative hypothesis.

### Associational Hypothesis

This type of hypothesis poses a prediction that identifies a relationship between two or more variables. For instance, example 1.8 is a predictive statement about the relationship between job satisfaction (independent variable) and absenteeism (dependent variable).

### Example 1.8

Job satisfaction is related to absenteeism.

A hypothesis can be stated in either a *non-directional* or a *directional* manner. A non-directional, associational hypothesis simply states that there is a relationship without explicitly stating the type of relationship (or how the variables are actually related to each other). The research hypothesis (example 1.8) is an example of a non-directional, associational hypothesis. In contrast, a directional, associational hypothesis (see example 1.9) explicitly states the nature of the relationship (i.e., whether the variables are positively or negatively related). The research hypothesis (example 1.9) states the exact nature of the relationship between job satisfaction and absenteeism, that is, there is a negative relationship between job satisfaction and absenteeism.

### Example 1.9
Higher levels of job satisfaction are related to lower levels of absenteeism.

In contrast, the research hypothesis (example 1.10) clearly indicates a positive relationship between work stress and absenteeism. For an associational hypothesis, stating a relationship in a positive or negative relationship results in a directional hypothesis statement.

### Example 1.10
Higher levels of work stress are associated with higher levels of absenteeism.

## Comparative Hypothesis

A comparative research hypothesis makes a prediction about how respondents in different groups statistically compare with respondents in other groups in relation to some quantitative variable. These types of hypotheses may also be stated in a non-directional or directional fashion. For example, a non-directional comparative hypothesis is presented in example 1.11.

### Example 1.11
There is a difference between male and female employees in relation to job satisfaction.

This type of research hypothesis makes a comparison between male and female employees (sex is the independent variable) in relation to their levels of job satisfaction (dependent variable). It is not clear whether we are expecting males to have higher satisfaction than females or vice versa. Hence, it is non-directional.

We could alternatively state our hypothesis as a directional, comparative hypothesis. In example 1.12, we are stating (in exact terms) that males are reporting higher levels of job satisfaction than females.

### Example 1.12
Male employees report higher levels of job satisfaction than female employees.

## Null vs Alternative Hypothesis

Traditionally, hypotheses were stated in two versions: a null hypothesis and an alternative hypothesis. A null hypothesis normally states that no relationship exists between two or more variables for an associational hypothesis or that there is no difference between groups of respondents for a comparative hypothesis. The null hypothesis normally runs counter to theory or empirical evidence, whereas the alternative hypothesis is the researcher's actual or primary hypothesis. However, this form of hypothesizing is not as popular as it was in the past. Today, researchers simply pose hypotheses on the basis of theory or evidence and engage in research to determine whether they can be supported or disconfirmed by the emerging evidence.

### Summary

> *Overall, hypothesis development is a practice that is crucial for certain quantitative research studies aimed at testing theories or statistical models. Not all quantitative studies require hypotheses. For example, quantitative studies on new and emerging topics (where there is insufficient literature, theory, or body of knowledge) do not rely on hypotheses but on research questions.*

> *The way in which results are written and presented are quite different when hypotheses are used instead of research questions. A common error made by many novice researchers is to use hypotheses, but report as if research questions were used. For instance, some novice researchers may forget to indicate whether hypotheses were supported or confirmed in their reporting of substantial findings.*

**TIP**

Hypotheses in quantitative research are only used for testing theories or statistical models.

Topic areas that do not have sufficient existing theoretical or empirical support cannot be investigated using hypotheses but rely instead on research questions.

# QUALITATIVE RESEARCH

 Qualitative Research is an exploratory approach which seeks to understand phenomena In in-depth and inductive ways.

## Focus of Qualitative Research

Qualitative research goes against the assumptions and tenets of quantitative research. Qualitative research typically seeks to understand how various phenomena operate in a naturalistic world or environment. Qualitative research focuses on in-depth, individual perspectives and experiences by exploring how participants make sense of their own *reality*.

Qualitative research does not seek to quantify reality or experiences or explain cause and effect or correlational relationships. Normally, a qualitative research study does not start with a clear or guiding theory or empirical body of evidence. Its focus is to uncover or explore new or novel topic areas and provide an interpretive or subjective assessment of various attributes of a topic space from the perspective of those who are under investigation. Qualitative research methods are typically unstructured, flexible, and fluid in nature and allows for deeper assessments of data.

## Critical Attributes of Qualitative Research

There are several attributes critical to a qualitative research study. Qualitative research:

- Performs an in-depth examination into a topic area.
- Does not specify variables but focuses on concepts or issues.
- Does not test theories or hypotheses but helps to build theories for further research.
- Focuses on the use of subjective, flexible, and unstructured methods of data-collection.
- Emphasizes smaller, non-random samples for exploration.
- Explores new areas of research.
- Does not rely on statistical or mathematical analyses but endorses the assessment of non-numerical data in the form of text or images.

## What Critics Say About Qualitative Research

Researchers who utilize qualitative research have fought a hard battle to gain recognition. Qualitative research is an intuitive approach which focuses on finding out *why* and *how* things occur. Qualitative research has been criticized by quantitative researchers because of its appreciation for smaller samples, subjective data, and the inductive (bottom-up) approach. Notwithstanding, qualitative research has been gaining momentum in certain fields such as sociology, psychology, and political science.

## Techniques Used in Qualitative Research

Qualitative researchers tend to use the following methods of data-gathering:

- One-on-one unstructured or open-ended interviews.

- Focus group interviews.
- Document analysis.
- Historical research methods.
- Participant and non-participant observations.

## Criteria Used to Assess Qualitative Research

Qualitative analytical techniques are flexible and rich in their ability to extract and uncover latent patterns, themes, and connections emanating from textual responses derived from a variety of participants and data sources. Consequently, qualitative research is assessed on criteria such as credibility (believability), dependability (based on the researcher's ability to account for inevitable changes in the research context), and confirmability (based on the ability to be corroborated by others). This contrasts with quantitative research which is judged on criteria such as validity, reliability, and objectivity.

However, many researchers and reviewers still mistakenly rely on quantitative based criteria to judge the appropriateness of qualitative research studies in many academic settings. It is important for researchers to appreciate the strengths and weaknesses of qualitative research as well as how it deviates from established conventions and standards traditionally set by the quantitative research paradigm.

Qualitative research typically deviates from conventional quantitative standards and protocols.

It should therefore be judged on different criteria.

Qualitative research, although unpopular in some disciplines, cannot be regarded as inferior to quantitative research. However, it might be more contextually appropriate for some topic areas than others.

# RESEARCH QUESTIONS IN QUALITATIVE RESEARCH

Research Questions in Qualitative Research are generally broader, more in-depth open-ended questions depicting the overall purpose of qualitative research studies.

## Nature of Qualitative Research Questions

Qualitative research questions are naturally open-ended, broad, and general expressions of the purpose of a qualitative study. These questions are more in-depth in nature and elicit textual (non-numerical) data. Most qualitative research questions may start with *What, Why,* or *How* to maintain their open-ended nature. Qualitative research questions are aimed at exploring and understanding different phenomena rather than explaining causes and relationships (as quantitative studies do). For example:

- How do teachers use information and communication technologies (ICT) within special needs classrooms?

- What are teachers' views regarding the use of corporal punishment in primary schools?
- How do teachers empower students with different learning styles in special needs classrooms?
- Why do teachers utilize different teaching approaches in special needs classrooms?

These questions cannot be answered by a simple 'yes' or 'no' response but invite a variety of textual responses and data that can only be assessed using qualitative (non-statistical) techniques. The purpose of a qualitative study may start with a broad, central research question followed by specific research questions or sub-questions. Example 1.13 presents a central qualitative research question, followed by three sub-questions. It is important that all sub-questions provide the level of specificity needed for readers and other research consumers to understand the key research objectives associated with the overall purpose of the research. These sub-questions also help researchers in the stages of formulating and designing their qualitative research instruments and their constituent items.

### Example 1.13

**Core Research Questions**

1. How are various educational ICTs implemented by teachers in special needs classrooms to promote learning?

**Sub-research Questions**

a. What types of ICTs do special needs teachers utilize in their classrooms?

b. What key opportunities and barriers are present for ICTs in special needs classrooms?

c. What key benefits do teachers and students enjoy through the application of ICTs within special needs classrooms?

## Specifying the Central Research Question and Sub-Questions

When specifying the central research question in qualitative research, it is important to recognize that this constitutes the overarching question and should follow the undermentioned conventions which are illustrated in example 1.14.

1. The question should start with a **what** or **how** to depict the need for exploration.
2. The question should specify the **core phenomenon** under study.
3. The question should highlight the **core participants** and the **research setting.**
4. The question should be neutral, open-ended and exploratory in nature.

When specifying the sub-questions, it is important to remember that these questions provide the necessary refinement for the central research question and should comprise the same properties (previously listed) as central questions, albeit more specific.

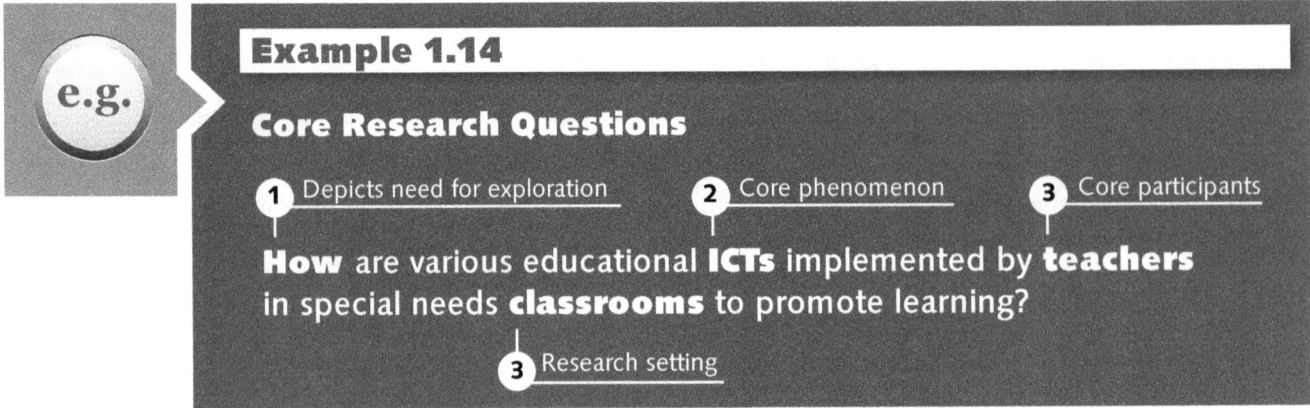

### Example 1.14

**Core Research Questions**

① Depicts need for exploration  ② Core phenomenon  ③ Core participants

**How** are various educational **ICTs** implemented by **teachers** in special needs **classrooms** to promote learning?

③ Research setting

## Qualitative Purpose Statements

Apart from research questions, the purpose of a qualitative research study can also be stated in the form of a purpose statement. Similar to qualitative research questions, this purpose statement should communicate the intent to explore or understand a central phenomenon under study (see example 1.15). In a qualitative purpose statement, consider the following:

- Start with...The purpose of this research is to....
- Mention the key or central phenomenon you are studying.
- Apply terms such as *explore, understand*, and *describe*.
- Include the type of participants and research setting.

### Example 1.15 – Purpose Statement

The purpose of this qualitative study is to explore the perceptions of educational ICTs among special needs teachers within Barbadian primary schools.

### Summary

> *Overall, qualitative research studies require either research questions or purpose statements to communicate its overall purpose to readers. It is not unusual for researchers to include both sets of these items within their introduction or opening paragraphs of their studies.*

Having a central research question followed by sub-questions is a useful way of communicating the purpose of a qualitative study.

Alternatively, you can use a simple purpose statement which incorporates the central and specific dimensions of your study's overall purpose.

# APPLIED VS BASIC RESEARCH

Applied versus Basic Research has a distinguishing feature such that applied research concerns work that is applied directly to real-life contexts or situations, whereas basic research concerns work that is more academic in nature.

## Overview

Research can be performed under one of two contexts or for one of two reasons. Research that is carried out to make direct applications to real-life scenarios and situations is referred to as *applied research*. However, research that is conducted for purely academic reasons such as building a theoretical understanding of some phenomenon or topic area is referred to as *basic research (or pure research)*.

## Applied Research

Applied research is about solving real-life problems or addressing practical needs of primary stakeholders, agents, and clients. Oftentimes, applied research is typically a methodology aimed at problem-solving as well as designing and implementing practical interventions for change. Applied researchers can also act as independent consultants attached to private sector organizations or government agencies to help management address emerging or persistent problems or issues affecting the workplace or wider industry.

A number of key characteristics and considerations of applied research are presented below:

- Applied research builds from theoretical knowledge and principles by applying these to actual real-life situations.
- Applied research goes beyond searching for and building on scientific knowledge. It aims to solve problems and enhance the manner in which things are done.
- Applied research is normally linked to the practical interests or needs of some institution, organization, or industry (whether private or public) and can manifest in the forms of specialized research consultancies or developmental funded research projects.
- Applied research almost always directly leads to implementation and evaluation of a practical set of recommendations or actions.

Key examples of applied research may include the following:

- Research seeking to improve the customer service profile of a local hotel whose customer intake has fallen over the years.
- Research seeking to develop an organizational strategic plan which identifies the existing and future strategic needs and actions for a university undergoing a serious financial crisis.
- Research seeking to identify the causes of some serious health condition (e.g., HIV/AIDs) with the aim of developing a cure or sustainable treatment plan for those suffering from the same condition.

## Basic Research

Basic research involves the pure attainment of knowledge (largely theoretical) on a given phenomenon or set of phenomena for the purpose of gaining greater understanding or addressing intellectual curiosity. Basic researchers are concerned about developing new theories, testing existing theories or models, and gaining further data or knowledge about particular conceptual, empirical, or logical concerns or propositions. Basic research is typically conducted within an academic setting by professors, research fellows, and students. Published work or journal manuscripts in various areas are key examples of basic research. Student research papers or assignments which simply serve to gain *knowledge for the sake of knowledge* (*or fulfilling the requirements of an academic programme*) are also prime examples of basic research.

A number of key considerations of basic research are presented below:

- Basic research is primarily concerned with developing or advancing theory.
- Consistent with its nature, basic research does not seek to provide any real-life applications but sets out the necessary foundation for applied research.
- Basic research is normally conducted within an academic (scholarly) environment and institution, with its typical outputs manifested as journal publications, books, or student research papers.
- The main motive for conducting basic research is to gain further knowledge, address intellectual questions, and to provide greater understanding on a given topic area.

Key examples of basic research may include the following:

- Research seeking to develop a sociocultural theory of entrepreneurship in developing countries.
- Research seeking to test hypotheses derived from an existing conceptual model depicting the consequences of workplace bullying for employees and managers in the services sector.
- Research seeking to identify and examine the key conditions that led to the formation of the universe and life on earth.

## Summary of Applied vs Basic Research

> *Overall, basic and applied research studies are vital to both methodologists and practitioners. As previously mentioned, basic research lays down the foundation for applied research in many contexts. Outside of the differences mentioned earlier, both categories of research follow the same principles, rigour, and stages inherent in scientific research.*

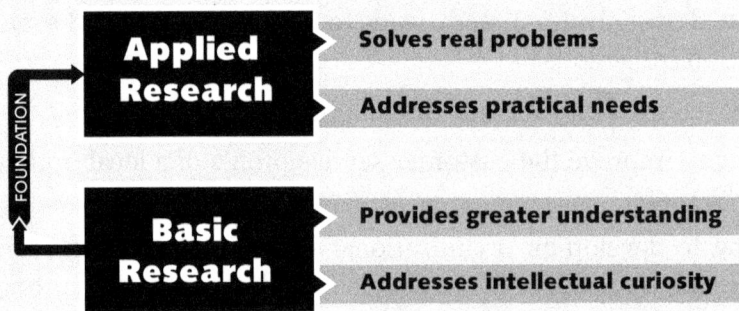

 **TIP** In order to decide whether you are doing a basic or applied research study, ask whether the research is seeking to make an impact on some practical context or situation in a meaningful and immediate way, leading to practical courses of action. If the answer is yes, you are probably doing applied research.

# 2 Literature Review

- The Literature Review or Review of Literature
- Sources of Literature
- The Literature Review Process
- Citations and Quotations
- References
- Plagiarism
- Searching for Sources
- Links to Useful Resources

## THE LITERATURE REVIEW OR REVIEW OF LITERATURE

The Literature Review or Review of Literature is a compilation of information that summarizes and evaluates what is already published or known about a topic of interest.

### Relevance of the Literature Review

A literature review can actually act as a standalone paper whereby you can evaluate what other researchers have done in an area of interest. For example, you can summarize and compare research, trace the progression of a theory and evaluate how it operates within different contexts, compare and contrast different research methodologies or practices used in a specific discipline (e.g., social sciences) or area (e.g., education), and provide a critique of the information. In addition, a literature review also forms the justification and foundation of a primary research investigation.

### Functions of a Literature Review

A literature review has several important functions:

1. It provides knowledge and insight so that both the researcher and the readers know what has occurred in an area of research over a particular time period, and highlights the work of researchers who have influenced the field. It also equips the researcher with insight into the terminology and theories that are used within that particular field.

2. It can be used to extend a theory, or add different interpretations to existing information.

3. It provides the foundation for the research question as an extension of, or gap in, the current literature. Consequently, it provides arguments for or against your research question, and frames your research question so that you can meaningfully contribute to the literature in your particular field.

4. It allows you to determine how to proceed with new or extended information. For example, you may not need to reinvent the wheel. If an efficient and effective way to gather data, or an approach to an issue has already been demonstrated to be useful, then you can reuse the method or practice and give credit to the initial author. Alternatively, the literature can also provide you with information about strategies that did not work so that you can avoid making the same mistakes.

5. It provides a backdrop for discussion of original/primary research. Here, original findings can be supported by, or differences in findings can be explained through comparisons to, past research.

## Literature Reviews
- Summarize the main points
- Look for relevant theories
- Examine best practices
- Compare/contrast methodologies
- Identify main contributors
- Use subject specific terminology
- Evaluate the information

## What is Missing?
## How can I add to the literature?
- Evaluate existing information
- Retest an existing method/strategy
- Fill the literature gap:
  - Add a twist/different context
  - Research a new theory/approach/strategy/method

**TIP**

A quality literature review provides the foundation for, and allows you to argue the importance of, your research question(s).

It is also incorporated in the discussion section of original research.

## SOURCES OF LITERATURE

Sources of Literature are generally classified into three categories: primary (original material), secondary (critique/interpretation of primary material), and tertiary (summarization of primary/secondary) materials.

### Does Source Matter for Academic Papers and Scholarly Manuscripts?

Before you actually begin to select published work on a topic area for your literature review, it is important to understand the various types of sources that can be tapped to inform your literature review. An important question that needs to be considered is whether source matters. For academic papers and scholarly manuscripts, researchers are expected to use credible sources. To determine credibility, researchers need to evaluate issues such as reliability of the actual article (e.g., Is the article published in a refereed journal or on reputable websites such as the World Bank or the United Nations?), as well as author affiliations, area of expertise, and so on.

### Sources of Literature

There are three sources that can be used to inform your review of the literature.

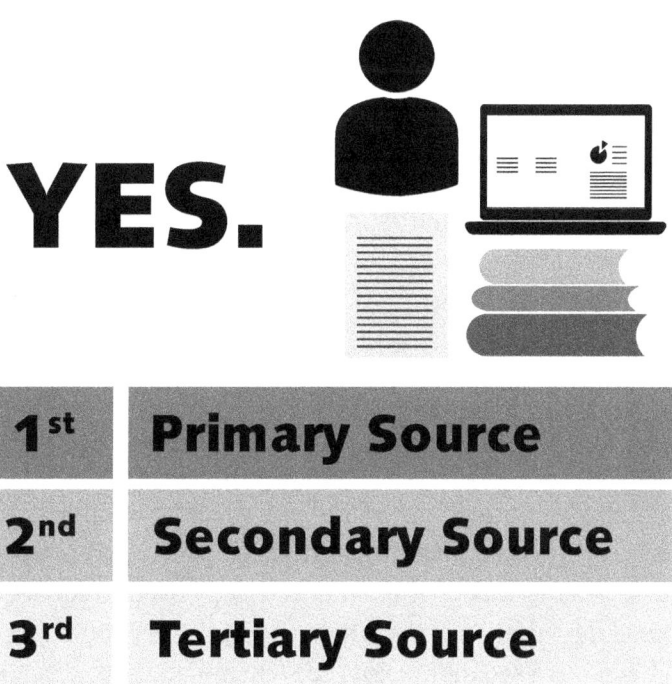

## Primary or Empirical Sources

Primary sources refer to articles where *original data* was gathered by the author (see table 2.1). In academia, for example, this is generally through systematic observations, experiments, or surveys. These types of articles are published in *peer reviewed academic journals* and provide a *first-hand account* of the research. Literature reviews prepared for scholarly purposes should be comprised of mostly referee journal articles. Referee journal articles follow a standardized format with specific sections:

*Abstract:* The abstract provides a brief summary of the salient aspects of the research. You can usually tell from an abstract if the article is a first account (i.e., if the authors gathered the data themselves). For example, key words used within the abstract (e.g., *participants, findings revealed,* and/or *statistically significant*) tend to signify that the article in question is a primary source.

*Review of Literature:* The literature review summarizes the relevant information in a particular field and informs the research question(s).

*Methods Section:* The methods section identifies the sample (number of participants, demographics), explains how the data will be collected (interviews, surveys, experiments, observations), and discusses the data analysis techniques that will be utilized. It also discusses challenges encountered and solutions used to mitigate challenges.

*Results:* The results section presents findings in many forms, including tables, graphs, and descriptions.

*Discussion:* This section interprets the results through comparisons to the literature review and research question linkages, highlights contributions to the literature in that field of study, gives implications of results, identifies limitations/weaknesses of the research and possible areas that can be examined in the future.

*Conclusion*: This section provides a general summary. It may identify limitations and future research if not already addressed in the discussion section.

*References:* This section provides thorough information on all in-text citations, so that readers can look up original sources used by the author(s).

## Secondary Sources

A secondary source (see table 2.1) provides a *second-hand account* and interpretation/critique of a primary source. Such information may or may not be accurate. Journal review articles are generally excellent examples of secondary sources as they tend to highlight the most current literature in a given area. Another great advantage of a review article is that the reference section can lead you to the actual primary source, which you can then review for your paper. You can search for possible review articles via key words such as meta-analysis, comparative analysis, and review of research. Sometimes even the title of a journal is a direct indication that the article is a review article (e.g., *Clinical Psychological Review, Educational Research Review*).

Secondary sources can provide very useful information and can be cost effective. Notwithstanding, it is important that before you use a secondary source that you determine information credibility. For example, if you are planning to use government statistics or statistics collected by a private sector organization, how were the statistics collected? Was a sound, robust methodology used to collect the data? Note that when an organization collects original data that the data is actually a primary source for the organization. However, when you use the data, it becomes a secondary source. When using secondary sources in scholarly writing, it is really important to do some fact checking to determine how credible the secondary sources are before you actually use them in your literature review. Look for things like the authors' names, authors' affiliations, reputation of the publisher, year of publication, and so on.

## Tertiary Sources

These sources (see table 2.1) *only summarize* information but do not interpret or critique information. Some tertiary sources are quite credible while others should be avoided completely. For example, dictionary definitions from sources such as Webster or Oxford will be considered as credible. However, a personal blog (unless it is by some well-known expert or organization) should be avoided. Tertiary sources that are based on opinion and not fact should be avoided at all costs. Like primary and secondary sources, tertiary sources also need to be properly cited and referenced.

To avoid problems, if evidence is supplied through a reference section or footnote, you should always try to track the source articles and review them before using them in your academic paper. This provides an opportunity for you to formulate your own interpretations based on original information. Many tertiary sources are online and therefore easily accessible. However, you should fight the urge to include too many tertiary sources in your paper. *Scholarly/academic writing relies mostly on primary sources.*

### Table 2.1: Examples of Primary, Secondary, and Tertiary Sources

| | Primary Sources | Secondary Sources | Tertiary Sources |
|---|---|---|---|
| | Refereed journal articles | Journal review articles | Dictionaries |
| | Empirical books | Textbooks | Fact books |
| | Legal documents | Monographs | Handbooks |
| | Historical records | Bibliographies | Manuals |
| | Dissertations | Newspapers | Databases |
| | Artefacts | Magazines | Personal blogs |
| | Field studies | Commentaries | Travel guides |
| | Letters and diaries (e.g., the diary of Anne Frank) | Political analyses | Wikipedia |
| | Statistics (e.g., census, credible organizations such as the United Nations, the World Bank) | Review of legislation | Opinion pieces in newspapers, magazines |
| Used for Academic/ScholarlyPapers? | Yes | Yes – but use sparingly and perform fact checking to determine credibility (e.g., reputation of author(s), publisher) | |

**TIP:** Do not use someone else's literature review and then cite and pretend that you have read the original articles yourself – this is unethical. You must return to the source so that you can ensure that both context and relevance to your topic is accurate.

A current review article on your topic is a good place to start your review of the literature. It offers up to date references on your topic that you can then locate, read, and incorporate into your literature review.

## THE LITERATURE REVIEW PROCESS

 The Literature Review Process is multifaceted. It includes reading and analysing the literature to construct the arguments pertinent to your research questions and/or theoretical framework.

### Things to Keep in Mind when Conducting a Literature Review

For many, the literature review process can be a daunting process. There is usually an abundance of literature on practically every subject area, and the sheer volume can be a bit overwhelming. Before you start to write your literature review, peruse the various sources discussed in the preceding section paying careful attention to credibility of source (look for primary and secondary sources) and year of publication (since outdated publications may be criticized). Keep in mind that the literature review process is a multistep process and your written literature review will require multiple revisions if you want it to read coherently. Your thought process must therefore have clear logical progression.

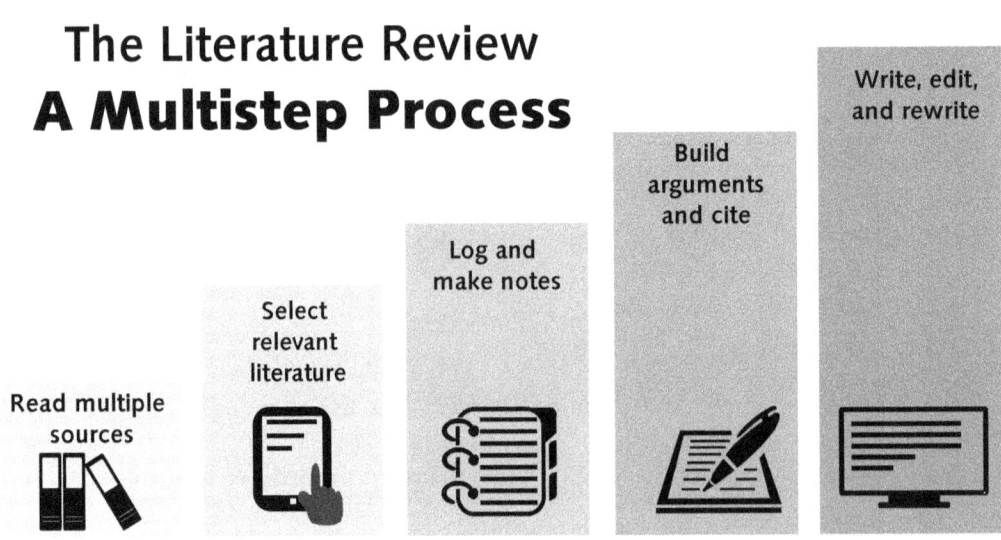

The Literature Review — A Multistep Process: Read multiple sources → Select relevant literature → Log and make notes → Build arguments and cite → Write, edit, and rewrite

## Guidelines for Preparing Your Written Literature Review

*Read Multiple Sources:* Read literature around the topic that interests you and begin to formulate your research question(s) (see chapter 1).

*Select Relevant Literature:* Select literature that is current/relevant/focused to your research area. Here, it might be useful to determine if there is a relatively recent review journal article (secondary source) in your area. The reference section will provide useful links to the primary sources.

*Log and Make Notes:* If your articles are accessed online, download them all and log the references. In the social sciences, the American Psychological Association (APA) citation/reference format is used, but, there are other formats depending on your discipline requirements. If some of your articles are accessed as hardcopies, record the reference information, page numbers, and library access numbers and make notes in your own words. Properly referenced articles cut down on the tedious task of formatting at the end of your paper, and can help you to gain quick access to the information again, thereby cutting down on frustration when you need to recheck information.

*Build Arguments and Cite:* Begin to build your argument(s) for each research question mainly from the primary sources and some secondary sources. For definitions you can use dictionaries (tertiary sources) where applicable. Keep checking information relevance to your research question(s) so that you maintain your focus.

If you are conducting an original (primary) investigation, then the aim here in your review of literature is to explain what has been done in this area and how and why your research fills a gap in the literature or extends the current literature, in order to lead up to your research question(s).

Alternatively, if you are doing a stand-alone review of the literature, then your aim may include tracing the progress of the field, examining/evaluating a theory, method, practice, or context.

As previously mentioned, as you write your notes and your literature review, put in-text citations next to the different ideas so that you do not forget where different information comes from or you will have a momentous and onerous task to figure this out later.

*Write, Edit, and Rewrite:* Be prepared to invest substantial time to write and edit your literature review. You should also make time allowances to leave the paper for a while and then return to it since you will see it with 'new' eyes. As you write, pay close attention to the citation and formatting style of your discipline. For example, the APA style is a common style used in the social sciences, business, and nursing.

- *Use headings and sub-headings* to jot down different findings from the literature that relate to your specific research questions. This will help to keep your literature review properly organized in a logical and coherent manner. Separate your arguments with a topic sentence for each paragraph and only put the information relevant to that topic sentence in that paragraph.
- *Use the following formatting guidelines when typing:*
    - Use a clear, readable font such as Times New Roman.
    - Use a font size of at least 12.
    - Double space your text since this will allow you to edit more easily.

- ***Use transition words and sentences*** so that your literature review reads coherently and flows well. Check the internet for lists of transition words that you can use. Some common transition words include words such as *first, second, third, finally, although, consequently,* and *similarly* (see example 2.1).

- ***Constantly backup your work and defy Murphy's Law!*** Save on multiple devices – your computer, your memory stick, your email. As you edit your work, it may be a good idea to save your file using daily dates especially if you plan on making substantial edits. When you overwrite, information cannot be salvaged. However, if you save under different dates, you can always go back to an earlier version to salvage something that may not have made much sense in a previous version.

**Example 2.1** (taken from Persaud & Persaud, 2016)

Research indicates that student enrolment status can affect stress levels. Gudrun, Covarrubias-Venegas, Simbrunner, and Janous's (2012) longitudinal study in Austria (2009–2011) found that more part-timers in comparison to full-timers (approximately 75% vs. 60%) usually work, and part-timers actually work longer hours compared to full-timers (40 hours vs. 20 hours). Consequently, part-timers experience more stress compared to full-timers when academic demands are added to their existing commitments.

You can use different colours to highlight different aspects of your topic that can be found in the literature. For example, you can use yellow for definitions, green for theories, etc. This helps you to quickly organize/categorize the information.

# CITATIONS AND QUOTATIONS

Citations in academic writing are necessary to avoid plagarism. In-text citations are used to refer to the author/organization whose idea/information you have incorporated into your paper.

Quotations are verbatim accounts taken from someone's work, which you have used to emphasize a point.

## Citation Styles

Numerous citation styles exist and you must use the correct citation style for your research paper. You will therefore need to check your discipline or university to figure out which citation style must be used for your paper. Relevant in-text citations are foundational, and speak to the credibility of your work. From this chapter, you already know that the most credible sources that you should use are primary sources.

This section will illustrate use of the APA citation style (see table 2.2) since this is one of the most widely used citation styles globally.

## APA In-text Citations

The APA manual is very handy, albeit tedious, when you first start to use this citation style. As you learn this formatting style, it becomes easier to accurately cite and reference information. Also, when you understand the APA citation and reference formats, you can then easily identify the source (e.g., journal articles, books, online sources).

When you provide in-text citations, the author(s) or organization can be used at the *beginning of a sentence*, *within a sentence*, or *at the end of a sentence*. Read the following examples (see table 2.2) taken or adapted from Persaud and Persaud (2016).

The APA Publication Manual is a necessary text for all persons who are required to use the APA citation and referencing format.

### Table 2.2: Basic APA Citations

| Basic Citation Guide | First Use in Your Document | Subsequent Use In Your Document |
|---|---|---|
| Beginning of the sentence<br><br>1 OR TWO AUTHORS | According to Adam and Epel (2007), persons who eat more as a means of dealing with stress actually use food to activate their physiological reward system.<br><br>**Note:**<br>▪ Year is enclosed in brackets.<br>▪ And is used between names since names are not enclosed in the brackets. | Adam and Epel (2007) further noted that...<br><br>**Note:**<br>▪ First and subsequent in-text citations of one or two authors remain the same. |

| Basic Citation Guide | First Use in Your Document | Subsequent Use In Your Document |
|---|---|---|
| **MORE THAN 2 AUTHORS** | Trockel, Barnes, and Egget (2000) noted that reduced sleep, late rising, and/or long hours of work were more likely to result in poor academic performance.<br><br>**Note:**<br>• Punctuation – commas between each author but not after author closest to the date. | According to Trockel et al. (2000), reduced sleep, late rising, and/or long hours of work were more likely to result in poor academic performance.<br><br>**Note:**<br>• First author's name followed by et al.<br>• Period/full stop between et al. and the date. |
| **End of the sentence**<br><br>**1 OR TWO AUTHORS** | Persons who eat more as a means of dealing with stress actually use food to activate their physiological reward system (Adam & Epel, 2007).<br><br>**Note:**<br>• When placed in brackets the ampersand (&) symbol is used between the two names.<br>• A comma is placed after the second name before the date.<br>• A period/ full stop comes after the bracket at the end of the sentence. | Persons who eat more as a means of dealing with stress actually use food to activate their physiological reward system (Adam & Epel, 2007).<br><br>**Note:**<br>• First and subsequent in-text citations of one or two authors remain the same. |
| **MORE THAN 2 AUTHORS** | Reduced sleep, late rising, and/or long hours of work were more likely to result in poor academic performance (Trockel, Barnes, & Egget, 2000).<br><br>**Note:**<br>• Each author's last name is separated by a comma.<br>• When placed in brackets the ampersand (&) symbol is used between the last two names. | Reduced sleep, late rising, and/or long hours of work were more likely to result in poor academic performance (Trockel et al., 2000).<br><br>**Note:**<br>• First author's name followed by et al.<br>• Period/full stop, followed by a comma between et al. and the year. |
| **Throughout the sentence** | Alternatively, other researchers found that regardless of sex, students had similar stress levels in relation to family-life changes, transition into new academic environments (Dyson & Renk, 2006), and problems with sleep (Waqas, Khan, Sharif, Khalid, & Ali, 2015).<br><br>**Note:**<br>• Punctuation in first and second citation.<br>• Note use of ampersand (&) symbol in both citations since both citations are placed in brackets. | This stress of unfamiliar environments (Dyson & Renk, 2006), may cause students to misuse sleeping pills (Zafar et al., 2008) …in order to combat day time fatigue and sleepiness (Waqas et al., 2015).<br><br>**Note:**<br>• For only two authors, both authors are used with an ampersand (&) symbol since the names are in brackets.<br>• For several authors, subsequent use entails the first author's name followed by et al.<br>• Period/full stop, followed by a comma between et al. and the year. |

| Basic Citation Guide | First Use in Your Document | Subsequent Use In Your Document |
|---|---|---|
| **Organization as the author** | United Nations Educational, Scientific and Cultural Organization [UNESCO] (2012) noted that… **Note:** <ul><li>Organization's name is spelled out for first usage. If organization's name has an acronym, it is placed in brackets.</li></ul> | UNESCO (2012) also explains that… **Note:** <ul><li>Acronym is used for subsequent use.</li><li>Never put a web link as an in-text citation.</li></ul> |
| **Several authors to support the same point** | Researchers have noted a negative relationship between stress and GPA (see Busari, 2012; Struthers, Perry, & Menec, 2000; Thawabieh & Qaisy, 2012). **Note:** <ul><li>Each citation is separated by a semi-colon.</li><li>Citations are arranged in alphabetical order – not by date.</li><li>The ampersand (&) symbol is always used when names are placed in brackets.</li></ul> | Researchers have noted a negative relationship between stress and GPA (see Busari, 2012; Struthers et al., 2000; Thawabieh & Qaisy, 2012). **Note:** <ul><li>Each citation is separated by a semi-colon.</li><li>Citations are arranged in alphabetical order – not by date.</li><li>The ampersand (&) symbol is used in brackets.</li><li>Subsequent use of more than two authors is written with et al.</li><li>Note punctuation between et al. and year.</li></ul> |
| **5 authors** | Anxiety caused by academic stress usually translates into students experiencing sleeping problems (Ahrberg, Dresler, Niedermaier, Steiger, & Genzel, 2012). **Note:** <ul><li>Each author's last name is separated by a comma.</li><li>When placed in brackets the ampersand (&) symbol is used between the last two names.</li></ul> | In conclusion, similar to previous research (see Ahrberg et al., 2012), we also found that anxiety from academic stress resulted in students experiencing sleeping problems. **Note:** <ul><li>For several authors, subsequent use entails the first author's name followed by et al.</li><li>Period/full stop, followed by a comma between et al. and the date.</li></ul> |
| **6 or more authors** | Additionally, younger students may be more inclined to drug use which can induce sleep directly (Zafar et al., 2008). **Note:** <ul><li>Here et al is used from the very first time because there are more than six authors.</li></ul> | Zafar et al. (2008) further noted… **Note:** <ul><li>Citation is written in the same manner as the first use (with et al.) when six or more authors are involved.</li></ul> |

Source: (Taken/adapted from Persaud & Persaud, 2016)

It is crucial that you place the correct in-text citations with the relevant information that you have paraphrased. Example 2.2 explains what you should and should not do.

**Example 2.2** (taken from Persaud & Persaud, 2016)

*However, stress is relative based on several factors which include <u>personality</u> (Rajasekar, 2013), <u>biological vulnerabilities</u> (Schneiderman, Ironson & Siegel, 2005), <u>social support</u> (Bland, Melton, Welle, & Bigham, 2012), and <u>stress relieving activities</u> (Ragsdale, Beehr, Grebner, & Han, 2011).*

- In one sentence, the authors use four different factors, each from a different source, and placed a citation next to the factor. **CORRECT**

- If the authors had placed all citations at the end of the sentence, it would indicate that the four factors are found in all four sources which they are not. **INCORRECT**

- If the authors had only put one, two, or three of the four citations, then all sources are not recorded. **INCORRECT**

## Quotations in APA

*Use Quotes Sparingly*: A literature review comprised of mainly quotations will be accurate but WILL NOT be your own work (even if you cite and put the page/paragraph numbers) and WILL BE marked down by your professor or may be rejected by a journal. **Example 2.3 explains what you should <u>not</u> do.**

**Example 2.3** (quotations taken from Persaud & Persaud, 2016)

Diana reads the journal article on stress from Persaud and Persaud (2016). She then puts the following information in her paper.

According to Persaud and Persaud (2016), "the three most common reasons expressed by students for less summer school stress were: (i) smaller class numbers which results in more individual attention from lecturer (20%), (ii) more time to focus on summer course since fewer courses are being taken (15%), and (iii) easier summer courses compared to semester courses (11%)" (p.17). These researchers further noted that "in contrast, the most common reason expressed for higher summer stress pertained to the shorter time period in summer which makes it more difficult to absorb material (39%). Table 1 highlights some of the verbatim responses provided by students on Question 2"

Literature Review

(p. 17). In addition, the authors found that "part-time students experienced higher levels of stress with summer courses compared to full-time students [(M = 6.79, SD = 2.41 vs. M = 5.72, SD = 2.62), t(102) = 2.17, p = .03]" (p .18).

- Diana has correctly cited the source. She has provided the authors' names, publication date, and page numbers. However, only 17 out of 149 words actually belong to her (see highlighted text). Diana has not plagiarized, but neither is this paragraph in her own words.

- Even if Diana had used quotes from different authors and put the full in-text citations, the work would not be hers. At best, it is only a copy of relevant research, minus any comprehension or evaluation on Diana's part.

- Using such a long quote or too many quotes indicates that Diana does not understand how to paraphrase and/or is too lazy to paraphrase and is indicative of poor writing skills.

- Diana also did not observe the rule pertaining to block quotes discussed hereunder.

***Use Quotes for Emphasis:*** Quotes should be used to emphasize really important information that is best kept in its original form.

   ***Short Quotes*** – When quotes are less than 40 words, structure it within the sentence, put in quotation marks, and cite (see example 2.4).

**Example 2.4** (taken from Persaud & Persaud, 2016)

Fox (2004) also noted that women are more likely to engage in crying as a stress relief mechanism and noted that crying can be "therapeutic, cathartic, de-toxing, [and] stress-busting" (p. 2).

***Block Quotes*** – When quotes are more than 40 words (see example 2.5) note the following:
- There are no quotation marks for a block quote. The entire quote is indented ½ inch from the left hand margin.
- The citation (authors' names and date) can be placed either before the start of the quote (see example 2.5) or after the quote (see example 2.6). Observe that the period/full-stop is placed before the page number in example 2.5 and before the full citation in example 2.6. No period/full-stop is placed after the bracket in either example.

**Example 2.5** (taken from Persaud & Persaud, 2016)

According to the literature, males and females used different coping strategies. For example, research by Persaud and Persaud (2016) highlighted these differences:

> Females tended to use comfort mechanisms such as eating more to de-stress while males tended to use more negative coping strategies such as smoking/drugs. We also found that full-timers tended to use more recreational/socializing strategies as stress relievers, and that younger students tended to sleep more which is an unusual finding. (p. 23)

**Example 2.6** (taken from Persaud & Persaud, 2016)

According to the literature, males and females used very different coping strategies:

> Females tended to use comfort mechanisms such as eating more to de-stress while males tended to use more negative coping strategies such as smoking/drugs. We also found that full-timers tended to use more recreational/socializing strategies as stress relievers, and that younger students tended to sleep more which is an unusual finding. (Persaud & Persaud, 2016, p. 23)

## Other Citation Styles

The preceding has focused on the APA citation style. It is important to reiterate at this point that there are many different citation styles and that you must use the citation style that is relevant to your field. If you are a student, note that failure to adhere to the correct citation style may result in your work not being accepted by your university or professor. In addition, if you are submitting a paper to a journal, the journal's editor may refuse to even review your paper if you do not comply with the journal's guidelines and formatting styles.

Table 2.3 provides a brief comparison of important differences among three common citation styles (APA, Chicago, and Harvard) to illustrate how a journal entry would be cited and how the reference for the journal would be typed. Table 2.4 provides a summary of citation styles used in various disciplines. The full list of disciplines along with the citation style can be obtained from the URL at the bottom of the table.

**Table 2.3: Illustration Showing How an In-text Citation and Reference would be done using APA, Chicago, and Harvard Styles**

| In-text citation | APA | Chicago | Harvard |
|---|---|---|---|
| Journal Article (several authors) from the Internet | **Example** Reduced sleep, late rising, and/or long hours of work were more likely to result in poor academic performance (Trockel, Barnes, & Egget, 2000). **Note:** <ul><li>*Each author's last name is separated by a comma.*</li><li>*When placed in brackets the ampersand (&) sign is used between the last two names.*</li></ul> | **Example** Reduced sleep, late rising, and/or long hours of work were more likely to result in poor academic performance (Trockel, Barnes, and Egget 2000, 3). **Note:** <ul><li>*Last name before the publication year does not carry a comma.*</li><li>*When placed in brackets the word **and** is used between the last two names and a page number is provided after the publication year.*</li></ul> | **Example** Reduced sleep, late rising, and/or long hours of work were more likely to result in poor academic performance (Trokel, Barnes and Egget, 2000). **Note:** <ul><li>*Punctuation marks in the citation.*</li><li>*When placed in brackets the word **and** is used between the last two names.*</li></ul> |
| Presentation of information in Reference List<br><br>Journal Article from the Internet | **Example** Persaud, N., & Persaud. I. (2016). The relationship between socio-demographics, stress levels, stressors, and coping mechanisms among undergraduate students at a university in Barbados. *International Journal of Higher Education, 5* (1), 11-27. doi: 10.5430/ijhe.v5n1p11 **Note:** <ul><li>*Punctuation.*</li><li>*Use of upper case and lower case letters.*</li><li>*The authors' last name is followed by the first name initial, and the middle name initial (if available).*</li><li>*Publication year is placed in brackets.*</li><li>*Article title is in script text.*</li><li>*Journal name and volume number are italicized.*</li></ul> | **Example** Persaud, Nadini, and Indeira Persaud. 2016. "The Relationship between Socio-Demographics, Stress Levels, Stressors, and Coping Mechanisms among Undergraduate Students at a University in Barbados." International Journal of Higher Education 5, no. 1: 11-27. http://doi.org/10.5430/ijhe.v5n1p11. **Note:** <ul><li>*Punctuation.*</li><li>*Use of upper case and lower case letters.*</li><li>*The first author's last name is followed by the first name and the second author's first name is placed before the last name.*</li><li>*Publication year is written without brackets.*</li></ul> | **Example** Persaud, N., and Persaud, I. (2016) 'The relationship between socio-demographics, stress levels, stressors, and coping mechanisms among undergraduate students at a university in Barbados', *International Journal of Higher Education*, 5(1) pp. 11-27. Available at: www.sciedupress.com/ijhe (Accessed: 1 June 2017) **Note:** <ul><li>*Punctuation.*</li><li>*Use of upper case and lower case letters.*</li><li>*The authors' last name is followed by the first name initial, and the middle name initial (if available).*</li><li>*Publication year is placed in brackets.*</li><li>*Article title is in script text and placed in single quotation marks.*</li></ul> |

| In-text citation | APA | Chicago | Harvard |
|---|---|---|---|
| Presentation of information in Reference List<br><br>Journal Article from the Internet (cont'd) | • *Issue number is placed in brackets in script text.*<br>• *Page numbers are provided.*<br>• *Digital Object Identifier (DOI) is provided.*<br>• *References are not numbered on the Reference List.*<br>• *References are arranged in alphabetical order on the reference list.* | • *Article title is in script text and placed in double quotation marks.*<br>• *Journal name is italicized.*<br>• *Volume and issue numbers are provided.*<br>• *Page numbers are provided.*<br>• *DOI is provided.*<br>• *References are not numbered on the Reference List.*<br>• *References are arranged in alphabetical order on the reference list.* | • *Journal name is italicized.*<br>• *Volume and issue numbers are not italicized.*<br>• *Page numbers are provided with the abbreviation **pp.** before the actual page numbers.*<br>• *URL address is provided.*<br>• *Date of retrieval follows the URL address.*<br>• *References are not numbered on the Reference List.*<br>• *References are arranged in alphabetical order on the reference list.* |

**Table 2.4: Discipline-specific Citation Styles**

| American University Citation Style Guide | Business | Computer Science | Education | History | Law | Linguistics | Literature | Mathematics | Medicine | Political Science | Psychology | Sociology |
|---|---|---|---|---|---|---|---|---|---|---|---|---|
| Association of Legal Writing Directors (ALWD) | | | | | ✓ | | | | | | | |
| American Mathematical Society (AMS) | | | | | | | | ✓ | | | | |
| American Medical Association (AMA) | | | | | | | | | ✓ | | | |
| American Political Science Association (APSA) | | | | | | | | | | ✓ | | |
| American Psychological Association (APA) | ✓ | | ✓ | | | ✓ | | | | | ✓ | |
| American Sociological Association (ASA) | | | | | | | | | | | | ✓ |
| Chicago Manual of Style | ✓ | ✓ | | ✓ | | | | | | | | |
| Harvard Business School Citation Guide | ✓ | | | | | | | | | | | |
| Modern Language Association (MLA) | | | | | | | ✓ | ✓ | | | | |

Source: http://subjectguides.library.american.edu/c.php?g=175008&p=1154150

## Still Unsure about which Citation Style to Use?

Based on what we have already discussed, here is what we suggest.

If you are a student:

- Check to see if your education institution has an official citation style. Most universities do. Moreover, they usually indicate which style should be used for submission of papers in different fields/disciplines.
- If your education institution does not have an official policy on citation style, check with your professor to find out which citation style you should use.

If you are submitting a paper for publication:

- Follow the journal guidelines and submit your paper using the citation style indicated in the guidelines.

Remember to correctly cite all ideas that you have taken from other researchers/writers using the correct citation style of your discipline/university.

# REFERENCES

A Reference is a list of all sources cited in your work.

## References vs a Bibliography

The term **References** refers to all primary, secondary and tertiary sources that you *actually cited* in your research paper. References differ from a **Bibliography**, which can also include sources (primary, secondary, and tertiary) that you may have consulted in order to obtain background knowledge for your topic, but did not actually cite in your paper. Academic research generally requires the use of a reference list, not a bibliography. If you are unsure, check with your professor.

When you create a reference list or bibliography, note that the title of the source document should be spelt in the exact manner as provided by the source. For example, in the reference list shown on the next page, the journal name is *Cyberpsychology, Behavior, and Social Networking*. If you were using standard British English, you cannot change the spelling of the word 'Behavior' to 'Behaviour'.

- Centred, **NOT** bolded
- Double spaced
- First line of each reference is hanging; the rest is indented by ½ inch.
- Include the Digital Object Identifier (DOI) if available.
- If you have more than seven authors, list up to six, then put three dots ... (ellipsis) and put the last author's name. Note that no ampersand is used either before or after the ellipsis.
- Reference list is arranged in alphabetical order (i.e., A to Z). References are not numbered in the list.

References

Jacobsen, W.C., & Forste, R. (2011). The wired generation: Academic and social outcomes of electronic media use among university students. *Cyberpsychology, Behavior, and Social Networking, 14*(5), 275-280. doi:10.1089/cyber.2010.0135

Zafar, S. N., Syed, R., Waqar, S., Zubairi, A. J., Vanqar, T., Shaikh, M.,...Saleem, S. (2008). Self-medication amongst university students of Karachi: Prevalence, knowledge and attitudes. *Journal of Pakistan Medical Association, 58* (4), 214-217.

## Referencing Tips for APA Format

Under APA formatting style, all in-text citations must be referenced and all references must be found as in-text citations. Each reference that you type indicates that you personally read the source and is a mark of your integrity. Writers who pad their references with sources they have not read, most likely copied someone's reference section/bibliography. Pretending that you have read something first-hand when you have not is dishonest. Additionally, you may likely reproduce inaccurate material or material that is out of context and therefore suspect. Learn the correct process and learn it thoroughly. This is especially important as you continue your tertiary education, publish in the field, present at conferences and even for your job.

References have a different format depending on the type of source (e.g., journal article, book, web page). Check the APA manual and the websites provided in the Links to Useful Resources at the end of this chapter for more information on referencing. The following examples illustrate how books (see examples 2.5, 2.6), and journal articles (see examples 2.7, 2.8) should be referenced when using the APA citation style.

# Literature Review

**Example 2.7** (Book with one author)

Donatelle, R. J. (2012). *My health: An outcomes approach.* San Francisco, CA: Benjamin Cummings.

| Author/Year | • Last name followed by a comma, then initial of first and middle names, followed by a full stop after each initial.<br>• Year of publication placed in brackets. Full stop after bracket. |
|---|---|
| Book Title | • Book title written in italics.<br>• Note punctuaton in book title, use of a capital letter after the colon, and full stop at end of the book title. |
| Publisher | • Address for publisher (generally city and state).<br>• Name of publisher.<br>• Note punctuation between city, state, and publisher. |

**Example 2.8** (Book with two or more authors)

Edmonds, E., & Gonzalez, M. (2010). *Caribbean religious history: An introduction.* New York, NY: NYU Press.

| Author/Year | • Last name followed by a comma, then initial of first and middle names followed by a comma and full stop.<br>• An ampersand (&) is used between the two names.<br>• Year of publication placed in brackets. Full stop after bracket. |
|---|---|
| Book Title | • Book title written in italics.<br>• Note punctuaton in book title, use of a capital letter after the colon, and full stop at end of the book title. |
| Publisher | • Address for publisher (generally city and state).<br>• Name of publisher.<br>• Note punctuation between city, state, and publisher. |

**Example 2.9** (Journal Article with one author)

Devonish, D. (2013). Job demands, health, and absenteeism: Does bullying make things worse? *Employee Relations 36* (2), 165-181. doi: 10.1108/ER-01-2013-0011

| Author/ Year | <ul><li>Last name followed by a comma, then initial of first and middle names followed by a full stop.</li><li>Year of publication is placed in brackets. Full stop after bracket.</li></ul> |
|---|---|
| Article Title | <ul><li>Article title in script font.</li><li>Note punctuaton in article title and use of a capital letter after the colon.</li></ul> |
| Journal Details | <ul><li>Journal name, followed by volume number, issue number, page number, and DOI.</li><li>Note punctuation. Journal name and volume are written in italics and the issue number and page number are in script font.</li><li>DOI is typed in lower case.</li><li>All words in the Journal title begin with a capital letter, except for prepositions and conjunctions.</li></ul> |

**Example 2.10** (Journal Article with two or more authors)

Persaud, N., & Persaud, I. (2016). The relationship between socio-demographics and stress levels, stressors, and coping mechanisms among undergraduate students at a university in Barbados. *International Journal of Higher Education, 5* (1), 11-27. doi:10.5430/ijhe.v5n1p11

| Author/ Year | <ul><li>Last name followed by a comma, then initial of first and middle names followed by a full stop and comma.</li><li>An ampersand (&) is used between the two names.</li><li>Year of publication is placed in brackets. Full stop after bracket.</li></ul> |
|---|---|
| Article Title | <ul><li>Article title in script font.</li><li>Note punctuaton in article title.</li></ul> |
| Journal Details | <ul><li>Journal name, followed by volume number, issue number, page number, and DOI.</li><li>Note punctuation. Journal name and volume number are written in italics and the issue number and page number are in script font.</li><li>DOI is typed in lower case.</li><li>All words in the journal title begin with a capital letter except for prepositions and conjunctions.</li></ul> |

Note also that DOIs identify journals in much the same way that books carry International Standard Book Numbers (ISBN). However, this is a relatively new trend and older journal articles may not have a DOI.

Edited books, chapters in an edited book, and those that have editions, web sources and newspapers are all referenced differently. You will need to check the APA manual to see how to reference these types of sources.

**TIP** If you learn the basic APA reference formats, when you look at the reference section provided by an author, you can immediately recognize, for example, which sources are books and which are journal articles.

## PLAGIARISM

Plagiarism occurs when a researcher uses any primary, secondary, or tertiary information source and does not give credit to the original author.

## What Constitutes Plagiarism

Plagiarism refers to when you use authors' ideas and/or words without giving them credit. It can take many forms (see table 2.5), and is considered a serious offence in the academic arena. According to the American Psychological Association (2007)

> Psychologists do not claim the words and ideas of another as their own; they give credit where credit is due. Quotation marks should be used to indicate the exact words of another. Each time you paraphrase another author (i.e., summarize a passage or rearrange the order of a sentence and change some of the words), you will need to credit the source. (p. 349)

Universities and research institutions have strict guidelines concerning plagiarism and the consequences of plagiarism. For students, consequences can include a zero for an assignment, suspension, dismissal from the institution, and/or payment of a fine. For staff, consequences can include a ruined career and/or termination of services. Therefore, researchers must avoid the temptation to commit plagiarism since it can now be easily detected with plagiarism software such as Turnitin.

Most academic institutions subscribe to professional plagiarism detection software that their staff and students can access to check their work. Always remember to check your work using your institution's plagiarism software before handing it in to your professors or sending it out for publication.

## Table 2.5: Types of Plagiarism

| Types of Plagiarism | Illustration |
|---|---|
| Quoting information without providing citations | **Example**<br>Diana reads the article from Persaud and Persaud (2016) and writes<br><br>*Research highlighted that females tended to use comfort mechanisms such as eating more to de-stress while males tended to use more negative coping strategies such as smoking/drugs.*<br><br>**Why is this Plagiarism?**<br>- Information is taken verbatim from Persaud and Persaud (2016).<br>- No citation is provided.<br>- Quotation marks are not included.<br><br>**Correct Way to Write (With a Quotation)**<br>"Research highlighted that females tended to use comfort mechanisms such as eating more to de-stress while males tended to use more negative coping strategies such as smoking/drugs" (Persaud & Persaud, 2016, p. 23). |
| Rephrasing sentences without citations | **Example**<br>Diana reads the following sentence in Persaud and Persaud (2016)<br><br>Additionally, younger students may be more inclined to drug use which can induce sleep directly (e.g., sleeping pills) (Zafar et al., 2008).<br><br>Diana then writes the following sentence in her paper.<br><br>*Less mature students may use medication to facilitate sleep.*<br><br>**Why is this Plagiarism?**<br>- Although Diana has paraphrased the information, she has not put a citation next to her sentence.<br>- Ideally, Diana should review the original source (i.e., Zafar et al., 2008). If Diana does not review the original source, she will have to cite the information in a different way.<br><br>**Correct Way to Write**<br>According to Zafar et al. (as cited in Persaud & Persaud, 2016), less mature students may use medication to facilitate sleep.<br><br>**Note:** You should avoid using too many *as cited in* sources. Always try to go back to the original source. |

| Types of Plagiarism | Illustration |
|---|---|
| Using cut, paste and rearrange (CPR) without providing citations | **Example**<br>Diana takes information from various sources, rearranges the information and writes:<br><br>*A strong social support network, in addition to improving campus mental health services and organizing peer counseling and self-help groups, help to beat stress experienced by students.*<br><br>**Why is this Plagiarism?**<ul><li>Diana took information from two web sources (MayoClinic, 2018)[1] and an executive summary of a book written by Whitman, Spendlove, and Clarke (1985).[2]</li><li>Three verbatim quotes from two sources are put together to form the sentence:<br>**A strong social support network**[1], in addition to **improving campus mental health services and organizing peer counseling and self-help groups**[2], help to **beat stress**[1] experienced by students.</li><li>No citation is given for any of the quotes.</li><li>Quotation marks are not used.</li><li>Note also that even if one citation was provided, this would still be considered plagiarism because the information came from two different sources.</li><li>Furthermore, Diana read only the summary, not the book.</li></ul>**Correct Way to Write (With a Quotation)**<br>"A strong social support network" (MayoClinic, 2018 ¶1), in addition to "improving campus mental health services and organizing peer counseling and self-help groups" (Whitman, Spendlove, & Clarke, 1985, p. 2) help to "beat stress" (MayoClinic, 2018, ¶1) experienced by students.<br><br>**Alternative Way to Write (Paraphrasing)**<br>Positive interactions with personal/significant others (MayoClinic, 2018), as well as the use of professional and peer counseling services offered by the university (Whitman, Spendlove, & Clarke, 1985), can help students to reduce stress.<br><br>**Note:** The symbol ¶ is used when information is quoted from an online source that does not contain page numbers. It means paragraph. You will need to manually count the number of paragraphs to get the paragraph number. |
| Reusing the same sentence structure as the original | **Example**<br>Diana reads the following sentence in Persaud and Persaud (2016)<br><br>The positive and negative aspects of stress can be visualized on a continuum.<br><br>Diana then writes the following sentence in her paper.<br>*The good and bad features of stress can be pictured on a field.* |

| Types of Plagiarism | Illustration |
|---|---|
| | **Why is this Plagiarism?**<br>- No credit (i.e., citation) is given to the original authors.<br>- Diana used the thesaurus and used replacement words out of context (e.g., **field** to replace the word **continuum**).<br>- Even if Diana cited the sentence she wrote, she has still plagiarized the sentence structure. Specifically, Diana has placed the adjectives, conjunctions, verbs, and nouns in her sentence in the same order as the original sentence.<br><br>| Original words | Parts of Speech | Diana's Words |<br>|---|---|---|<br>| The | definite article | The |<br>| positive | adjective (positive) | good |<br>| and | conjunction | and |<br>| negative | adjective (negative) | bad |<br>| aspects | noun | features |<br>| of | preposition | of |<br>| stress | noun | stress |<br>| can be visualized | verb | can be pictured |<br>| on | preposition | on |<br>| a | indefinite article | a |<br>| continuum | noun | field |<br><br>**Correct Way to Write**<br>According to Persaud and Persaud (2016), varying levels of stress can have a good, bad, or little to no effect on students.<br><br>| Diana's Paraphrase | Parts of Speech |<br>|---|---|<br>| According to | prepositional phrase |<br>| Persaud and Persaud (2016) | nouns+ conjunction |<br>| varying | adjective |<br>| levels | noun |<br>| of | preposition |<br>| stress | noun |<br>| can have | verbs |<br>| a | indefinite article |<br>| good | adjective (positive) |<br>| bad | adjective (negative) |<br>| little to no effect | adjectives |<br>| on | preposition |<br>| students | noun |<br><br>As you can see, the sentence structure of Diana's correct paraphrase is very different from the authors' original sentence and what Diana had initially written. Diana has cited her source and now she has not plagiarized the sentence structure. |

| Types of Plagiarism | Illustration |
|---|---|
| | The addition of the words *on students* in this paraphrase is acceptable based on the context of the journal article, while the descriptors good, bad, and little to no effect are captured within the original word continuum. |
| Self-plagiarism | • Reusing your own work from one course in another course without the permission of your lecturer/professor, and without changing the structure and wording is considered self-plagiarism.<br>• For example, if Diana decided to turn in the same paper that she wrote in her undergraduate Year 1 Management class for an assignment in her Year 2 Management class, she is guilty of self-plagiarism.<br>• Similarly, if she has published a paper and then sends much of the same content, without restructuring her sentences to a different publishing company, she has self-plagiarized.<br>• In either case, Diana can be sanctioned by her professor and/or an ethics board. |
| Buying or copying someone else's work and submitting it as your own. | This is cheating and is also known as authorship plagiarism. Your goal should always be to learn the correct process. You should always adhere to high ethical and professional standards. |

## Strategies to Avoid Plagiarism

The best strategy to avoid plagiarism is to use your own words and cite. Many persons find this challenging. However, there is a process that can help you to avoid the plagiarism pitfalls.

- Read the source (remember to use mainly primary sources).
- Select/highlight the information that relates to your research question(s). Here you can use colour coding if you have more than one research question. For example, use one colour to consistently highlight literature for research question 1 and another colour for research question 2. This visually separates information within the same source and among different sources.
- Read the highlighted information again and close the source.
- Write the relevant main points in your own words or take out your phone and record yourself.
- Type out what you have written or recorded and cite. Record the source reference in the citation style of your disciple/institution.
- Go back to the source and check that the meaning/context is similar, and that you have not used the same sentence structures.
- Put similar information together in paragraphs, under topic sentences. Ensure that you have all citations and references.
- Check for grammar. Poor grammar and poor spelling may cause some anti-plagiarism checkers to not pick up some plagiarism issues, but most likely, your professor will be able to spot plagiarism issues that the plagiarism checker did not catch.
- Run each section through a plagiarism checker (e.g., Turnitin). Make edits where necessary.
- After your final edit, use a plagiarism checker on the completed paper and make corrections again if necessary.

- Recheck your university/discipline citation style to ensure that you are adhering to the correct rules.

Do not procrastinate. The less time you have or give yourself to complete a paper, the more you can become frustrated. Frustration/anxiety is more likely to cause you distress and you may then begin to justify plagiarism and/or cheating.

More time means that when you run into challenges, you have the time to iron out the problems, edit multiple times, and present your best effort.

Where possible, choose a topic that you are really interested in doing. This promotes motivation, focus, and enthusiasm.

## SEARCHING FOR SOURCES

Searching for Sources requires the use of concepts, keywords, and refinement of such search terms.

## Search Strategy

There is no global best practice for conducting searches for literature. If you were to open any web browser and start to type some key words, it would probably bring up a hundreds, thousands, or even millions of results on your topic. You may therefore need to set some parameters to refine your search.

### Using your General Topic to Identify Key Concepts

Suppose you were interested in reviewing literature on the topic *aggression* and you opened the **Google** search engine and typed in this word. If you really do not know which aspect of *aggression* you would like to research, then a quick scan of the topics that pop up within one or two pages on your **Google** search may help you to make a decision. The bottom of the **Google** search engine home page also provides a list of more specific searches pertaining to the topic *aggression*.

### Google

**Searches related to aggression**

| | |
|---|---|
| causes of aggression | aggression antonym |
| types of aggression | **aggression examples** |
| aggression quotes | theories of aggression |

At this point, you may decide to choose *aggression examples* which will provide examples of physical and verbal aggression. This may cause you to think about other concepts (e.g., bullying, domestic violence, gangs). You can then narrow your search by (1) doing a manual brainstorming activity or (2) providing more specific key concepts/phrases for the search engine (e.g., physical bullying on the playground, theories of domestic violence, aggression in young children). If you type 'pdf' after the key concepts/key phrases, you can then access peer reviewed articles that pop up, which you can scan/read. Similarly, you can type in the term aggression in a database such as EBSCOhost and use the limiters to refine your search.

**DATABASE**

- When you type the word aggression in the box, a number of possibilities appear in a drop down box (e.g., aggression in children, aggression and violent behavior, aggression in sports).

- You can refine your search at this point or just continue. This will bring up over 50,000 possibilities on **'aggression'**.

- If you limit your search to full text and scholarly peer reviewed journals, you will now get about 10,000 articles on **'aggression'**.

- If you further refine your search to say **'aggression in young children'**, about 50 peer-reviewed full articles pop up. This is definitely a more manageable number from which to start.

- If you type the words **'review of aggression in young children'** or **'aggression in young children review'**, one peer-reviewed article comes up about television viewing and video games. You might decide that this will be your topic. At any rate, you now have a 2009 article whose reference section can be helpful.

Databases such as EBSCOhost also use Boolean phrases such as **'aggression in young children'** and limiters to help you refine your searches. You can also use advanced searches of databases. For example, in EBSCOhost, the advanced search provides additional fields where you can add words to refine your search even more.

## Using your Research Question to Identify Key Concepts

If you already have a research question, it should signify that you have already read relatively extensively on your topic of interest. Therefore, you can use key words from the research question to access further information and try to access articles and books from the reference section of material you have already gathered. There are also keywords found on peer-reviewed articles that you might also put into a search engine/database for more information on the topic.

You can also type in actual journal titles and then within those journals you can also type keywords to access the articles. The only problem here is that in a database like EBSCOhost, you will get many articles from that journal so you will need to use the advanced search feature. Type the name of the journal in the top field box. Then type in your keywords in the other boxes. Limit your search by date to the more recent articles/books since limiting by date helps you to find the most recent literature on the topic.

## Popular Databases

There are numerous databases that researchers can use to find information. Academic institutions subscribe to many databases so that students and staff can have access to scholarly resources. Notwithstanding, institutions do have different contract agreements regarding what types of materials can be downloaded free of charge by students and staff at the institution. Table 2.6 provides information on popular databases used by many colleges and universities.

### Table 2.6: Databases by Discipline

| Discipline | EBSCOhost | ERIC | ProQuest | Sage Journals | WorldCat |
|---|---|---|---|---|---|
| Business | ✓ | ✓ | ✓ | ✓ | ✓ |
| Criminology | ✓ | ✓ | ✓ | ✓ | ✓ |
| Economics | ✓ | ✓ | ✓ | ✓ | ✓ |
| Education | ✓ | ✓ | ✓ | ✓ | ✓ |
| Geography | ✓ | ✓ | ✓ | ✓ | ✓ |
| History | ✓ | ✓ | ✓ | ✓ | ✓ |
| Law | ✓ | ✓ | ✓ | ✓ | ✓ |
| Linguistics | ✓ | ✓ | ✓ | ✓ | ✓ |
| Medicine | ✓ | ✓ | ✓ | ✓ | ✓ |
| Management | ✓ | ✓ | ✓ | ✓ | ✓ |
| Nursing |  | ✓ | ✓ | ✓ | ✓ |
| Political Science | ✓ | ✓ | ✓ | ✓ | ✓ |
| Project Management | ✓ |  | ✓ | ✓ | ✓ |
| Project Evaluation | ✓ |  | ✓ | ✓ | ✓ |
| Psychology | ✓ | ✓ | ✓ | ✓ | ✓ |
| Sociology | ✓ | ✓ | ✓ | ✓ | ✓ |

 **TIP** Learn about and use the library resources that are available at your college/university. The more you know about what is available and how to access these resources before you have any major assignment, the less stress you will experience. Use as many relevant databases as you can to find the most up to date material.

## LINKS TO USEFUL RESOURCES

| Type of Resource | Link |
| --- | --- |
| APA Citation Format | <ul><li>http://www.apastyle.org/learn/tutorials/basics-tutorial.aspx</li><li>https://owl.english.purdue.edu/owl/resource/560/02/</li><li>**Sample Paper:** https://owl.english.purdue.edu/owl/resource/560/18/</li></ul> |
| Chicago (Author-Date) Citation Format | <ul><li>http://www.chicagomanualofstyle.org/home.html</li><li>http://www.chicagomanualofstyle.org/tools_citationguide.html</li><li>https://www.cavehill.uwi.edu/cermes/getdoc/4115ae89-95554b41-ae32-b28739335d34/cite_chicago_style_dec2013.asp</li><li>**Sample Paper:** https://owl.english.purdue.edu/owl/resource/717/11/</li></ul> |
| Harvard (Author-Date) Citation Format | <ul><li>https://intranet.birmingham.ac.uk/as/libraryservices/library/referencing/icite/referencing/harvard/index.aspx</li><li>https://www2.le.ac.uk/library/help/referencing/author-date</li><li>**Sample Paper:** http://dkit.ie.libguides.com/harvard/sample</li></ul> |
| Plagiarism Software | <ul><li>**Turnitin Plagiarism Checker** – http://turnitin.com/gateway/index.html Check for access at your university</li><li>**Plagiarism Checker** – http://smallseotools.com/plagiarism-checker/</li><li>**Advanced Plagiarism Checker** – https://searchenginereports.net/plagiarism-checker</li></ul> |
| Transition Words | <ul><li>http://www.smart-words.org/linking-words/transition-words.html</li><li>https://owl.english.purdue.edu/owl/resource/574/02/</li></ul> |
| Grammar Checker | <ul><li>https://www.grammarly.com/</li><li>https://www.paperrater.com/</li></ul> |
| Free Citation Software | <ul><li>http://www.citethisforme.com/citation-generator/apa   (All Styles)</li><li>http://www.zotero.org/</li><li>http://www.bibme.org/</li></ul> |

# 3 Methodology and Study Designs

- Research Methodology
- Experiments
- Observations
- Surveys
- Interviews
- Focus Groups
- Case Studies
- Document Review and Analysis
- Mixed Methods Approach

## RESEARCH METHODOLOGY

Research Methodology refers to a set of rules/ideas/principles that guide research within a specific discipline.

### Basic Overview

The term research methodology generally refers to how the research is conducted with regards to data collection types and procedures. From chapter 1 you learned how to formulate your research question(s) (most likely based on a specific theory), but how do you now determine which research approach is best for gathering your data? Actually, you will need to have at least a basic understanding about various types of research methodology, identify which aspects seem to be more appropriate and/or beneficial for your research and then do more advanced reading on each type before you can make an informed decision.

You will also need to determine if your research question(s) will be best answered through quantitative

and/or qualitative methods (see chapters 7 and 8 respectively). Your final decision will need to be balanced against realistic considerations such as the time frame for the study, budget, availability of a suitable sampling frame (see chapter 5), your data collection and analyses competencies (see chapter 5, 7, 8), and most importantly, your research question(s) (see chapter 1).

If you cannot decide which methodology to use, you can check the literature to find out the research methodology of those who have published in your field and topic area. Based on their findings and methodological limitations, you can then make a better determination of which methods will best fit in with your topic area while bearing in mind your own skills and knowledge in social science research methodology. Table 3.1 provides a brief overview of the various research methods along with their pros and cons. The remainder of the chapter provides more explanation on each of the various methodologies presented in table 3.1.

### Table 3.1: Pros and Cons of Various Research Methods

| Method | Quantitative | Qualitative | PROS | CONS |
|---|---|---|---|---|
| Experiments | ✓ | x | - Cause and effect principles establish that the independent variable affects the dependent variable.<br>- Both the experimental and control groups have the same characteristics except for the independent variable(s).<br>- Better results since extraneous variables are controlled.<br>- Internal validity is much higher. | - Can be expensive when specialized lab equipment is required, and when participants have to be paid.<br>- Demand characteristic issues – participants may change their behaviour to please the researcher.<br>- Researcher effect/experimenter bias issues – researchers may consciously or unconsciously look for what they wish to find or indicate to the participants what they wish as the outcome, thereby biasing the results.<br>- Artificial setting – a lab is not a real world setting.<br>- May lack real world application (low external validity). |
| Observations | ✓ | ✓ | - Descriptive – provides detailed information on what is observed.<br>- If done covertly, there is no researcher effect on observed behaviour.<br>- Useful when an experiment is unethical or impractical.<br>- Has ecological and external validity. | - May lack real world application.<br>- May lack objectivity or standardization of observations.<br>- Lacks scientific rigour. Inability to control variables may cause results to be unreliable.<br>- If done overtly, social desirability biases may occur.<br>- There may be ethical issues such as lack of consent and deception as well as legal implications.<br>- Poor inter-observer reliability will result if observers are not properly trained. |

| Method | Quantitative | Qualitative | PROS | CONS |
|---|---|---|---|---|
| Focus Groups | x | ✓ | <ul><li>Rich, in-depth descriptive information.</li><li>Can identify possible patterns in responses between/among focus groups.</li><li>Allows researcher to gather data in a shared and interactive setting.</li></ul> | <ul><li>Small groups lack generalizability.</li><li>Some members may dominate the discussion and there is a risk of going off topic if the moderator is not skilled.</li><li>Possible inappropriate questions if not piloted.</li><li>Participants may not respond to sensitive questions.</li></ul> |
| Surveys | ✓ | ✓ | <ul><li>Standardized questions.</li><li>Can have both close-ended and open ended-questions.</li><li>Easy to administer.</li><li>Useful for large samples.</li><li>Especially cost-effective for online surveys.</li><li>Can be both descriptive and correlational.</li></ul> | <ul><li>Possible inappropriate questions if not piloted.</li><li>Non-response to specific questions possible.</li><li>Socially desirable answers possible.</li><li>Participants may not respond to sensitive questions.</li><li>Higher costs for paper-based surveys, for follow-up, and replacement surveys.</li><li>May have poor survey completion and return rate.</li></ul> |
| Interviews | ✓ | ✓ | <ul><li>Flexible as it can be face-to-face, online, telephone, group, individuals.</li><li>Rich, in-depth data is obtained.</li><li>If face-to-face, you can use both verbal and non-verbal information/cues.</li><li>Can be formal or informal depending on topic and research goals.</li><li>Can gain additional information through probing.</li></ul> | <ul><li>Can be costly in time/effort/resources depending on type of interview.</li><li>Usually a small sample size which limits generalizability unless the population is small (e.g., persons who have had corpus callosum surgery for chronic epilepsy).</li><li>Socially desirable answers possible.</li><li>Phone interview cannot capture non-verbal cues.</li><li>Untrained interviewers compromise standard practices and affect results.</li></ul> |
| Case Studies | ✓ | ✓ | <ul><li>Rich, in-depth descriptive information.</li><li>Generally qualitative, but there can also be quantitative aspects.</li><li>Utilizes multiple methods of data collection.</li><li>Relies on multiple perspectives within a single case.</li></ul> | <ul><li>Usually one case so it lacks generalizability.</li><li>Time consuming.</li><li>Focus is on one case which provides depth, but not breadth.</li><li>Subjective as it is based on the interests of the researcher and based on what the participant/group/organization has indicated. May require objective collaboration/evidence (e.g., via medical records, tests, eyewitnesses, etc. to authenticate information).</li></ul> |

# Methodology and Study Designs

| Method | Quantitative | Qualitative | PROS | CONS |
|---|---|---|---|---|
| Document Analysis | ✓ | ✓ | • Cost effective.<br>• Relies on objective documented sources.<br>• No researcher effect on findings. | • Time consuming.<br>• Researcher may be subjective in terms of document choices.<br>• Sources may be dated or unavailable. |
| Mixed Methods | ✓ | ✓ | • If properly done, it can lead to more credible and robust results.<br>• Vast array of data that complement each method to give a more holistic picture. | • Cost in time, effort, and other resources.<br>• Requires that researcher be knowledgeable in both quantitative and qualitative methodologies.<br>• Requires researcher's competence to handle all required areas from implementation to analyses. |

## Types of Research and Common Research Methods

| | |
|---|---|
| **Descriptive**<br>• Case Studies<br>• Observations<br>• Surveys | If I want to find out how polar bears survive harsh winters I might choose a descriptive study. |
| **Causal**<br>• Experiments | If I want to find out if consumers will purchase more of a product depending on if it is attractively packaged or not, I might want to conduct an experiment to examine cause and effect. |
| **Exploratory**<br>• Observations<br>• Focus Groups<br>• Case Studies<br>• Surveys | If I want to find out what consumers think about a new product, I might want to consider an exploratory research study. |

**TIP**: The research methodology used must be suitable to your discipline, your research question(s), and the nature of your study. An inappropriate methodology will result in skewed/biased or inaccurate results and cannot be compared to past research. Its value and use will therefore be questioned.

# EXPERIMENTS

Experiments are used to determine cause and effect.

## Basic Overview of Experiments

Within an experiment, a hypothesis about the relationships between variables under investigation is stated. Then, you manipulate one variable (i.e., the independent variable), while holding another constant to determine what, if any, changes occur in the dependent variable (refer to chapter 1). The results will either confirm/support or disconfirm/not support your hypothesis.

The Social Scientist studies people

## Types of Experimental Designs

There are generally two types of experimental designs. The first type is the independent measures design (or the between groups design) which involves testing the effects of one or more independent variables on a dependent variable through the creation of separate participant groups representing different levels of the independent variable. The second type is the repeated measures design (or the within group design) which involves repeated testing of the same group of participants to examine effects on a dependent variable (e.g., a pretest-posttest).

Many variants of independent and repeated measures designs can be used. Researchers should assess the strengths and weakness of both the independent measures design and the repeated measures design before choosing a design. For further discussion on the variants of the two designs, researchers should refer to the dated but invaluable resource by Campbell and Stanley (1963).

## Aspects that Need to be Considered when Conducting an Experiment

Many different aspects need to be considered if you plan to conduct an experiment. For example, what are your sample demographics? Which sampling method would be most suitable to the nature of your particular study? How will your variables be operationalized (i.e., measured)? Are there likely to be placebo effects? How will your independent variables be manipulated? Are there external (i.e., extraneous) variables that can influence your experiment? What procedures will be used? These aspects, among others, all require careful thought since all sample aspects affect the generalizability of your results. Example 3.1 will be used to discuss these aspects.

### Example 3.1

Suppose you wish to test the effectiveness of a new energy drink (independent variable) on the attention span (dependent variable) of young adults.

## Sample Demographics

Your sample demographics provide fundamental criteria for your sample selection but should be relevant to your overall hypotheses or research questions. Some demographics that you may wish to consider for the research question in example 3.1 might include:

- Age – which specific age range to include (anybody or young adults aged 18–20)?
- Sex – males and females or just one group?
- Race/Ethnicities – all races/ethnicities or only one group?
- Occupation – any group or a particular group such as university students?

## Sample Method

The best way to choose participants in a true experiment is when you use a probability sampling methodology (e.g., simple random selection). This sample selection method allows everyone in the target population to have an equal chance to participate in the experiment. In example 3.1, it was specified that the researcher is interested in learning about the effect of an energy drink on young adults. Since the researcher has a specific criterion (i.e., young adults), the researcher will be unable to use a simple random selection method to select his/her participants from the general population. However, s/he can randomly choose a sample from a list of young persons enrolled at a university campus. Chapter 5 provides more discussion on various probability sampling methodologies.

From a scientific perspective, probability sampling methods are the most robust type of methodology. However, there are certain instances in which the use of a probability sampling methodology may not be suitable and may actually raise ethical concerns. For instance, if you are interested in customer feedback regarding a new alcoholic beverage in a particular town, all persons in this town might not qualify as the target population since non-drinkers and children cannot be classified as consumers of alcoholic beverages. Including them would therefore be a violation of research ethics and practices.

## Conceptualizing and Operationalizing of Variables

Put simply, operationalizing refers to how your variables will be measured (see chapter 4). When conducting research, it is important that the researcher and readers know what your variables are and how they are measured? For instance, in example 3.1, the dependent variable is *attention span*. However, attention span can mean different things to different researchers. Thus, it is important that the researcher provides a definition for *attention span* so that everyone can interpret the variable in the same way. This will facilitate accurate measurement of the variable. With reference to example 3.1, you could use the completion time for various tasks or the measurement of brain wave patterns as your participants engage in structured tasks. Note that standardized measures should be used for all dependent variable(s).

## Placebo

Oftentimes, participants in an experiment may try to determine what the experimenters want and deliberately behave in that manner. This is referred to as *demand characteristics*. For instance, in example 3.1, your participants may say that they are more focused after they drink the new energy drink because they may have picked up the reason for the experiment and wish to help you, the researcher.

A placebo helps to determine if the independent variable is really effective. It is really a non-treatment presented as the legitimate treatment – a deception to guard against demand characteristics. For a placebo to be useful, the placebo group has to have all the characteristics of the experimental group, except for the actual treatment.

If you get similar results for the placebo and the new energy drink, then the energy drink is ineffective. If the placebo group demonstrates a higher attention span, there might be a possibility of social desirability. If the energy drink produces better results, then your hypothesis is supported.

## Manipulation of Independent Variables

One of the principal activities of an experiment is to manipulate the independent variable. In example 3.1, the independent variable is *consumption of a new energy drink* and the dependent variable is *attention span*. There are two ways in which an experimenter can manipulate the independent variable. One method involves using an independent measures design. In this method, the researcher may divide a group of participants into two separate groups, an experimental group and a control group. The experimental group receives the experimental treatment (e.g., the energy drink itself) while the control group receives a placebo (e.g., flavoured water) or nothing (see figure 3.1). After the treatment, the dependent variable (i.e., attention span) is observed for both groups.

**Figure 3.1: Independent Measures Design**

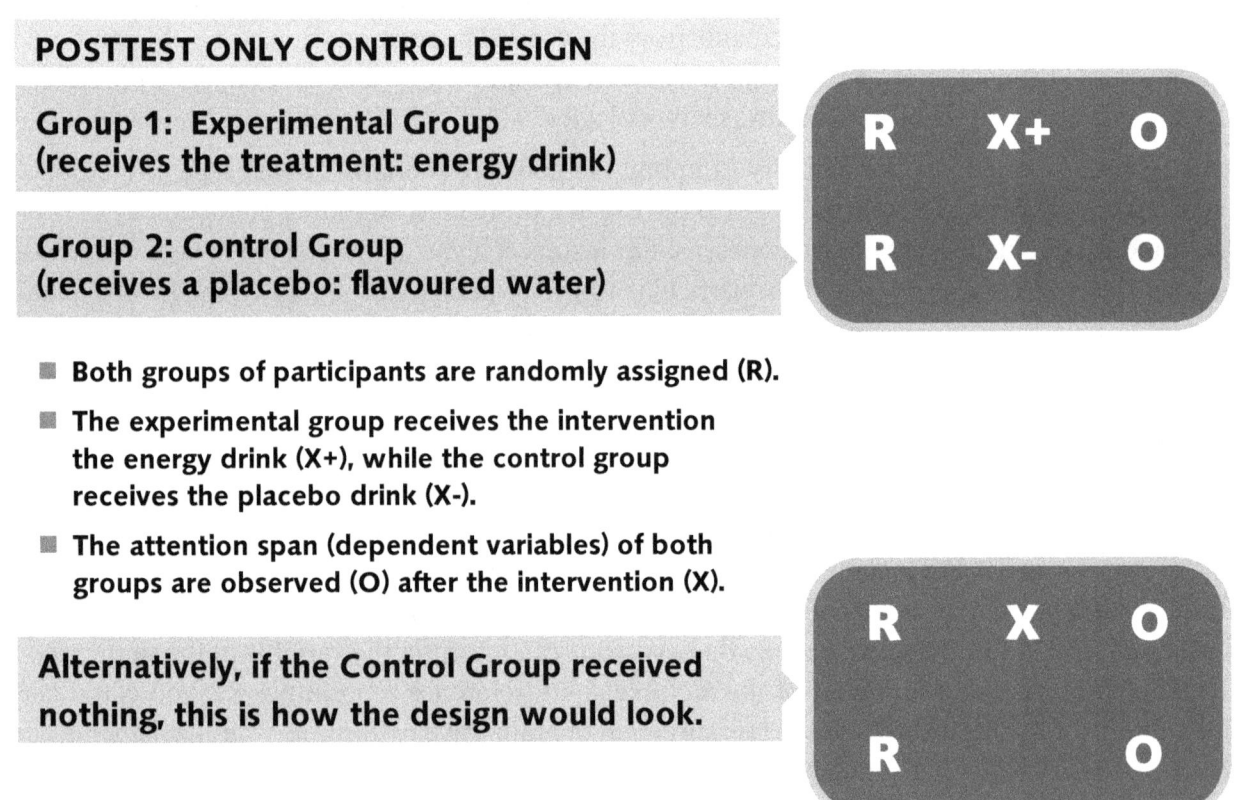

The other approach is a repeated measures design. In its simplest form, the same group of participants receives one pretest and one posttest (see figure 3.2). For example, the dependent variable (attention span) is observed before and after the experimental treatment is administered for the same group of participants. The major advantage of a repeated measures design is that fewer participants are required since a separate control group is not needed. Essentially, the control and treatment group is the same group of subjects since all subjects are exposed to all treatments at different times.

## Figure 3.2: Repeated Measures Design

### PRETEST AND POSTTEST GROUP DESIGN

**All subjects are exposed to all treatments. Essentially, the same group of participants functions as both the experimental and control group.**

- Participants are randomly assigned to the group (R).
- All participants are given a pretest and posttest. The pretest $O^1$ (i.e., the measurement of attention span before the treatment) is conducted at the start of the experiment.
- All participants receive the same stimulant or treatment X (i.e., the energy drink).
- The posttest $O^2$ (i.e., the measurement of attention span after the treatment) is conducted at the end of the experiment.
- Comparisons are made between the pretest and the posttest.

$$\text{Group} \quad R \quad O_1 \quad X \quad O_2$$

## Extraneous Variables

These are variables that can influence the outcome of an experiment that you did not deliberately control, thereby skewing the outcome. To control for such effects in example 3.1, you may need to control for time of day. This is important because individuals' attention spans may change according to the time of day. In the morning, people generally tend to have more energy. Using an energy drink in the morning may not have the same effect as using an energy drink in the afternoon when persons may be tired. To further gauge the true effects of the energy drink on attention span, the researcher may also need to control diet.

For instance, the researcher may ask participants to refrain from drinking caffeine some hours before the experiment because if participants consume caffeine, the researcher will not be able to determine if it is the energy drink or the caffeine that is influencing his/her participants.

## Single Blind vs Double Blind Procedure

One of two procedures is commonly used in experiments. In a single blind procedure, the participants alone are unaware of the conditions whereas the research staff members are aware of the conditions. In a double blind procedure, neither the research staff nor the participants are aware of the conditions and treatment. The latter approach guards against any conscious or unconscious experimenter bias or demand characteristics.

**TIP:** When you identify cause and effect through experimentation, there should be little likelihood of an alternative explanation, and other researchers should be able to replicate your study and findings.

# OBSERVATIONS

**Observations are used to record data in a systematic way without attempting to influence the outcome.**

## When to Use Observational Research?

Observational research can be used in any discipline but is widely used in the fields of marketing, psychology, and criminology. Researchers turn to observational techniques when they want to study some phenomenon in great detail in its natural environment. Observational techniques can be either overt (i.e., participants know that they are being observed) or covert (participants are unaware that they are being observed). Overt approaches may cause participants to change their behaviour since they are aware that they are being observed, whereas covert approaches can have ethical implications.

## Observational Techniques

There are a variety of settings in which observations can be used including naturalistic, ethology, laboratory, and field settings.

### Naturalistic

A naturalistic observation is where you objectively observe people and animals in their natural habitat without interfering with these participants. For example, you can record how many times young people (ages 18–30) actually smoke cigarettes in a bar, note the interaction of children on a playground, or film or record information about drug activity in a specific area.

As a naturalistic researcher you need to consider the following: First, you might be observing, recording, and/or filming persons without their consent which may raise ethical concerns. Second, you will need to ensure that you do not call undue attention to yourself since this will cause those under observation to change their behaviour (i.e., Hawthorn Effect). Therefore, you should try to dress and behave in a manner which allows you to blend into the environment to avoid drawing unnecessary attention to yourself or you may be challenged, verbally abused, or physically assaulted. You will also need to determine your course of action if you see a situation where a person you are observing will be hurt or killed. Do you have an ethical, moral, and/or legal obligation to at least call the police? In all situations, you need to be cautious and diplomatic.

Another form of naturalistic observation refers to the study of animals in the wild (e.g., gorillas, chimpanzees, lions). Documentaries about animals are naturalistic observations as long as the videographer did not try to interfere with the day-to-day life of the animals. Although seemingly cruel, if a baby chimp is attacked, killed and eaten, the videographer is not supposed to make any attempt to stop the predator (e.g., by firing a gun).

### Ethology

Ethology is a type of naturalistic observation of both humans and animals. However, the researcher's goal is to identify common adaptive/evolutionary behaviours among, rather than within, species. For example, work by Lorenz (1970) on birds and other mammals allowed Lorenz to determine that animals instinctively use imprinting as a survival mechanism.

## Laboratory Setting

To gain more control, you can observe using a more controlled environment. For example, using a one way mirror, you can observe children engaging in play activities inside a room that you set up with toys. This allows the researcher to observe without being detected, thus avoiding the common issues inherent in participants who recognize that they are being observed.

## Field Studies

This technique is a compromise between the naturalistic and the laboratory study. Here, the researcher applies a level of control and manipulation within the naturalistic setting. For example, you might wish to test the cost and reward theory from Piliavin, Rodin, and Piliavin's (1969) 'Good Samaritanism: An Underground Phenomenon' in a less controlled setting. You may solicit an accomplice to pretend that s/he is drunk, ask the person to fall in a public park on a Sunday afternoon, and sit back and observe if any one helps, who (male or female) helps, how long it takes, and if another accomplice had to first model the helping behaviour.

## Ethical Concerns with Observational Research

Observational research can provide rich insight into behaviours which cannot be obtained by any other means. However, critics argue that covert observation involving humans may raise ethical concerns since participants are not aware that they are under observation and that their behaviour is being recorded. There is some debate that even though certain behaviours, for example, kissing and fondling, are performed in the public domain, that they should not be recorded by others without the permission of the persons involved. Others contend that once a behaviour is performed in the public domain, the 'actors' have given up their right to privacy as long as you do not infringe on their actual space. This dilemma may be cleared up with a judgment call, your ethics board, and/or speaking with colleagues.

Naturalistic observation has both ecological and external validity due to the real world setting. Consequently, findings can be generalized to the wider population.

# SURVEYS

**Surveys are one of the most common ways of gathering data in the social sciences.**

## Overview

In its most basic form, a survey is comprised of a number of questions that elicit information from a group of people (respondents). It is a common data collection instrument used by various sectors of the society and for different reasons. For example, surveys can be used to identify and solicit the extent of certain health behaviours and health care concerns, to garner information about the effects of socio-economic issues, to improve business by testing customer satisfaction of a new product, or soliciting feedback on customer care.

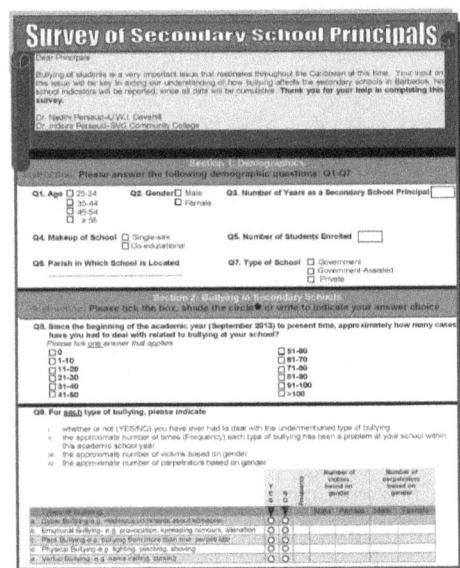

## Surveys Characteristics

Surveys have the undermentioned characteristics suited to data gathering:

### Versatility

Surveys are quite versatile. They are exceedingly useful for collecting information on a wide range of issues. Common types of information include views, attitudes, behaviours, preferences, and experiences. Surveys generally use two types of questions (closed-ended versus open-ended) depending on the research objectives (see table 3.2).

Close-ended questions can be dichotomous (two categories) or can have more than two categories (multinominal). For example, a question can take a yes/no format or may have several choices such as hair colour. Alternatively, close-ended questions can be classified into ordinal (e.g., Likert scales), interval (e.g., Slider scales), or ratio (e.g., annual income). In contrast, open-ended questions are free response or qualitative in nature.

### Anonymity

Surveys provide a platform for possibly more honest and less socially desirable answers, although this may not always be the case especially for controversial issues (e.g., sexual behaviour and preferences).

### Coverage, Convenience, and Costs

Surveys are used for large samples since they can reach a large number of persons within the target population with relatively low costs in time/effort/money.

## Table 3.2: Types of Survey Questions

| Survey Question Type | Example |
|---|---|
| **Close-Ended Nominal Question** (order has no meaning) | Have you counselled repeat perpetrators of bullying?<br>☐ Yes<br>☐ No |
| **Close-Ended Ordinal Question** (based only on ranking order) | On the scale below (**1** denotes **Very Unlikely** and **5 Very Likely**), indicate how likely you are to buy the A to Z Energy Bar again.<br><br>1 — 2 — 3 — 4 — 5<br>Very Unlikely ............ Very Likely |
| **Close-Ended Interval Question** (based on ranking order and equal interval) | At which outdoor temperature (°C) do you feel most comfortable?<br><br>-5  0  5  10  15  20  25  30  35  40  45  50  55 |
| **Close-Ended Ratio Question** (ranking order, equal intervals, and absolute zero) | How many years have you held a job? |
| **Open-Ended Question** (free response answer) | In your opinion, what should be done to address the issue of chronic littering throughout the country? |

## Stimuli Control

Surveys can assist with stimuli control, that is, each respondent receives the same stimulus from each question in the same way and can respond individually without the bias/influence of the survey administrator.

## Issues to Consider when Using Surveys

Surveys are convenient and elicit rich information providing that they are well thought out, properly designed and administered, and accurately analysed. A good survey requires an effective approach throughout the entire process (inception, administration, and data analysis). Your survey questions must be in keeping with your research questions/objectives. You should already know which tests you will be using to analyse the data in order to determine whether you will use close-ended or open-ended questions (see chapter 4), and what coding you will use in order to make data analysis efficient and effective (see chapter 6). All questions should be piloted (see chapter 5) to determine clarity, ease of navigation, and suitability/appropriateness. This is especially important when sensitive issues (e.g., sexual behaviour, illegal drug use) are surveyed, and/or vulnerable groups (e.g., children, at risk teens, the elderly, patients) make up the sample. Table 3.3 provides a list of pros and cons of common survey types.

## Table 3.3: Pros and Cons of Common Survey Types

| | PROS | CONS |
|---|---|---|
| **Paper Based Mail Survey** | <ul><li>Standardized appearance.</li><li>Sample can be large.</li><li>Convenient to the respondent.</li><li>Wider access to population.</li><li>Gathers a large amount of information in a relatively short time.</li></ul> | <ul><li>Time consuming.</li><li>Response rate may be low and may require constant follow-up.</li><li>Costs may be high.</li><li>May not be able to easily track respondents.</li><li>Not ecologically friendly due to quantities of paper.</li><li>May appear crowded due to fact that all tick boxes have to be visible.</li></ul> |
| **Electronic Survey** | <ul><li>Response rate may be high and quick.</li><li>Cost is low.</li><li>Sample can be large.</li><li>More user friendly and less crowded due to drop down boxes.</li><li>Able to redirect respondents to questions based on their responses.</li><li>Easy to track respondents.</li></ul> | <ul><li>Appearance may differ depending on the screen used for viewing.</li><li>Difficult/impossible for those who are computer illiterate.</li><li>Online surveys can crash.</li><li>Some participants may be excluded because they do not have a computer or access to the internet.</li><li>Low response rate.</li></ul> |
| **Telephone Survey** | <ul><li>More convenient to reach certain groups like the elderly.</li><li>Response rate may be high and quick.</li><li>Some respondents prefer to speak with someone rather than write.</li><li>The questioning phase is guided and supervised by the interviewer and not dependent on the participant's literacy level.</li></ul> | <ul><li>Phone calls can be expensive.</li><li>Many phone numbers are unlisted, which means that certain participants are excluded.</li><li>It may not be possible or affordable to get a sampling frame for mobile phone numbers.</li><li>Participants may not feel comfortable discussing sensitive matters over the phone.</li><li>Participants may not be free to engage in dialogue.</li></ul> |

**TIP** Surveys are great for research involving large populations. Surveys that use close-ended questions are relatively simple to code and analyse.

# Methodology and Study Designs

# INTERVIEWS

**Interviews refer to conversations between the researcher and persons of research interest.**

## Formal vs Informal Interviews

Interviews can be either formal (structured) or informal (unstructured). Each type has its pros and cons (see table 3.4). In a formal interview the researcher uses a standardized instrument which permits no deviation. The researcher can use either closed-ended questions, and/or open-ended questions. However, the researcher must strictly follow a predetermined format and record the responses. In contrast, an informal interview is one that is conversational in nature and permits flexibility. This type of interview allows the respondent to give totally free style responses (i.e., questions are open-ended) and permits the researcher to add or delete questions depending on the conversation.

**Table 3.4: Pros and Cons of Formal vs Informal Interviews**

|  | PROS | CONS |
|---|---|---|
| Formal | <ul><li>Easy to replicate.</li><li>Easy to analyse data with close-ended questions.</li><li>Less time consuming than an informal interview when the majority of questions are close-ended.</li></ul> | <ul><li>No flexibility allowed.</li><li>Loss of clarifying data if only close-ended questions are used.</li></ul> |
| Informal | <ul><li>Flexible.</li><li>Allows researcher to probe to better understand an issue.</li><li>Moves at the pace of the interviewee.</li></ul> | <ul><li>Time consuming to conduct.</li><li>Time consuming to analyse mostly free response data.</li><li>May be more expensive in comparison to a formal interview comprised of only close-ended questions.</li></ul> |

## When are Interviews Used?

Interviews are suited to a variety of situations. You may use interviews to explore a new research topic or to help you refine/decide on your research questions. Interviews can also be used to gather multiple perspectives from different stakeholders, and access more details about a specific aspect. Such conversations may be formal or informal.

## Interview Modes

Interviews basically take one of two modes. Face-to-face interviews can be conducted with both the interviewer and interviewee in one location, or can be conducted from a remote location using technology such as video conferencing or Skype. Face-to-face informal interviews allow you as the researcher to rely on non-verbal cues to gauge if clarification needs to be sought for a particular question, if questions need to be asked in a different way, or if certain questions should be left for later in the interview. Telephone interviews are another popular way to conduct interviews. These interviews are usually more formal in nature with structured responses.

## Costs Associated with Interviews

Costs are an important consideration for all types and modes of interviews. Informal interviews may be more costly compared to formal interviews if they require more time for the actual interview, more training for the interviewers, and more time for data analysis. The interview mode utilized also has cost implications. For instance, in-person face-to-face interviews are more costly compared to face-to-face interviews conducted using a social media platform such as Skype. The number of responders who are interviewed will also impact cost. Therefore, cost considerations always have to be balanced against benefits.

## Issues to Keep in Mind when Conducting Interviews

Overall, when you decide on conducting an interview, you should exude professionalism in dress, manner, and interview skills (see chapter 6 and Persaud, 2010). You also need to be personable and diplomatic, yet remain objective. Otherwise, your respondent will not be comfortable in the interview and may decline to answer certain sensitive questions.

Ensure that you have piloted, and then practised the questions.

Check your equipment (e.g., tape recorder).

Dress professionally, or in keeping with your environment, depending on what is likely to put your participant at ease.

Do not make judgmental remarks.

Body language is important. You can nod to encourage your respondent to continue but always try to remain objective.

# FOCUS GROUPS

**Focus Groups are sessions facilitated by a moderator which bring together small, diverse groups of persons who provide insight into an issue.**

## Purpose of a Focus Group

The purpose of any focus group is to get answers to specific questions. Therefore, if the focus group is to be truly effective, you the researcher, as the focus group moderator, have to be quite skilful in managing the focus group discussion. The goal of a focus group is to get group members to freely interact with each other and to actually carry the session. However, in a focus group setting, it is quite possible (particularly if a controversial topic is being discussed) for a few individuals to try to dominate the conversation and perhaps even try to intimidate other participants. As the moderator, you will need to ensure that this does not happen. It is important that all voices are heard – not just the most powerful, wealthiest, and/or loudest.

Sometimes you may also need to ask persons to clarify their stance on a specific issue (e.g., a product, a new health care policy), provide solutions (e.g., more effective care of the elderly), and give feedback (e.g., about behaviours, views, and experiences). The success of any focus group depends on the moderator's skills to keep the group members focused and interactive, to ensure that the conversation does not stray from the topic, to solicit contributions from all participants, and to control the time response of any one participant. Focus group moderators need to be firm, but diplomatic, in order to ensure that useful discussion takes place in the focus group forum.

## Key Issues to Consider when Thinking about a Focus Group

Here are some questions you need to consider before you attempt to use a focus group in your research:

- Why have you decided on this data gathering method for your research?
- Is this your best choice?
- Have you formulated clear and suitable open-ended questions to maintain interest in the topic?
- Have you piloted the guided questions for clarity, sensitivity, and overall acceptability?
- Are the questions relevant to your research question(s)?
- What criteria (e.g., demographics, participants' experiences with the issue, topic or product) will you use to select the group members?
- How many members (e.g., five to ten) will comprise the group?
- What is the length of time for the focus group session? It is generally recommended that focus group sessions should not exceed three hours. If more time is needed, a second session may need to be convened.
- Where will the focus group be held? Do you know if your group members will need transportation or incur any other costs in order to attend your session?
- Will participants be reimbursed for costs to attend your session? How?
- Will refreshments be provided?
- Will incentives be provided for taking part in the focus group? If so, what type of incentive and what are the costs?
- How will you record the session (e.g., pen and paper, video/tape recording, independent observers behind a two-way mirror, an observer in the same room but apart from the group)?
- How will you address ethical issues (e.g., confidentiality of material, sharing of information among group members) associated with sensitive questions?

- Will the focus group be held in a face-to-face setting or via technology from various remote locations? Face-to-face interaction allows for the moderator or observer to note non-verbal cues and adds that dimension to the data collection. However, if your focus group is on an online forum, this dimension will be absent.

> The moderator's skills are key to the effectiveness and success of the focus group.

# CASE STUDIES

> Case Studies are in-depth descriptions about whom or what you are studying/treating over a period of time.

## Overview of the Case Study Approach

A case study approach is useful in situations where you want to get a holistic picture of what is taking place. A case study can be exploratory (used to learn about some relatively unknown phenomena), explanatory (used to explain trends), or descriptive (used to collect information). It can comprise one individual, a group, a situation in an organization, or a particular event for the purpose of description and/or exploration of a phenomenon. You can use existing case studies to inform your research, help you to better understand some issue, or to assist with providing content for your research.

For example, the Malden Mills case study by Nohria, Piper and Gurtler (2006) has been lauded by many as a demonstration of excellence in employer-employee relations and is likely to be frequently referenced in emerging research on company values and philosophy. This case illustrates the owner's extraordinary principles, values, and concern for the welfare of his employees. Aaron Feuerstein, chief executive officer of the company, paid full wages to his 3,000 employees for several months while his factory was being rebuilt following destruction by fire. Feuerstein gained fame for his actions. Unfortunately, the story did not have a happy ending. Malden Mills was forced to file for Chapter 11 bankruptcy in 2001.

Likewise, Thigpen and Cleckley's (1954) study explored the claims of Chris Sizemore (portrayed as Eve White) who had multiple personalities. The doctors cross-checked her personal history with family members, used the electroencephalogram (EEG) to record brain wave patterns of the different personalities, administered psychometric tests (e.g., an independent intelligence test and the Rorschach projective test), and noted differences in mannerisms and eye problems. They concluded that their patient did have multiple personalities. Although the findings from the Nohria et al. and the Thigpen and Checkley case studies cannot be generalized to the wider population, they can be used to formulate, confirm, or challenge a theory, and/or highlight an unusual practice or behaviour.

In addition to using existing case studies to inform or gain better insight, a researcher may opt to use a case study approach for his/her research because s/he wishes to obtain in-depth information on a particular issue and/or when financial resources are limited. For example, if a funding institution (Agency A) was conducting an evaluation of its borrowing member countries in a particular region (10 countries) and Agency A did not have the financial resources to visit all 10 countries, Agency A could choose two or three countries as case studies and collect in-depth information from those countries. Agency A can use several different strategies to select its sample (e.g., loan size: large, medium, small; country size: population or square miles; type of project financed: roads, airports).

## Information Sources for Case Studies and Types of Case Studies

The objective of any case study is to get a comprehensive picture on an issue. Therefore, all variables are generally of interest (e.g., demographics, socialization, culture, attitudes, and behaviours) because they may all contribute to the understanding of the case. Consequently, information for case studies can come from a variety of sources such as interviews, reports, records, documents, and observations. The sources for a particular case study may utilize both quantitative and qualitative information. For example, researchers may use a quantitative approach such as EEG to record brain wave patterns, test reaction times, or assess the ability of their participant to do specific activities. In addition, researchers may use a qualitative approach that includes interviewing family and friends of the participant, as well as observing the participant in a particular setting.

## Criticisms of the Case Study Approach

Although case studies can be very useful and informative, and provide flexibility for you to explore/examine a specific topic area within a given context, case studies are greatly criticized for being unscientific due to its weaknesses of subjectivity and its lack of generalizability. A case in point is Freud's (1909) case study of Little Hans as support for his Oedipus complex theory. Freud's research was heavily criticized because alternative explanations were quite apparent. Similarly, criticisms were levelled against Thigpen and Cleckley's (1954) work. Specifically, critics questioned the validity and reliability of many of the tests and findings; some critics even accused the researchers of fudging the results, and/or noting only those aspects that confirmed their diagnosis.

## Issues to Keep in Mind When Thinking about Using a Case Study

To conduct a case study, keep the following aspects in mind:
- Your research topic, questions, and objectives.
- Your sample and reasons for your choice.
- Data collection methods (multiple methods are better).
- Relevance of data to your research questions and objectives.
- Data analyses and interpretations.

> More confirmation among different data sources means better authentication of case study findings.

# DOCUMENT REVIEW AND ANALYSIS

Document Review and Analysis refers to the use of documents from a variety of sources (e.g., public documents, media sources, journal articles, recordings, and biographies) in order to collect and analyse data to offer insight into or provide evidence for a specific research topic.

## Why do Document Review and Analysis?

Document review and analysis is suited to all types of research but is widely used in the social sciences and legal professions. In any specific field or discipline, numerous documents exist that can be reviewed to better inform your research. Document review and analysis can help you to refine your research question(s) and/or topic. It can help you to build a case in the legal profession. It can even help with making links between your research and previous research.

## How to Conduct Document Review and Analysis

Document review and analysis involves substantial reading with the ultimate aim of finding similarities, themes, patterns, number of occurrences, and so on. It can be either qualitative, quantitative, or both. The qualitative approach tends to use techniques such as thematic, discourse, narrative, grounded theory, interpretative phenomenological, and conversation analyses (see chapter 8). The objective of the qualitative approach is to try to understand and make sense of the data. In contrast, the quantitative approach focuses on content analysis. With respect to content analyses, you may choose keywords/themes/phrases, and then search and select all the documents that highlight those content areas within the given context or topic area. Through content analysis, you then count the number of times the key words/themes/phrases appear in the documents. The results from both types of analyses can be presented in narrative write-up and/or via tables/charts/graphs.

## Skills Needed to Conduct Document Review and Analysis

Document review requires considerable reading. Therefore, any individual tasked with this job must enjoy reading. Additionally, the person must possess some important characteristics such as being meticulous, systematic, dependable, conscientiousness, and ethical. Furthermore, the person must have good work ethic, discipline specific knowledge, and good critical thinking/analytical skills.

This methodology is relatively inexpensive and provides good information for corroboration. However, it is extremely time consuming. Additionally, documents may be dated/incomplete.

## MIXED METHODS APPROACH

**Mixed Methods Approach** refers to the collection of both quantitative and qualitative data that can provide a more holistic picture of your research topic

### Why Choose a Mixed Methods Approach?

Mixed methods approaches are now quite popular and are used by many researchers globally. This approach combines quantitative and qualitative data collection strategies and can help with triangulation, as well as strengthen and improve a research design. The mixed methods approach can therefore be seen as the best of both worlds since it can improve the robustness of your research study, including your analysis and conclusions.

### Challenges with Mixed Methods Approaches

A major challenge with a mixed methods approach is that some researchers may not be sufficiently skilled to conduct both qualitative and quantitative research. Researchers may therefore need to get additional training or collaborate with other researchers skilled in specific methodologies so that the mixed methods approach can be effective. Of course, one challenge with collaboration and using different strategies may be philosophical differences between researchers. You therefore need to carefully consider the implications of using a mixed methods approach and pay special attention to issues such as expertise, how data collection will be managed, cost implications, timing, data analysis and reporting to determine if a mixed methods approach should really be pursued.

### Questions to Consider Before Adopting a Mixed Methods Approach

1. Do your research topic and research questions require more than one design (e.g., a mixture of quantitative and qualitative questions)?
2. How will your research benefit from a mixed methods approach (e.g., from incorporating a survey with an observation)?
3. Do you have the skills to successfully conduct a mixed methods study?
4. How will the study be managed?
5. When will the different approaches be conducted? Will the various approaches have a particular sequence?
6. Will you be able to address challenges (e.g., differing sample sizes, procedures, ethics) in a timely manner?
7. Do you have time to invest in a mixed methods approach?
8. Can the quantitative and qualitative data be combined for analysis and reporting purposes to provide logical conclusions?
9. What are the cost implications of doing a mixed methods study versus the benefits to be derived from such a study?

### Examples of Mixed Methods Approaches

**Scenario 1:** Suppose you were systematically observing the same children on a playground over a four-week period to determine how often they help/look out for each other. You note the frequency with which a child helps another who has fallen down, hugs a crying child, stops bullying from another child, and/or seeks help from an adult if another child gets hurt. Here you have quantitative data about what has occurred and how often it has occurred. If you are able to interview (using qualitative methods such as focus groups or in-depth interviews) the children, their parents, and perhaps their teachers about the possible reasons or motives for helping, you will be collecting qualitative data. Now you will have a better idea about not only the frequency of helping behaviours but also the possible motives and reasons behind such behaviours. In this mixed methods scenario, the quantitative and qualitative data complement each other to give a better overall picture of the children's helping behaviours.

**Scenario 2:** Suppose you wanted to determine the effectiveness of training on employees' punctuality at work. You may record the number of training sessions an employee attends and the number of days (in the last six months) that an employee was punctual. Statistics may show that although an employee attends many training sessions, that employee is less punctual than others who did not attend as many training sessions. You might therefore (erroneously) conclude that the training sessions are ineffective in promoting employee punctuality. However, you may decide to interview employees, managers, and training facilitators of the sessions and realize that the training sessions might be perceived as too demanding and unsatisfactory thereby explaining the reasons behind their ineffectiveness. The qualitative aspect of your research (interviews) clarified the statistics (punctuality records) and challenged the incorrect assumption about the poor impact of training sessions which was based on the statistics alone.

These two illustrations show that mixed methods can either complement findings of each data collection instrument (as noted in scenario 1) or highlight the differences between findings based on the strengths and weaknesses of each approach used (as noted in scenario 2). A real world example of a mixed methods design in the education sector is shown in table 3.5. In this study, a mixed methods design was used to gather data on gender, teacher praise and criticism, and student motivation in St Vincent and the Grenadines (SVG). The research was conducted using a four-stage process (see Persaud, 2017). Four different data collection strategies were utilized: classroom observations, a survey of students, interviews with students, and document analysis of end of term grades.

## Table 3.5: Illustration of a Mixed Methods Approach in Education

**MAIN ASPECTS OF THE RESEARCH:**
- **Psychological Perspective:** Social Psychology
- **Sample Frame:** Co-educational secondary schools in SVG
- **Sample:** Third Form students aged 13–17
- **Research Questions:** Pertained to praise and criticism in terms of amount, types, interpretation, and source (male or female teachers)
- **Mixed Methods:** Classroom observations, student surveys, random student interviews, and review of end of term grades
- **Research Ethics:** Approval from Institutional Review Board, Ministry of Education, principals, teachers, and parents

| Phase 1 – Classroom Observations (Qualitative) | Phase 2 – Student Survey (Quantitative) | Phase 3 – Review of Final Grades (Quantitative) |
|---|---|---|
| - Four schools, two classes each (Mathematics + English Language).<br>- Neither teachers nor students had any knowledge about research goal (i.e., teacher praise and criticism and student responses) to avoid behaviour changes.<br>- Focused on amount, types, and source of praise and criticism.<br>- Specific criteria were used to avoid teacher gender conflation, and for practical purposes.<br>- Four classes were purposely selected based on specific criteria. However, there was no prior knowledge of which schools would fit the criteria.<br>- Used observation seating chart and key descriptors for on task, distracters, number of times teachers used positive and negative feedback, and positive or negative student response. | - Nine classes (original four classes + five additional).<br>- Total students n=245.<br>- Students not aware of research goal based on survey questions.<br>- Focused on amount, types, interpretation, and source of praise and criticism.<br>- Employed cognitive interviewing and pilot testing of instrument.<br>- Approval from parents obtained during a Parents/Teachers' Day.<br>- Thank you and debriefing letters sent out. | - Obtained all grades from the four original classes in Mathematics and English to check academic outcomes by teacher sex.<br><br>**Phase 4 – Random Interviews with Students (Qualitative)**<br><br>- Parental permission obtained.<br>- Forty-eight random interviews from the original four classes were conducted.<br>- Focused on amount, types, interpretation of praise and criticism the students received. |

Source: Persaud (2017).

**TIP:** A mixed methods approach allows you to compare at least two types of data. This comparison can paint a more accurate picture of the issue under investigation.

# 4 Instrumentation and Measurement

- Conceptualization and Operationalization
- Measurement
- Questionnaire Design
- Closed-ended vs Open-ended Questions
- Reliability
- Validity
- Validated Instruments
- Scale Construction
- Interview Schedule Design

## CONCEPTUALIZATION AND OPERATIONALIZATION

Conceptualization in research is necessary so both the researcher and the readers clearly understand how concepts in the research are defined.

Operationalization determines how the researcher will measure the concepts.

### Why is Conceptualization Important?

Embedded in the word *conceptualization* is the term *concept*, which can be relative. This means that what I may understand from, or how I interpret a concept, is not necessarily the same as someone else. For example, the concept *happiness* may mean something different depending on our perspective such as contentment, enjoyment, and/or pleasure. Individually, it could mean going on a dream vacation or things are going well in your life. It could even be stretched to include something negative if happiness for a person means humiliating others or engaging in and getting away with illegal activities.

From these examples, you can see that there are different meanings attached to one term. To avoid misunderstanding, conceptualization means that you need to clearly define your concepts so that everyone can interpret your concept in a like manner. Example 4.1 provides one definition of the concept *happiness*. The next section will show how this definition can be operationalized.

# Instrumentation and Measurement

**Example 4.1:** (Original Definition of Happiness)

Happiness is a condition in life that consists of contentment, delight, and satisfying positive experiences which promote a positive outlook.

## Linking Conceptualization and Operationalization

Operationalization works hand in hand with conceptualization. Not only must you clearly define the concept, you also need to determine *how the concept will be measured*. For instance, if you are measuring speed and distance, you can check the speedometer and use a stopwatch. However, oftentimes, concept measurement is not that simple.

Suppose you wanted to measure the concept of *happiness* in terms of its impact on health, specifically that of stress. You would need to modify the original definition of the concept *happiness* to make it appropriate to your specific study on stress. One possible modification is shown in example 4.2.

**Example 4.2:** (Happiness Modified for Specific Study on Stress)

For the purpose of this study, *happiness* is a condition in life that consists of contentment, delight, and satisfying positive experiences which reduces stress levels of young adults in the workplace.

Note that in the revised definition *happiness* is now linked to reduced stress levels, and the sample has also been specified (i.e., young adults). This modified definition also indicates that that the stress will be workplace related. Note however, that you may still have to define descriptors used within the happiness definition and discuss what are satisfying positive experiences.

## Ways to Operationalize the Concept of Happiness in the Workplace

Happiness is an intangible concept, so you will need to specifically identify how happiness measured through stressful experiences at work will be operationalized. To *operationalize* the concept of *happiness* based on your revised definition, you may decide to do one or several of the following:

- The literature indicates that stress is associated with increased blood pressure, heart attacks, stress hormone levels, and frequent/chronic pain. Therefore, you can chart the number of absenteeism workplace cases for health reasons. The number of sick days taken by each employee within a given month or year can point to work stress related issues.

- Chart employee general absences and punctuality records which can be influenced by workplace stress.
- Interview employees to find out about their workplace stress and levels of job happiness. Are deadlines generally met? Is teamwork productive or is it ineffective because some persons do not pull their weight and the burden is placed on others to get the job done? Check worker productivity levels over a time period.
- Administer and analyse an established happiness and workplace stress survey instrument.

**TIP**
Each concept needs to be clearly defined.
Even adjectives used to describe a concept may need to be further clarified to avoid misinterpretations.
Clear operationalization of each concept is needed to ensure that the measurement used is appropriate.

## MEASUREMENT

**Measurement refers to a body of rules that is used to categorize information using a numerical assignment for the purposes of comprehension and/or comparison.**

## Levels of Measurement

Measurement levels or scales are classified into four tiers, namely, nominal, ordinal, interval, and ratio. The nominal level of measurement is the lowest in the hierarchy while the ratio is the highest. It is critically important for a researcher to understand all four levels of measurement so that s/he can select the level of measurement best suited for his/her research (see table 4.1).

In general, it is better to collect data at a higher level of measurement since a higher level can be described at a lower level but not vice versa. For instance, age (ratio level) can be described at the ordinal level since it can be grouped into categories of young, middle-age, and old using some universal definition. Likewise, income (ratio level) can also be described at the ordinal level (i.e., societal status – upper, middle, lower).

It is also important to note that statistical techniques that may be appropriate for one measurement level might be quite inappropriate for another level. For example, the variable religion is measured at the nominal level. Suppose you numbered Christian denominations in Jamaica as follows: Anglican = 1, Catholic = 2, Methodist = 3, Other = 4. These numbers do not mean anything; they are merely labels. You cannot add a Catholic and a Methodist to get an Anglican. Neither can you take the average of the four denominations. You therefore need to have a good idea beforehand about the types of analyses you would like to report. If it is possible to collect some types of data at a higher level, this may be quite advantageous since it will permit more flexibility for reporting purposes.

## Table 4.1: Basic Overview on Levels of Measurement

| Level | Characteristics | Examples | Types of Statistical Analyses |
|---|---|---|---|
| Nominal | • Distinct unordered categories or groups.<br>• Discrete.<br>• Can be dichotomous or multinomial.<br>• Labels have no meaning even if a number is assigned to a category.<br>• No ordering is implied. Favourite colours can be 1= Blue, 2 = Red. Red is not twice as important as blue. Could label 1 = Red, 2 = Blue. | • Sex (dichotomous)<br>• Marital status (multinomial)<br>• Religion<br>• Hair colour<br>• Occupation | **Non-Parametric**<br>• Descriptive statistics – only mode<br>• Chi-Square test<br><br>**Parametric**<br>• Logistic Regression |
| Ordinal | • Distinct categories.<br>• Categories can be rank ordered.<br>• Distance has no meaning.<br>• Cannot quantify differences between one value and the next.<br>5. Strongly Agree<br>4. Agree<br>3. Neutral<br>2. Disagree<br>1. Strongly Disagree | • Socio-economic status (e.g., lower, middle, upper class).<br>• Education level<br>• Likert scales<br>• Age (when grouped into categories) | **Non-Parametric**<br>• Descriptive statistics – only median, mode<br>• Wilcoxon Test<br>• Mann-Whitney<br>• Spearman's Rank Order Correlation |
| Interval | • Numerical.<br>• Continuous.<br>• Can be ordered.<br>• Equal intervals.<br>• Quantitative distance between one value and another is known. For instance, when you use a ruler, you know the value of two inches and ten inches, as well as the difference of eight inches between the two values.<br>• No true zero point. There is no such condition as the absence of temperature. Consequently, 90°C is not three times as hot as 30°C because no zero point exists that can quantify such a claim. | • IQ scores<br>• Temperature | **Non-Parametric**<br>• Descriptive statistics – mean, median, mode.<br>• Spearman's Rank Order Correlation<br><br>**Parametric**<br>• ANOVA<br>• Regression<br>• T-tests (independent and paired) |
| Ratio | • Numerical.<br>• Continuous.<br>• Absolute meaningful zero point.<br>• Facilitates meaningful ratio or fraction comparisons (e.g., one runner can be twice as fast as another runner; $100 is twice as much as $50). | • Salary<br>• Age<br>• Number of children<br>• Weight<br>• Most count variables | **Non-Parametric**<br>• Descriptive statistics – mean, median, mode.<br>• Spearman's Rank Order Correlation.<br><br>**Parametric**<br>• All quantitative tests for continuous data (e.g. correlation, regression, T-tests). |

## Measurement and Statistical Tests

The types of statistical tests that can be conducted and the types of data analyses that can be done will depend on your level of measurement. Statistical tests are classified as either *parametric* or *nonparametric*. Significant differences between the two are that parametric tests are used for data with a normal distribution and equal variance, while non-parametric tests are used when the data do not have a normal distribution, and/or equal variance. This may be true of even interval or ratio levels when the homogeneous variance assumption is violated.

Some statistical tests can be run solely from data within a specific scale. For example, you can run a Chi-Square from data gathered from categorical (nominal) data. However, you also need to take into consideration that some statistical tests are dependent on aspects from different measurement levels, that is, categorical (nominal or ordinal) and continuous data (interval or ratio). For example, a two way ANOVA requires two categorical variables (e.g., sex from a nominal scale, and age group from an ordinal scale), as well as one continuous dependent variable (e.g., test scores from a ratio scale).

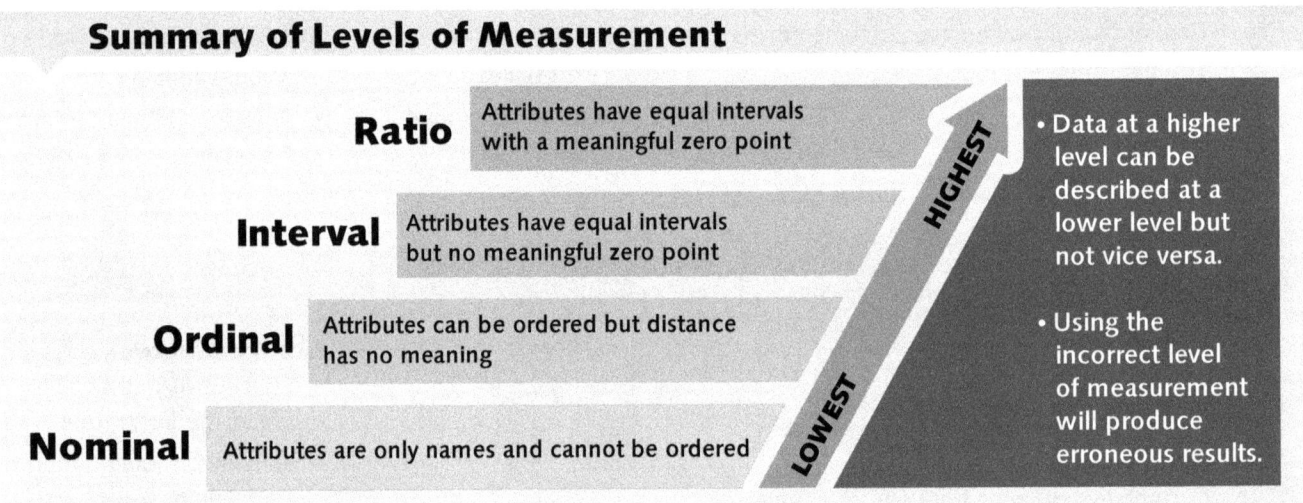

Readers must be able to understand your measurement process/procedure and be able to replicate it. Therefore, you need to be clear and provide a step by step measurement methodology.

# QUESTIONNAIRE DESIGN

Questionnaire Design is a multifaceted process that requires a lot of thought and attention to detail for the instrument itself.

## Instruments and Instrumentation

In order to collect quality data, researchers must determine which instrument is best suited to their research goals. Instruments refer to the array of tools and devices (e.g., thermostats, blood pressure monitors, tests, surveys) which can be used to collect data. Instruments can be used solely by the researcher (e.g., checklists, observation charts, interview schedules) or the participant (e.g., personality inventories, surveys).

All instruments go through a process referred to as instrumentation which essentially involves developing, piloting, and administering the instrument. One of the most common types of instruments used in social science research is the questionnaire or survey. The instrumentation of the questionnaire is a multifaceted process. You will recall that in chapter 3, pros and cons of surveys were highlighted along with basic examples of types of questions. In this section, a more in-depth look at questionnaire design is provided to complement the information presented in chapter 3.

## Steps in Questionnaire Design

Questionnaire design refers to how you set up and design your questionnaire in terms of the types and sequence of questions, instructions for completing the questionnaire and for skipping questions, and in the case where people will see the questionnaire (face to face, mail, or online), the layout/presentation. All aspects of questionnaire design are important; however, the attractiveness of the questionnaire and the user-friendliness of the instrument are perhaps the deciding factors for many respondents about whether or not they will complete the questionnaire. Therefore, although substantial time may need to be invested to ensure that your questionnaire is attractive, this effort will pay off when respondents complete the survey.

There are a few important points that you need to consider as you design a basic paper questionnaire:

1. Your research questions must guide your questionnaire development.
2. Questions need to be clear, user friendly, and properly sequenced, that is, there must be logical progression from one topic to the next. Be cognizant that question order can affect answers. The following pointers are helpful for question writing:

    - ***Easy versus Hard Questions:*** Start with easy questions and progress to harder questions. Demographic questions are relatively easy. Many researchers place these questions at the start of their survey. However, others may place these questions at the end of the survey. There is no right or wrong approach. Placement is simply a personal preference.

    - ***Specific versus Categorical Responses:*** Think carefully about whether or not you want to use specific responses for certain demographics such as age and income since these demographics are considered sensitive and many participants may omit these demographics if only a space is provided for them to give exact information. It may therefore be best to use categories for these demographics (see example 4.3). Note, however, that the categories used will depend on the group of participants being surveyed.

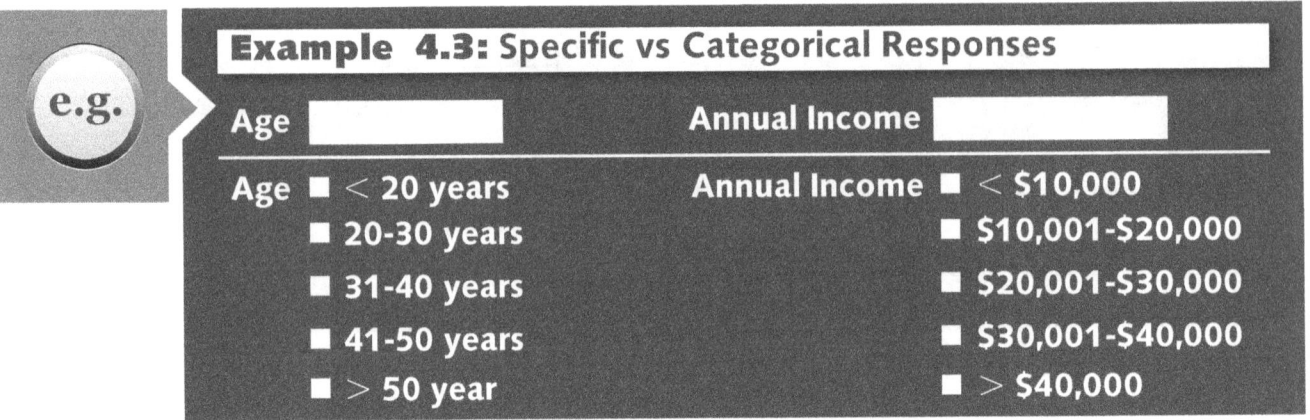

**Example 4.3:** Specific vs Categorical Responses

Age ▭   Annual Income ▭

Age ▪ < 20 years
▪ 20-30 years
▪ 31-40 years
▪ 41-50 years
▪ > 50 year

Annual Income ▪ < $10,000
▪ $10,001-$20,000
▪ $20,001-$30,000
▪ $30,001-$40,000
▪ > $40,000

- ***Close-Ended Versus Open-Ended Questions:*** Survey questions can either be close-ended or open-ended (see further discussion in next section). Close-ended questions are easier to analyse but limit responses to predetermined categories provided by the researcher. The nature of your research will determine what type of questions is best suited to your research endeavour. Many researchers find it advantageous to include at least one open-ended question which gives the participant an opportunity to share important information which the researcher may not have considered. For example, the final question on your survey could be: *Is there anything else which you would like to share about bullying in secondary schools in Barbados which was not captured on this survey?*

- ***Inclusion of 'Other' as a Category in Closed-Ended Responses:*** When close-ended questions are used, the researcher provides several possible choices. However, citing every conceivable choice may simply not be practical. Therefore, a choice of 'other' could be effectively used (e.g., using 'other' in demographic questions such as race or nationality) so that the respondent can provide an open-ended response.

- ***Match Vocabulary and Survey Design with Audience:*** Ensure that your vocabulary is in keeping with your target audience. Avoid the use of slang, discipline specific jargon (unless defined), and complex words. Also, if you are surveying children, keep in mind that graphics may help to make the survey more user-friendly for this group.

- ***Font:*** Use a font that is easy to read (e.g., Ariel, Times New Roman). Also use a font size between ten and 12. A font size larger than size 12 may also be desirable if some participants are elderly.

- ***Questionnaire Length:*** Many respondents tend to be turned off by lengthy questionnaires unless they are interested in the topic. They generally perceive such questionnaires as requiring too much time and effort and they are less likely to start, much less complete, the questionnaire. A questionnaire that does not require too much of the respondent's time and effort will be less likely to be rejected.

3. Following completion of the draft questionnaire, you will need to get some preliminary feedback from colleagues to fine-tune the instrument. Ask your colleagues if the questions are clear and if they understand the meaning as you intended. If the answer is 'no', edit and solicit feedback again. Ensure that respondents can easily navigate your questionnaire and that the layout will motivate

respondents to answer the questions. Think about it this way, a colourful, nicely presented new dish will entice people to try the dish, whereas, a dull, unappetizing dish will not have many takers. Similarly, a well thought out, attractive questionnaire will motivate respondents to complete it. Keep in mind that colour can be attractive but expensive to reproduce. Alternatively, a well-designed black and white questionnaire can be very effective.

4. After refinement of your instrument, you will now need to pilot the instrument using similar participants to your actual sample (see chapter 5 Pilot Study) and modify your instrument using the feedback from the pilot study. If the modifications are extensive, you may need to conduct a second pilot before actual execution to your sample.

> **TIP** It is usually advantageous to develop your code book in conjunction with your questions. It helps with your data analysis.

## CLOSE-ENDED QUESTIONS VS OPEN-ENDED QUESTIONS

**Close-Ended Questions** generally provide a number of response choices. Most often, respondents only need to select one answer choice.

**Open-Ended Questions** allow respondents to detail/expand their answers; they may also give free response answers.

### Should Close-Ended Questions or Open-Ended Questions be Used?

Your research objectives and questions will dictate the types of questions that are best suited to your research endeavour. Close-ended questions are used in many types of survey research. Such questions are relatively easy to code and quantify and are therefore suitable for large samples. These questions are designed with specific response choices which can be either dichotomous or multinomial.

In contrast, open-ended questions allow respondents to provide responses and/or explanations which are not influenced by the researcher. Such questions can provide rich insight into an issue which the researcher may never have conceptualized. Open-ended questions are however very difficult to code and can be quite expensive to use if the sample is large.

In addition to the cost consideration, researchers also need to think about the time factor, and its impact on the participants who must fill out the survey or complete the interview. Close-ended questions are likely to get many more takers. A compromise may therefore be to use mostly close-ended questions with one or two open-ended questions. Having looked at questionnaire design, we will now focus on the actual construction of close-ended and open-ended questions.

## Construction of Close-Ended Questions

Close-ended questions require that the questionnaire creator has, at the very least, a good grasp of the issues related to the topic, and knows how to translate that knowledge into crafting good, relevant responses. When constructing close-ended questions, the researcher needs to ensure that important choices are not omitted. The researcher also needs to think carefully about the types of scales that will be used. For instance, many Likert scales carry the category 'Neutral'. A scale that includes this category may indirectly encourage many participants to choose 'Neutral' without really thinking about their position on the topic. If a large percentage of your sample chooses the 'Neutral' choice, you could end up with data that is virtually useless.

Researchers do not need to reinvent the wheel when it comes to the type of response choices that could be provided for close-ended questions. The Internet abounds with dozens of Likert scale response choices and other types of close-ended question choices. Therefore, you should use the web as your first source to see if you can find a suitable scale. When selecting a scale, keep in mind that a shorter scale may be better than a longer scale because it is easier for participants to read. A good rule of thumb is a scale with 5 choices.

The instructions for completing close-ended questions can take many forms depending on the nature of the question. For example, a Likert scale response simply requires that the participant circle, shade, or tick his/her response. Another type of question may require that the participant selects all that apply from a list of possible choices. Close-ended questions can even take the form of multiple choice or true/false answers.

Sometimes it may be even be advantageous to use a blended approach and include a choice of 'other' in a close-ended question so that the respondent can include what the questionnaire creator has missed. Example 4.4 illustrates how the 'other' option is utilized in question 7.

**Example 4.4:** Example of a Close-Ended Question with Other Category

**PLEASE READ BEFORE PROCEEDING TO QUESTION 7**
Question 7 has <u>several</u> parts. There are four catergories of reasons presented.
- Under each category please **tick all** that apply.
- Then, **rate all** selected choices on the Likert Scale provided (Lowest = 0 to High = 10). For example

| Category 1: Enhancing Earning Capablities | Low 1 | 2 | 3 | 4 | 5 | 6 | 7 | 8 | 9 | High 10 |
|---|---|---|---|---|---|---|---|---|---|---|
| a. ☑ A better job | ☐ | ☐ | ☐ | ☐ | ☐ | ☐ | ☑ | ☐ | ☐ | ☐ |
| b. ☑ Higher pay | ☐ | ☐ | ☐ | ☐ | ☐ | ☐ | ☐ | ☐ | ☑ | ☐ |
| c. ☑ A promotion | ☐ | ☐ | ☐ | ☐ | ☐ | ☐ | ☐ | ☐ | ☑ | ☐ |

7. Why have you enrolled at UWI to pursue an undergraduate degree?
   Category 1: I have enrolled at UWI to enhance my earning capability.

| Category 1: Enhancing Earning Capablities | Low 1 | 2 | 3 | 4 | 5 | 6 | 7 | 8 | 9 | High 10 |
|---|---|---|---|---|---|---|---|---|---|---|
| a. ☐ A better job | ☐ | ☐ | ☐ | ☐ | ☐ | ☐ | ☐ | ☐ | ☐ | ☐ |
| b. ☐ Higher pay | ☐ | ☐ | ☐ | ☐ | ☐ | ☐ | ☐ | ☐ | ☐ | ☐ |
| c. ☐ A promotion | ☐ | ☐ | ☐ | ☐ | ☐ | ☐ | ☐ | ☐ | ☐ | ☐ |
| d. ☐ Job security | ☐ | ☐ | ☐ | ☐ | ☐ | ☐ | ☐ | ☐ | ☐ | ☐ |
| e. ☐ Perks that go with the job | ☐ | ☐ | ☐ | ☐ | ☐ | ☐ | ☐ | ☐ | ☐ | ☐ |
| f. ☐ Other, please specify_____ | ☐ | ☐ | ☐ | ☐ | ☐ | ☐ | ☐ | ☐ | ☐ | ☐ |

Observe in example 4.4, that six response choices (a–f) are provided under Category 1 and respondents are asked to tick **all** that apply. In choice (f) provision is made for a free response by the use of the word 'Other'. The question also employs the use of a ten-point Likert scale. This question has in effect combined use of a Likert scale, multiple responses, and an open-ended response all in one question.

When constructing close-ended questions, ensure that your question stems avoid emotionally charged words, that meanings are clear, and that questions make sense. To illustrate, although question 10 in example 4.5 has several choices, some of the choices are poorly worded and thereby defy logic, while others are ambiguous or vague. For instance:

**Example 4.5:** Critique of the Question 10 Response Choices

Q9. Do you think that the current City Council's proposal to demolish the Community Centre and construct low income apartment buildings is a good idea?
- ■ Yes ⟹ Please go to Q10
- ■ No ⟹ Please go to Q11

Q10. Why do you think that demolition of the Community Centre and the construction of low income apartment buildings is a good idea?

Please tick <u>all</u> that apply.
- a. ☐ The community centre is an eye sore.
- b. ☐ Better housing is needed.
- c. ☐ The area is unsafe as there are always gang activities around the community centre.
- d. ☐ It blocks the view.
- e. ☐ Other (please specify) _____

Q11. If you answered *No* to Question 9, please provide a reason for your response.

- A major problem with question 10 is that it is a double barrelled question. It is asking reasons for the demolition of the Community Centre, as well as reasons for the construction of a low income apartment building in the same question.
- Choice (c) defies logic. Replacing a community centre with an apartment complex will not prevent gang activites.
- Choice (d) is ambigious. This response seems to point to the reason for having the demolition done and not necessarily the construction.

## Construction of Open-Ended Questions

Open-ended questions collect qualitative data and are useful when the researcher needs to explore issues related to and/or receive added insight into the research topic. Such questions encourage respondents to provide their own free response answers without influencing the response.

When considering the use of open-ended questions, the researcher needs to keep in the mind that open-ended questions tend to be quite time consuming. Too many open-ended questions may require too much respondent effort and may not be completed, which can skew results and limit generalizability. In order to get the most effective responses, and bearing in mind that free response answers are harder to code, you may want to consider the use of a series of close-ended questions with a check all that apply option, combined with an 'Other' choice as the last option (see example 4.5), rather than a totally open-ended response (see example 4.6).

### Example 4.6: Open-Ended Question

**Q10. How do you view the current City Council's proposal to demolish the Community Centre and construct low income apartment buildings?**

Like close-ended questions, open-ended questions also need to be properly constructed since they require that people reflect and think. Consequently, such questions usually begin with an adverb such as *how/what*, or a verb such as *describe*. Example 4.6 shows how question 10 in example 4.5 could be presented as a totally free response open-ended question. In an interview setting, the participant's response in example 4.6 may also allow the researcher to probe further to gain deeper understanding if a flexible interview schedule guide is being used. Probes can be used to clarify a point, or to get more detail on something that the respondent mentioned.

The construction of some types of open-ended questions will also require that the researcher construct the question so that some boundaries are placed within the question to help to keep the participant focused so that s/he does not digress from the research question. For example, if you are interested in learning about which specimens of flowers are the most popular for Valentine's Day, you will need to specify the words

# Instrumentation and Measurement

'Valentine's Day' in the question, or the florist will just name the most popular flowers sold throughout the year.

Finally, when open-ended questions are placed on surveys, adequate space should be provided for the participants to respond (see example 4.7). Keep in mind that some people have very large handwriting and if sufficient space is not provided, you will get very little information.

**Example 4.7:** Open-Ended Free Response Question

Q10. Please list all of the reasons, <u>by order of importance</u> (1= most important and 8 = least important), to show why you enrolled at this university for an undergraduate degree.

1. _____
2. _____
3. _____
4. _____
5. _____
6. _____
7. _____
8. _____

Your research questions will determine if close-ended or open-ended questions are most suited to your particular study.

Keep in mind that open-ended questions are more time consuming for the participant and more costly for the researcher.

Note however that open-ended questions can enrich data analysis especially when verbatim quotes are included.

Many researchers find it advantageous to use both question types.

# RELIABILITY

**Reliability refers to the consistency of a measure.**

## Overview on Reliability

Reliability which refers to the consistency, stability, and uniformity of a measure is a critical concern in research since instruments (e.g., surveys, tests, scales, blood pressure monitors) with low reliability are worthless. An instrument is unreliable if you get totally different results each time it is used on similar samples and under similar conditions. Think about something as simple as a scale. Suppose one of the scales used to weigh baggage at one of the American Airlines counters in Miami was not working properly. Imagine the problems that would be caused if the scale minuses 20 pounds from each bag. The aircraft could end up with substantial overweight which could be detrimental to the safety of the flight.

In general, researchers strive for high reliability (at least .70). Reliability can be affected by several issues. For example, poorly constructed questions and/or unclear instructions can affect the reliability of a survey instrument or test. If a pilot test reveals that particular questions can be interpreted in several ways by your pilot sample, the questions should either be rewritten or tossed out.

Reliability of a survey or test instrument is also affected by the number of items on the instrument. Note that reliability is computed for a scale – not individual items. Therefore, more items will result in higher reliability. For instance, a test on ten topics would have higher reliability compared to a test with just five topics. A test with a legitimate longer duration will also have more reliability (e.g., a two-hour comprehensive test versus a 15-minute pop test). Reliability on a test can even be affected by participants' anxiety or fatigue since they will not perform at their optimal levels.

## Types of Reliability

Researchers need to be concerned with four types of measurement reliability:

### Test-Retest Reliability

This approach requires that the researcher administer the same instrument twice to the same participants. The expectation here is that if the same people take the identical test at Time $X^1$ and then again at Time $X^2$ they will get a similar score. This would demonstrate that the test items are consistent, or have measurement reliability, and are stable over time.

Test-retest reliability can be affected by several issues (see next page). Notwithstanding, researchers can guard against problems by ensuring that their tests or surveys are well constructed with clear instructions, unambiguous questions, consistent administration, and proper scoring.

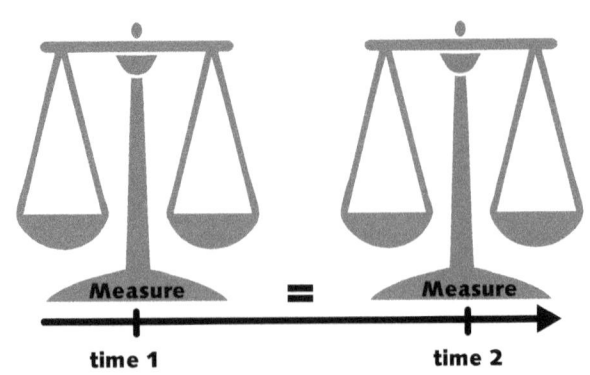

- Practice gained doing the test at Time $X^1$ can influence the score at Time $X^2$.
- If the time period is very short, test scores can be affected by increased memory and practice effects. In contrast, if the time between the two administrations is lengthy, respondents may forget answers. Alternatively, the opposite may occur and respondents may actually perform better due to maturity and learning. Determining the appropriate time span between Time $X^1$ and Time $X^2$ can therefore present some challenges.
- The construct may have changed over the time period. For example, suppose you did an attitude test on obesity in Time $X^1$. Shortly after, the government launches extensive publicity and education programmes on obesity. When the second attitude test is done, many of the original participants may have changed their views on obesity due to exposure on the issue.

## Observer or Inter-Rater Reliability

Accurate systematic observations require that all observers/raters record or judge the same phenomena in a like manner. For example, if the behaviours of John Smith are recorded by three independent observers using the same observation chart format, all raters should have similar things ticked or written onto their observation charts. Inter-rater reliability refers to the percentage of consistency (or agreement) these observers show in their recording of the number and types of behaviours displayed by John Smith. If a comparison between the raters shows large differences between the raters, this would indicate the procedure utilized is unreliable and inter-observer reliability of John Smith would not be considered as being credible. In general, researchers strive for high inter-observer reliability (at least .80). A perfect score would be 1.00.

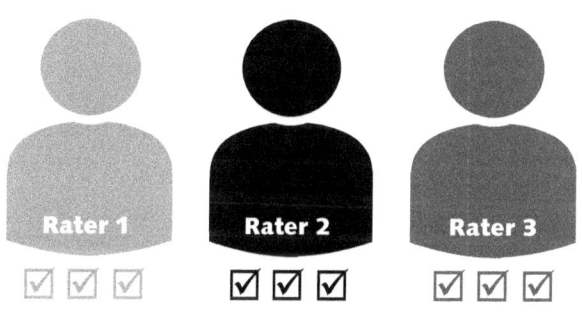

Inter-observer reliability can be affected by a number of issues such as distracted raters (e.g., checking email while observing), the actual research setting (e.g., noisy environment), and poorly designed instruments. Therefore, it is important that raters/observers be properly trained and observed prior to actual data collection to avoid low inter-observer reliability. A good detailed training manual is also critical to the success of high inter-observer reliability.

## Internal Consistency Reliability

Internal consistency reliability seeks to determine the extent to which items in a scale or test measure the same thing or construct. For example, if a programme was implemented to improve reading for ten-year-old children, then a test to gauge reading improvement should measure reading improvement (from the baseline), not quantitative skills.

Cronbach's alpha is used to check for internal consistency reliability. An alpha of greater than .70 indicates good internal consistency reliability. Having measures that are consistent is important. Unfortunately, you can have a test that is very reliable but lacks validity.

You can also use split-half reliability. Here, you divide your test or scale into two equal halves and administer it to the same group simultaneously. Pearson's Correlation Coefficient is used to measure the correlation between the two halves. If participants' performance is basically the same regardless of which half of the questions they received, then we can say that we have high correlation or good split-half reliability.

Your test or scale can be divided in a number of different ways such as even versus odd questions or purposively balancing the split by level of question difficulty. Note that your coefficient will be affected by the manner in which the split is done. In general, reliability is improved with more questions.

## Parallel Forms Reliability

When you need to determine which questions provide the most consistent results, one strategy is to use parallel forms. Parallel form reliability requires a pretest posttest application using the same participants. You prepare two tests where the phrasing of questions are different but test the same construct. The questions are divided randomly into two tests. From the responses, you can then determine which one of the two tests shows more consistency, or you can then determine if both have similar consistency.

Parallel form reliability is quite similar to split-half reliability. The major difference is that the test is administered to all participants in the group at two time periods compared to the split-half where different participants within the same sample take one or the other form of the test. Parallel forms reliability requires a relatively large question bank with all questions testing the same construct. As such, it can be quite difficult and time consuming to create questions that relate equally to a particular construct.

**TIP** Depending on your time frame, it may be helpful to use an established instrument as long as it is relevant to your research questions and you can obtain the necessary permission to use it.

# VALIDITY

**Validity refers to whether an item or instrument actually tests or measures what it is intended to test or measure.**

## Overview on Validity

Like reliability, validity is also of critical importance in research for ascertaining if an item or instrument actually measures what it claims to measure. If a researcher wants to find out about stress and workplace productivity, then the instrument being used should be in keeping with other measures of stress and workplace productivity. Note that while a valid instrument is always consistent (i.e., reliable), the converse is not always true. For instance, an instrument suited for measurement in one population (e.g., children) may not be suited to measuring the same construct in another population (e.g., adults). Likewise, an instrument created for one culture, setting, or environment may not be suited to another culture, setting, or environment.

## Internal vs External Validity

**Internal Validity** is specific to how well cause and effect research, that is, experiments are carried out in terms of controls established to deal with confounding extraneous variables. The greater the controls, the better the internal validity. For example, suppose you set up an experiment to test study strategies where one randomly assigned (experimental) group will engage in practice testing (independent variable), while the other randomly assigned (control) group uses another strategy such as self-explanation. You test both groups. Here, a confounding extraneous variable is that participants will have various degrees of knowledge about the topic which can affect performance. However, since you have randomly assigned group members, you have tried to minimize the systematic error (i.e., issues with the independent variable) of this confounding extraneous variable as best as possible.

Besides confounding extraneous variables, there are several other issues which can affect internal validity. For instance, internal validity can be affected by a host of threats which can be either participant related or measurement related (see figure 4.1). As such, it is important when designing your research study to take account of potential threats that can affect your study so that you can put mechanisms in place to control them. For example, history can be controlled through use of a laboratory environment, while maturation can be controlled by ensuring that the time frame between the pretest and posttest is not too long, and so on. While all threats may not be relevant to your particular study, you should be familiar with the different types of threats so that you can determine if they are relevant to your study and take measures to prevent them.

### Figure 4.1: Common Threats to Internal Validity

**Threats to Internal Validity**

**Participant Related**
- **ATTRITION** – loss of participants (e.g., death, relocation, boredom, tiredness, loss of interest).
- **COMPENSATORY RIVALRY** – comparison group competes with treatment group because of jealousy.
- **TREATMENT DIFFUSION** – intergroup communication leads to treatment diffusion.
- **HISTORY** – some event other than the intervention caused the outcome.
- **MATURATION** – participants' maturity caused the difference.
- **RESENTMENT DEMORALIZATION** – the comparison group gets discouraged because the group is aware of what the treatment group is getting.
- **SELECTION** – group differences due to kinds of participants used (e.g., volunteers are likely to respond differently compared to a random sample from the general population).

**Measurement Related**
- **INSTRUMENTATION** – changes in instrument between pretest and posttest. For example, two different tests are used so it is impossible to determine if the treatment caused the difference between the pretest and posttest scores.
- **STATISTICAL REGRESSION** – caused by some participants starting out in extreme positions (e.g., entire sample from an Ivy League University) and is not representative of the general population.
- **TESTING EFFECT** – taking the same test twice may change scores because participants were previously exposed to the questions.

***External Validity*** refers to whether or not you can generalize your research findings beyond your immediate participants and settings. External validity can be affected by three threats: people (e.g., perhaps you choose participants who are unique on some characteristic compared to those in the wider population), place (e.g., the area selected may have participants with the same attribute), and/or time (e.g., the time when the study was executed may coincide with something that could directly influence how participants respond). Researchers therefore need to guard against these three threats by ensuring that studies are done at different times and in different places using a random sampling methodology (see chapter 5).

## Types of Validity

Researchers need to be concerned with four types of validity which are discussed in this section.

### Face Validity

Face validity essentially involves asking colleagues and/or experts to peruse an instrument and provide feedback on whether the instrument is measuring what it purports to measure. For example, if a review of a Project Management test indicates that the test has only Project Management questions, then the test has face validity since it measures the concept of Project Management. Face validity is simple, easy, and inexpensive to ascertain. However, face validity by itself is not sufficiently rigorous in establishing an instrument's true validity.

### Content Validity

Content validity infers that the instrument thoroughly cover/measure the intended content area or domain. More specifically, it is concerned with the extent to which the questions are representative of the domain. For example, are the six specific belief domains of obsessive compulsive disorder (i.e., inflated personal responsibility, over-importance of thoughts, control of thoughts, overestimation of threat, intolerance of uncertainty and perfectionism) (see Obsessive Compulsive Cognitions Working Group 1997) covered by the questions on the Obsessional Beliefs Questionnaire (OBQ-44)?

**Content Validity**

Similar to face validity, content validity by itself is not sufficient to establish a scale's true validity. Content validity uses a similar process to face validity where experts are asked to peruse the instrument to ensure that questions cover the entire concept. This type of validity requires that the researcher first defines the concept(s) prior to question development. Definition of the concept usually comes from the literature. In many cases, researchers may even use an established statement and highlight that a particular theory was used.

### Construct Validity

Construct validity is concerned with ascertaining if a data collection instrument measures what it purports to measure (i.e., the constructs of interest), and if the measures are in keeping with the theory that underlies that particular construct (i.e., operationalization of the variables – see topic 1 in this chapter). For example, Bandura, Ross and Ross (1961) tested the social learning theory of aggression by imitation via the Bobo doll experiment. Construct validity can be established in several ways including factor analysis and score correlation on measures that measure and do not measure the same construct.

## Criterion Related Validity

Here, the researcher seeks to establish if the instrument is effective for identifying specific abilities. Criterion related validity can be established either through concurrent validity or predictive validity. In the former approach, the researcher compares his/her instrument with another well established instrument on the same construct and examines the correlation (agreement) between the two instruments. For example, if you compare your test with an established standard (e.g., your test against an established IQ test standard) and a high correlation is obtained, then this indicates that your instrument has concurrent validity. In contrast, predictive validity is essentially forecasting. Performance (on a test or scale) is used to predict the future. For example, universities generally use the Graduate Record Examination (GRE) scores to predict success in graduate programmes.

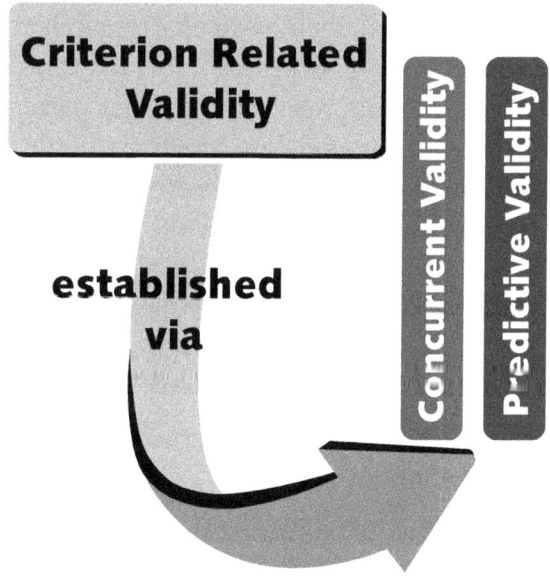

**TIP:** Issues related to validity can render your findings null and void.

# VALIDATED INSTRUMENTS/SCALES

Validated Instruments/Scales are typically reliable and valid. Scales that have been tried and tested are easier to use and more credible, but may not always be relevant to your research.

## Using Existing Instruments and Scales

In this section, the term scale refers to a previously validated instrument that was designed to measure one or more variables. The web abounds with numerous scales so researchers do not necessarily need to reinvent the wheel when thinking about designing a scale. Using an existing scale provides a good alternative to making your own and can save considerable time and money. However, it is important that as researchers you actually select a scale that is suited to your research, since scales can affect both the reliability/validity of your research.

A common problem that researchers may encounter when using an existing scale is that all of the items on a scale may not be suited to their particular research and/or population. In many instances, the researcher may need to modify a scale to make it more relevant to his/her particular study. If you are adopting or modifying an existing scale, you will generally need to request permission from the original developer to use the scale unless it is in the public domain with a note stating that the scale is freely available for public or academic use, and pilot any additional questions.

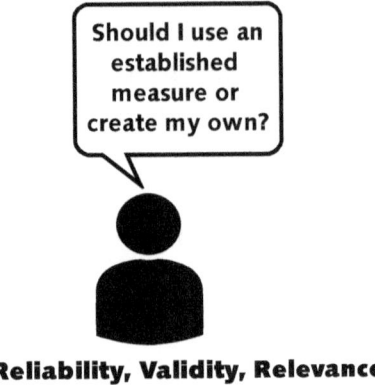

**Reliability, Validity, Relevance**

## Issues to Keep in Mind when Modifying an Existing Scale

If you think that you need to modify a scale to make it more relevant to your research/population/culture, keep the following in mind:

1. Before modifying the original scale, conduct a pilot test of the original scale with a sample from your population to gauge which items or wording may or may not need to be modified. You should also conduct your own personal review of scale items.

2. If you find that some of the items are unclear and could be better worded, bear in mind that:
   - If you make substantive changes, your items may be clearer, but the reliability and validity for that scale might be affected. You may therefore have to conduct your own reliability/validity assessment after revisions.
   - In order to compare and contrast a modified instrument with other similar studies that used the original instrument, the scales need to comprise the exact or similar item content or structure. Otherwise, such comparisons might be misleading.
   - Items of previously validated instruments might require revisions to ensure that the language (e.g., certain cultural concepts, jargon, phrases) is reflective of the environment in which the research is being conducted. For example, the term *professor* might have been used in an original instrument applied in a cultural context in which a professor is considered to be a teacher. However, in another culture the term *professor* may be reserved only for a senior academic employed at a university with a reputable track record in publications. Hence, it is important that researchers pay special attention to the relationship between the language used in scale items and the cultural environment under study.

3. You may also find that an established scale may need to be modified because it does not capture an important component of your research. Relevance of any scale to your research is paramount. However, note that if you decide to add another dimension to an established scale, it might be important to ensure that the value of this new dimension is examined in relation to the overall scale. Hence, it will be important to reassess the overall validity and reliability of this newly developed scale. You may also need to explain in your methodology section that you have added a new dimension and state the advantages and limitations therein.

4. Finally, you might decide to shorten the length of your scales but still be able to measure the constructs under your current research. You may do this to eliminate irrelevant items so that greater focus can be placed on more important aspects of the constructs. However, note that shorter scales may not possess the same properties as their longer counterparts and may not have the same interpretations.

**TIP:** Your choice of measurement will be dependent on issues of reliability and validity balanced against your research goals and population characteristics.

New scales need to be pilot tested using a similar sample as your targeted population.

# SCALE CONSTRUCTION

Scale Construction refers to how the different scales are designed and developed.

## Overview of Measurement Scales in Research

In the context of research, scales measure differences among choices or levels. As discussed in the preceding section, reliability and validity of a scale are critical. There are many different types of scales that can be used in research such as Likert, Thurstone, and Semantic Differential Scales which will be discussed shortly. The type of scale used must be suitable to your research questions. Oftentimes, a researcher may choose to use an existing scale. However, in many instances, researchers will need to create their own scales since no existing scale may be suited to their research. Writing good scale items comes with practice. Scale construction is therefore regarded as an art.

## Types of Scales and Scale Construction

*Likert Scales* are the most common scales used in many types of research to measure attitudes. Choices on a Likert scale differentiate among levels of agreement or disagreement with a statement and/or item. Likert scales are comprised of a number of Likert items which can be summed together to get an overall score or analysed independently. The web abounds with dozens of different Likert scales generally ranging from four to seven response choices. Example 4.8 presents a typical Likert scale used on many instruments.

### Example 4.8: Likert Scale

9. Over the past year, the number of crimes in my community has increased?

- ☐ Strongly Agree
- ☐ Agree
- ☐ Neutral ← Think carefully before using a scale with neutral as a choice.
- ☐ Disagree
- ☐ Strongly Disagree

If you are considering a Likert scale, keep in mind the following:

1. Participants may select choices that illustrate social desirability.
2. Participants may shy away from using the more extreme choices (e.g., strongly agree or strongly disagree), which could result in central tendency biases.
3. Likert scales are primarily ordinal in nature although there are special circumstances where nominal scales (e.g, attitudinal surveys to determine standard deviation) or interval scale properties may be present (e.g., use of a 12-point Likert scale to measure group data of job satisfaction).
4. Providing a neutral category may encourage many respondents to not take a position on an issue.
5. When you construct a Likert scale, you also need to know how you will code each choice. For example, you may code from 5 (Strongly Agree) to 1 (Strongly Disagree).

**Thurstone Scales** are essentially a rank order attitudinal scale used to determine how participants view indicators on a particular dimension, with two choices (Agree or Disagree) for each item. Thurstone scales tend to be time consuming and expensive since an extensive number of statements (generally between 80 and 100) initially need to be created. The process using the Equal-Appearing Intervals Approach is as follows:

1. Identify and define the concept in a question. An example is the concept *respect* which can be defined as the esteem of, and deference towards, someone we admire.
2. Create possible items (equal numbers of positive and negative statements that can possibly be used for the concept. Recall that a large number of statements (between 80 and 100) need to be created. Start generating your statement list (see possible examples below):
   - Adults do not have to respect children.
   - Children must always respect adults.
   - I only respect those who respect me.
   - If you want respect, you must earn it.
   - Respect does not exist anymore.
   - Respect is a two way street.
3. Ask an initial panel of judges to rank each statement generated in (2) above using an 11-point effectiveness scale, with 11 representing the most favourable attitude, and one representing the least favourable attitude.
4. Use the judges' rankings and create a more manageable shortlist of *respect* statements. To get this list, compute the median score and interquartile range for each *respect* statement. Now select the 'best' items from the judges based on least variability. At this point it is also a good idea to compute the mean for each *respect* statement since you will need this information in Step 6.
5. Give this shortlist to your sample participants and ask them to indicate whether they 'Agree' or 'Disagree' with each statement.
6. Finally, calculate the mean score for the concept *respect* for each participant. Suppose your shortlist comprised 10 respect statements. To get the mean for Participant 1, add the mean (already calculated in 4 above) for each statement that got an 'Agree' rating from Participant 1.

For example, if Participant 1 rated statements 1, 4, 7, 8, 9 as 'Agree', and the means were 8.6, 5.9, 10, 9.5, and 5 respectively, the mean for Participant 1 would be 7.8.

***Semantic Differential Scales*** provide adjectival opposites/extremes to describe attitudes. The researcher asks participants to circle (see example 4.9) or tick (see example 4.10) the value that is closest to how they feel about the issue (e.g., direction and intensity). Five or seven ratings are generally provided to describe the particular attitude.

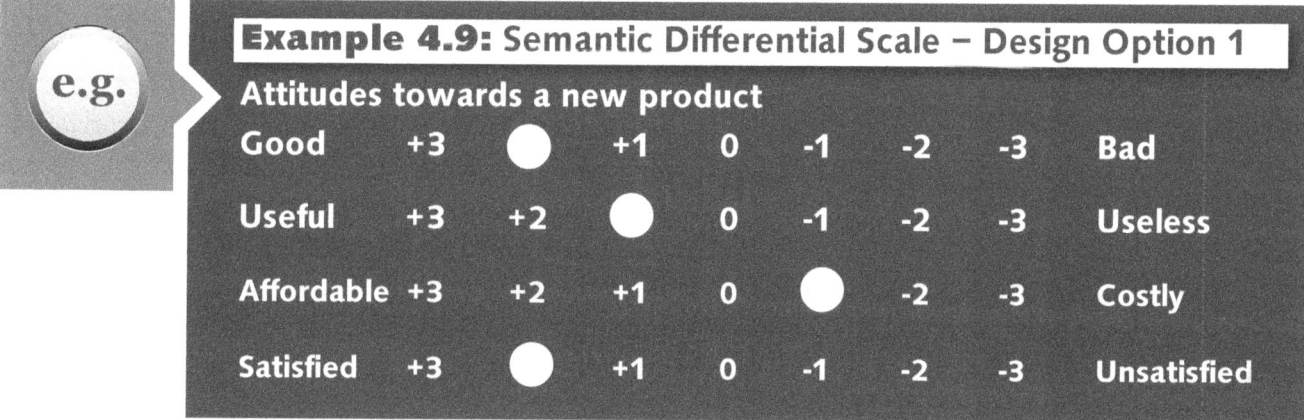

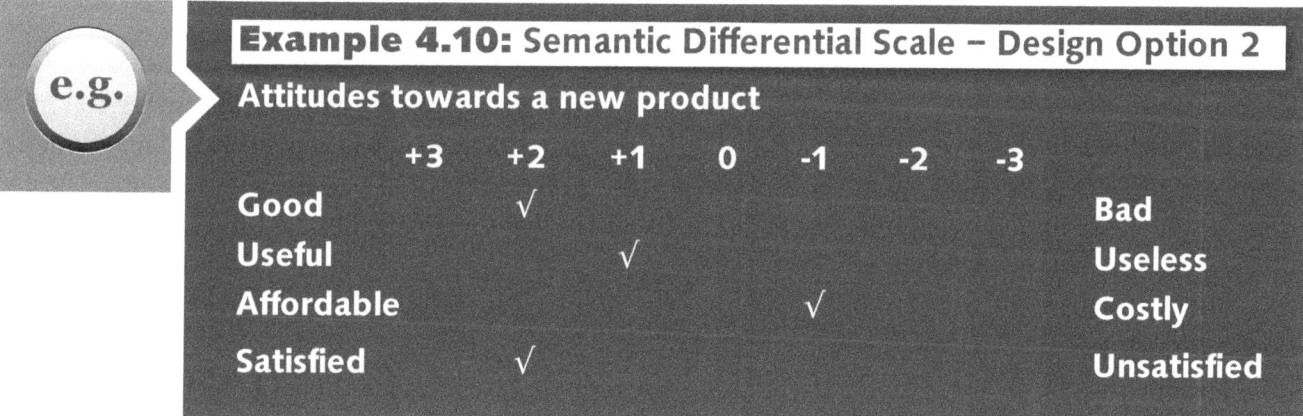

Semantic Differential Scales have many advantages over Likert scales:

- As previously mentioned, they provide direction and intensity of attitudes, whereas Likert scales only solicit the extent of attitudes.
- They tend to be clearer in terms of meaning and interpretation. As such, they are considered to be more robust, reliable, and valid.

Measurement scales must be suited to your survey questions.
It is advisable to review the literature to see what types of scales other researchers have used in similar research before deciding on a scale.

# INTERVIEW SCHEDULE DESIGN

Interview Schedule Design refers to the sequence and structure of questions that the interviewer will ask his/her participants.

## Importance of an Interview Schedule

Most researchers will use interviews at some point in their careers. When conducting interviews, interviewers need to be well prepared because interviews generally take a reasonable amount of time and you will not want to annoy or irritate your interviewees by being either unprofessional and/or unprepared. To avoid these problems, it is always recommended that an interview schedule be designed and used, especially when multiple interviewers will be conducting similar interviews. Designing an interview schedule is therefore a critical component of a good interview since it permits those involved in the research to think through the process in advance of the interview and design a schedule that will allow the interview to progress in a structured and logical manner.

## Issues to Consider When Designing an Interview Schedule

The questions in your interview schedule will be based on your overall research questions. Regardless of whether you are conducting a telephone interview or an in-person interview, logical progression from one point to another is important. In addition, when in-person interviews are being conducted, etiquette, mannerisms and the like are important issues that need to be considered (see chapter 6 Conduct in the Field and Interviewing Skills). Interview schedules tend to have three common design aspects similar to how you plan and write an essay:

1. **Introduction**

    The start of an interview is paramount to set the tone:
    - First, greet your interviewee with a smile and a handshake and introduce yourself.
    - Second, explain to the interviewee the purpose of your research, and how the interviewees were chosen.
    - Third, let the interviewee know the approximate time for the interview.

    To illustrate, suppose you conduct an interview to determine major changes in the community over time. Your introduction script may look something like example 4.11.

### Example 4.11: Introduction Script

- Good morning (smile, shake hands), my name is John Smith and I am so happy to meet you.
- I was speaking to Pastor Duke about community evolution since Independence and he highly recommended that I talk to you. He said you have been a member of this community for 73 years. Today, I will be asking questions about your background and your observations about how this community has changed over the years.
- This information is being used for the Government Information Series on 'How our Communities have evolved since Independence'.
- The interview should take approximately 40–60 minutes of your time.

Note that you will need to work this introductory information into the conversation giving your participant sufficient time to respond.

## 2. The Interview

The actual interview is where you will gather most of your research data. Therefore, invest sufficient time to ensure that your questions are sequenced in a logical manner so that all questions pertaining to one topic are grouped together. In this section you will learn about your participant through demographic information. Things to keep in mind include the following:

- Subdivide your topics into different headings. Ensure that your transitions are smooth and logical.
- Start with easy, non-sensitive questions and work your way up to more challenging and sensitive issues.
- The majority of questions tend to be open-ended. This gives your respondent sufficient leeway to respond and thereby provide rich data.
- Set a pace that does not unduly hurry the participant and one that will ensure that you get your questions thoughtfully answered.

After your introduction, you need to gather some *background information* before getting into the main interview questions. Example 4.12 provides a sample of questions that you might ask to gather opening background information.

### Example 4.12: Interview Body

**Background Information**

1. How long have you lived in Paradise Cove?
2. How old were you when you moved to Paradise Cove?
3. Did you always live in Paradise Cove?
4. How many persons made up your family here in Paradise Cove?

**Hint:** From your initial discussion with Pastor Duke, you already know this respondent moved to Paradise Cove when she was young and has since lived in Paradise Cove most of her life. You may use this information to segue into more in-depth questioning. Oftentimes, you may receive the answers to several related questions if the participant gives a more lengthy answer. You just need to record the information under the relevant questions in each section and skip to the next relevant question. After you have dealt with background information, you can then move to the central interview section which may be titled *Changes Over the Last Fifty Years* (see example 4.13).

### Example 4.13: Interview Body contd

**Changes Over the Last Fifty Years**

5. How has the family structure changed/evolved over the last 50 years?

6. What other changes have you witnessed over the last 50 years with regards to the following?

- Attitudes towards the environment
- Churches (role of the church in the community)
- Community attitudes in general (unity, togetherness)
- Crime
- Diversity of the population
- Dress
- Growth of the town (number of businesses, number of houses, expansions)
- Governance
- Infrastructure development (roads, utilities)
- Range of goods and services now available
- Trade diversity (if any)
- Schools (e.g., the education system)

It may also be useful to ask a final question that allows the interviewee a chance to contribute something beneficial to the topic of discussion which you may not have thought about and therefore was not captured in your interview schedule. For example, your final interview question could be the question shown in example 4.14.

### Example 4.14: Final Interview Question

Mrs Tony, is there anything else that you think is important about how Paradise Cove has changed/evolved over the last 50 years which was not discussed during the interview that you would like to share?

## 3. Conclusion

Thank your participant for his/her time (see example 4.15). You may follow up with results after your research.

**Example 4.15: Thank You**

Mrs Tony, it has been a real pleasure speaking with you this afternoon.

Thank you so much for taking time to share your thoughts on how Paradise Cove has been transformed over the last 50 years.

The Government Series on community evolution over the last 50 years will be aired later this year (sometime during October). It will be aired on Multi-Choice TV.

I will contact you as soon as I know the exact date so that you can view the series in its entirety.

Have a wonderful afternoon.

A skilled and personable interviewer can surmount many of the disadvantages associated with interviews.

Remember that successful interviews depend on
- Scheduling at a time and location that is convenient for the interviewee.
- Your professionalism.
- Your punctuality.
- The manner in which you interact with the interviewee.
- The time allocated for the interview.

# 5 Sampling

- Sampling Frame
- Sample Size
- Probability Sampling
- Sampling Error
- Sampling Bias
- Non-Probability Sampling
- Response Rate
- Pilot Study
- Incentives

## SAMPLING FRAME

**Sampling Frame is a list/file/directory of the population of interest from which potential sample respondents will be drawn.**

### Why Use a Sampling Frame?

Ideally, it would be fantastic if every member of the population (e.g., people, things, items etc.) to which the researcher would like to make an inference could be selected for a study; however, in reality this is neither practical nor economical. Thus, a sampling frame, a list of the population of interest, is used to extract a subset of the population. Using an existing sample frame can save considerable time, effort, and money. Thus, researchers rely on existing sampling frames since it can expedite the research process.

### Attributes of Good Sampling Frames

There are three essential attributes that researchers should consider when they opt to use an existing sampling frame:

*Completeness*: Is the complete population represented. If not, how much bias will be created by the portion that is unrepresented? For example, a poll of public opinions in a particular area could use the local telephone directory as the sampling frame. Note, however, that although a telephone directory would provide a good representation of the population, some members of the population will still be excluded because telephone directories only publish landline phone numbers, not cellular phone numbers and many people have only a cellular phone. Additionally, some persons who have a landline may have requested an unlisted number, or some persons may not have any type of phone. A primary criterion for probability sampling is therefore violated because not everyone has an equal chance for selection.

*Accuracy*: How accurate is the recorded information? If 2,000 names of persons with residential telephone lines were accidently omitted from the telephone directory, then the telephone directory would not be an accurate sampling frame. Likewise, if names were duplicated, this would again create inaccuracy. A small number of omissions/duplications would not be a cause for great concern; however, a large number of omissions/duplications would be quite problematic.

*Up to date:* Is the sampling frame current? Using a list that is dated can create potential biases since some members of the current population would not get a chance to participate. Further, some members may have moved, died, or migrated, thereby compromising random selection.

## Creating a Sampling Frame

Where no suitable sampling frame exists, the researcher will have no alternative but to create one. To do this, the researcher will need to identify the entire population (e.g., people, organizations) and assign a unique identifier to each element in the population (e.g., a population of 100 organizations could be numbered 1 to 100). If the population needs to be divided into strata, first divide the population into your desired strata (e.g., age, sex), and then assign the unique identifier to each element in each stratum.

## Updating an Existing Sampling Frame

Sometimes, it may be necessary for the researcher to update an existing sampling frame. To do this, the researcher should start with the baseline data available, then revise. For instance, if a researcher was interested in the marketing practices of business firms, suitable sampling frames would either be the yellow pages in the telephone directory or the membership list maintained by the local chamber of commerce. Suppose the researcher decided to use the chamber of commerce's membership directory which is two years dated. The researcher should start with the old list and speak with chamber of commerce officials to get a list of new companies that joined over the two-year period and companies that discontinued membership over the same two-year period. The membership directory would then be updated by adding the new companies and deleting any companies that are no longer members.

### Examples of Sampling Frames

*Opinion Polls* - electoral registers, telephone directories

*Businesses* - chamber of commerce membership list, telephone yellow pages

*Employees* - organization's list of employees

*Students* - university/college/school list of students

**TIP:** Use of an existing sampling frame saves time and money. However, be cognizant that an existing sampling frame may contain errors which could lead to sample biases depending on the magnitude of the errors.

# SAMPLE SIZE

Sample Size refers to the number of observations in a sample.

## Sample Size for Quantitative vs Qualitative Research

Sample size determination for quantitative versus qualitative research takes quite different approaches since sample representativeness is more important in quantitative studies than in qualitative studies. In the latter case, the researcher has a great degree of flexibility in choosing the sample size. For example, 40 cases in a qualitative study would be considered as relatively large, but quite small for a quantitative study. For comparative qualitative studies, a good rule of thumb is at least ten cases per group. In contrast, in quantitative studies, sample size needs to be considered in the context of expected variation in the data. A larger sample size will provide more accuracy; however, this accuracy comes at a price.

## Issues to Consider When Determining Sample Size for Qualitative Studies

The objective of quantitative research is to gain statistical validity, whereas the objective of qualitative research is to gain in-depth understanding. The issues that require consideration for determination of sample size between the two types of methodologies are therefore quite different. To date, much controversy still exists regarding a suitable sample size for a qualitative study. To assist with this dilemma, think about the following when trying to determine the sample size for a qualitative study:

*Data Saturation:* No golden rule exists regarding the sample size needed to attain data saturation in qualitative studies. The guiding principle is that data saturation is reached when new data does not result in the creation of any new categories/themes for a qualitative research study. Data saturation is important since it will impact content validity.

*Type of Qualitative Research:* Qualitative research can take a variety of forms, each of which usually has different assumptions and procedures. Consequently, it cannot be concluded that the same sample size needed to achieve data saturation in one form of qualitative research will be the same sample size needed to achieve data saturation in another form of qualitative research.

*Similar Research*: Your best option is to review the literature to see what sample size has been used in similar research. Typically, qualitative research studies in the literature rely on sample sizes ranging from one participant to 30 participants. If you are a student, you should also check with your professor.

## Issues to Consider when Determining Sample Size for Quantitative Studies

Determining the sample size for your study is a critical question that needs to be addressed from the outset. However, before you can figure this out you will need to consider four issues:

*Margin of Error:* The margin of error is a small amount of error that is usually tolerated to cater for any miscalculation when researchers seek to infer from a sample to a population. The margin of error is an indication of the accuracy of your results. The margin of error is also referred to as the confidence interval. A common rule of thumb used by researchers is +/- 5%.

*Confidence Level*: The confidence interval chosen will depend on the level of confidence with which you would like to generalize and the type of tests you are conducting. Common confidence levels used by many researchers are 90 per cent, 95 per cent, and 99 per cent. The most frequently used confidence level is 95 per cent.

*Population Size*: Figuring out your population size requires that you first know your population demographic (e.g., university students). Next you need to know the actual count of your population demographic. However, this may not always be possible to ascertain. Thus, you will need to approximate your sample size. A good rule of thumb for large populations is 20,000 since sample sizes do not increase substantially for populations greater than 20,000.

*Response Distribution:* What amount of variance do you anticipate in your responses? A good rule of thumb is generally 0.5 (50 per cent).

## Sample Size Calculator for Quantitative Samples

The advent of technology has made the process of sample size calculation which was previously primarily performed by statisticians practically obsolete. Today, even novice researchers can compute the sample size required for their study in mere seconds. For example, the Sample Size Calculator by Roasoft is exceedingly simple to use and will generate your sample size in a few seconds. This image shows the data fields required when using the Roasoft calculator.

| What margin of error can you accept? | % |
| What confidence level do you need? | % |
| What is the population size? | |
| What is the response distribution? | % |

Source: http://www.raosoft.com/samplesize.html

To illustrate, if you maintain *the margin of error rule of thumb at* five per cent and *the response distribution rule of thumb at* 50 per cent you will only need to enter two numbers, namely, a number for your confidence level and another for your population size. Suppose you want a 95 per cent confidence level and you input 20,000 for your population since it is large and you do not know the actual population size. The calculator will generate a sample size of 377, which is the minimum sample size that you would need for such a study.

| What margin of error can you accept? Rule of Thumb 5% | 5 % |
| --- | --- |
| What confidence level do you need? Common Choices 90%, 95%, or 99% | 95 % |
| What is the population size? If you do not know, use 20000 | 20000 |
| What is the response distribution? Leave this as 50% | 50 % |

Source: http://www.raosoft.com/samplesize.html

Table 5.1 provides an illustration of the sample size that would be required for four population sizes using confidence intervals of 95 per cent and 99 per cent respectively. As you can observe from Table 5.1, sample size does not increase in proportion to the increase in the targeted population. In fact, as the targeted population increases, sample size actually flattens out.

### Table 5.1: Sample Size Illustration

| Confidence Interval 95% | | Population | Confidence Interval 99% | |
| --- | --- | --- | --- | --- |
| Sample Size | 80 | 100 | 88 | Sample Size |
| Sample Size | 278 | 1,000 | 400 | Sample Size |
| Sample Size | 370 | 10,000 | 623 | Sample Size |
| Sample Size | 383 | 100,000 | 660 | Sample Size |

> In empirical studies, sample size is important since the aim of such research is to make generalizations from the sample to the population of interest.
>
> Many statistical tests have minimum sample size requirements. If these minimum requirements are not met, the statistical tests will generate biased output.

# PROBABILITY SAMPLING

Probability Sampling refers to a sampling methodology where every member in the population of interest/sampling frame has an equal chance of selection. This method uses a random sampling technique and statistically implies that the sample is representative of the population under study. Findings can therefore be reasonably generalized.

## When to Use a Probability Sample?

Probability sampling is scientific in nature and is the only option that can be used when a researcher is interested in making generalizations to the population of interest. This sampling method can be used in any discipline and allows the researcher to say with a certain degree of accuracy that findings from the research study are reasonably representative of the reality. Probability sampling is the choice for quantitative research.

## Probability Sampling Methodologies

Researchers can choose from several probability sampling options when conducting research. The option selected will be largely dependent on the nature of the research.

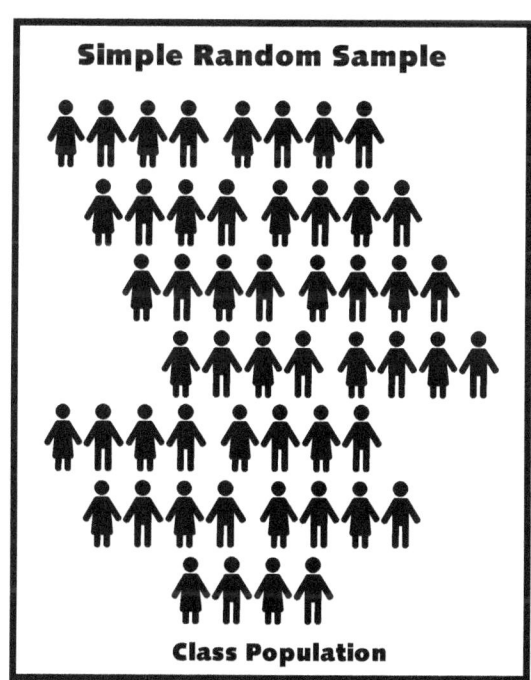

*Simple Random Sampling:* The most common probability sampling method is a simple random sample where each member of the population of interest has an equal chance of selection. For example, if you assign a number to each student in a class of 52 and use a random number generator to generate ten numbers between one and 52 to shortlist students for a trip, then you have used a simple random selection technique. While this technique is relatively simple, it may not be suited to some research situations since it might not capture the correct demographics needed for the study.

*Systematic Random Sampling:* Systematic sampling involves choosing every $n^{th}$ element in the targeted population. The sampling interval $n$ is mathematically determined by the researcher. For example, if a researcher was conducting research on undergraduate student stress and s/he wanted a sample of 400 students, and the total undergraduate student population was 20,000, then the researcher would have to use a sampling interval of 50 to get a sample of 400 (i.e., total population 20,000 / desired sample size 400 = sampling interval 50). The starting point to initiate the selection of these 400 students should be randomly selected (anywhere between 1 and 50).

*Stratified Random Sampling:* This method is used when the researcher wishes to collect data on different subgroups. It requires two steps. First, the total population is divided into different strata/subgroups based on the hypotheses/research questions. Second, simple or systematic random selection is then used to select participants from each stratum. Thus, if the researcher wants to measure university student stress levels by undergraduate degree programme, sex, and age (under 25, older than 25), the process would be as follows:

1. Identify all undergraduate students.
2. Stratify (divide) students by degree programme.
3. Stratify students in each degree programme by sex.
4. Stratify males and females in each degree programme into the two age groups 'under 25' and 'over 25'.
5. If simple random sampling is being used, use a random number generator to extract the desired sample. If systematic random sampling is being used, determine your sampling interval and randomly select every $n^{th}$ male and $n^{th}$ female in each age group from each programme until the desired sample size is obtained.

The major advantage of this method is that each subgroup as well as the overall population will be accurately represented. The major disadvantage is that the population will need to be fairly large so that a sufficient number of participants can be obtained from each subgroup since most statistical tests require a minimum number in order for the test results to make sense.

***Cluster Sampling:*** This method is suitable when the population of interest is scattered over a wide geographical area such as an entire country. Using our example on student stress, assume that the researcher decides to use only cities with populations of greater than 500,000 people as a cluster. Also, assume that Country X has 1,000 cities with populations of greater than 500,000. The process would be as follows:

1. **Obtain Sampling Frame**: The researcher will first need to get a listing of the 1,000 cities with a population of greater than 500,000 people in Country X.
2. **Determine Sample Size**: Next, the researcher must determine if a one stage cluster or two-stage cluster sample will be used. Let us assume that the researcher decides to use a two stage cluster sample and s/he determines that sufficient participants can be drawn from universities in 20 cities. The researcher has two options to select the 20 cities. If simple random sampling is used, the researcher will use a random number generator to select 20 cities (clusters) out of the 1,000 cities. If systematic random sampling is used, the sampling interval would be 50 (i.e., total population 1,000/desired sample size 20). The sample would comprise every $50^{th}$ city. If the researcher starts the initial count at one, the sample would comprise city 1, city 50, city 100...city 1,000. If the researcher starts the initial count at 15, the sample would comprise city 15, city 65, City 115, city 165, etc.

   Now that the researcher has 20 randomly selected cities, the researcher must make a decision on whether s/he will survey all university students in the 20 randomly selected cities (this would be a one stage cluster) or a subset of the university student population from those cities (this would be a two stage cluster). Recall that we initially said that the researcher would use a two stage cluster sample. Therefore, the researcher will need to select a sample of university students from the 20 randomly selected cities. To obtain the subset of university students for the second stage, the researcher will have to obtain a sampling frame comprising all university students across the 20 cities and use a similar process as was used for the selection of the cities (i.e., either simple or systematic random sampling).

Note that the *n* for both the random selection of universities and the university student populations would be determined based on the actual sample size that you need for your study.

## Probability Sample Selection Process

Probability samples can be selected using a variety of strategies, ranging from rudimentary to sophisticated. For small simple random samples, every element can be numbered and placed in a box. For example, if you had 100 elements, number each element from one to 100. Fold the 100 slips of paper and place them in the box. Ask someone to mix up the slips of paper in the box and pick out 20 slips of paper.

A more sophisticated approach would be to use the RAND function in the Microsoft Excel program to randomly select the 20 elements for your study. A random number generator can also be used where 20 randomly generated numbers can be selected from a list of 100 numbers. For example, if you use the free random number generator available at http://random.org and select *Sequences* under the *Numbers* tab you will get the box on the left.

**Part 1: Sequence Boundaries**
Smallest value [ 1 ] (limit - 1,000,000,000)
Largest value [ 100 ] (limit + 1,000,000,000)
Format in [ 1 ] column(s)

| Sample Count | 1st Try | 2nd Try | 3rd Try | 4th Try |
|---|---|---|---|---|
| 1 | 66 | 61 | 55 | 92 |
| 2 | 18 | 71 | 84 | 10 |
| 3 | 44 | 62 | 96 | 14 |
| 4 | 2 | 76 | 38 | 70 |
| 5 | 6 | 78 | 72 | 11 |
| 6 | 88 | 48 | 28 | 48 |
| 7 | 92 | 35 | 32 | 13 |
| 8 | 65 | 2 | 42 | 64 |
| 9 | 51 | 16 | 95 | 55 |
| 10 | 38 | 96 | 37 | 49 |
| 11 | 67 | 46 | 36 | 99 |
| 12 | 41 | 91 | 77 | 82 |
| 13 | 14 | 18 | 3 | 72 |
| 14 | 20 | 32 | 90 | 33 |
| 15 | 78 | 81 | 66 | 74 |
| 16 | 50 | 9 | 35 | 2 |
| 17 | 99 | 17 | 20 | 90 |
| 18 | 91 | 83 | 44 | 52 |
| 19 | 80 | 72 | 16 | 26 |
| 20 | 74 | 33 | 22 | 34 |
| 21 | 43 | 31 | 53 | 20 |
| 22 | 57 | 84 | 1 | 32 |
| 23 | 36 | 75 | 68 | 39 |

Recall, that we said that our population is comprised of 100 elements. Therefore, our largest value will be 100 and our smallest value will be 1. In Part 1 of the Sequence Boundaries, enter '1' and '100', set format to 1 and then select 'Get Sequence' under part 2. A list of 100 randomly generated numbers will appear. Note that no duplicates are in the list. All 100 members of the population have an equal chance of selection.

Select the first 20 randomly generated numbers in the list since our sample size is 20. Note that if you were to repeat the process, each time you would get an entirely new ordering of random numbers as shown here. Try it for yourself and repeat the process several times. You will see that you get a completely different sequence compared to our numbers.

When using random sampling, you should always cater for possible non-response by selecting a slightly larger sample than you actually need (e.g., you could select the first 23 randomly generated numbers).

## Cost Associated with Probability Sampling Methodologies

Probability sampling will definitely cost more compared to non-probability sampling methods. This is because the full population of interest has to be accessed and this can be quite costly especially if a sampling frame has to be created or modified to make it current.

## Summary of Probability Sampling Methodologies

**Simple Random Sample** → Determine sample size. Use a random number generator to select the sample from your sampling frame.

**Systematic Random Sample** → Determine sample size. Set sampling interval $n$. Choose a random start number then choose every $n^{th}$ element in population until the desired sample size is achieved.

**Stratified Random Sample** → Determine sample size. Divide total population into desired strata. Use either simple or systematic random sampling to select participants from each stratum.

**Cluster Sample** → Determine sample size. Select cluster(s) using either simple or systematic random sampling. Determine if a one stage cluster will be used (i.e., all participants in the cluster), or if a two stage cluster will be used (i.e., a subset of the population in the cluster). If a two stage cluster is being used, select the subset using either simple or systematic random sampling.

**TIP** Scholarly work in many disciplines requires that the researcher must use a probability sampling technique.

Therefore, check your discipline to see what type of sampling was used for the type of research you are conducting.

# SAMPLING ERROR

Sampling Error is a statistical term associated with random sampling and arises because it is not possible to say with absolute certainty that any sample is perfect (i.e., the sample will always be slightly different from the population). Sampling error is therefore the variation between the sample and the true population.

## Is Sampling Error Inevitable?

Sampling error which results from observing a sample rather than the entire population is also commonly referred to as sampling variability or random error. It is a normal occurrence when random sampling techniques are used to extract a sample from a population and provides some idea of the precision of our estimated statistic. No matter how proficient a researcher is in designing a study, sampling error is inevitable. Specifically, no sample can be a perfect representation of the targeted population.

For example, if a sample of 100 is drawn from a population of 1,000 students in social sciences and the mean sample student mark is 60, the possibility exists that the mean mark may not be a completely accurate representation of the average mark of all students in social sciences. This could occur because the sample of 100, although randomly selected, may have included either an exceptional number of students carrying a high mark or alternatively an exceptional number of students carrying a low mark. Although improbable, it is not impossible. Consequently, the mean mark could either be overstated or understated. For any research utilizing random sampling therefore, a small percentage of the sample size variation will always be attributable to sampling error.

## Ways to Reduce Sampling Error

Researchers have a few options that can help to reduce sampling error:

- Observe every element in the population. If this is done you will have no sampling error. However, this may only be cost feasible if your population is relatively small.
- Use a sample size calculator to get an accurate sample size.
- Increase sample size. The larger your sample size, the smaller your sampling error. If you add more numbers to your sample, the sample size variance becomes smaller (less variation) thus providing a more precise approximation of the population parameter. However, bear in mind that a larger random sample will come at additional cost which may be quite prohibitive.
- Ensure that you have a good probability sampling design. If there are some specific demographics that you are looking for, ensure that your study is designed in such way that your sample captures a fair representation of the demographics of interest.

## Sampling Error Rule

In statistics, a general rule prevails in probability theory which allows researchers to estimate how close a sample statistic is compared to the true value. This rule is applicable as long as we observe a normal (bell-shaped) distribution. According to the rule, approximately 68 per cent, 95 per cent, and 99 per cent respectively of mean sample values will fall within +/- 1 to 3 standard deviations of the true population mean. The statistical terminology used to describe sampling error is referred to as the standard error of the mean. Using our previous example where our mean sample student mark was 60, if our standard deviation was ten, our normal distribution curve would look like this and we can conclude as follows:

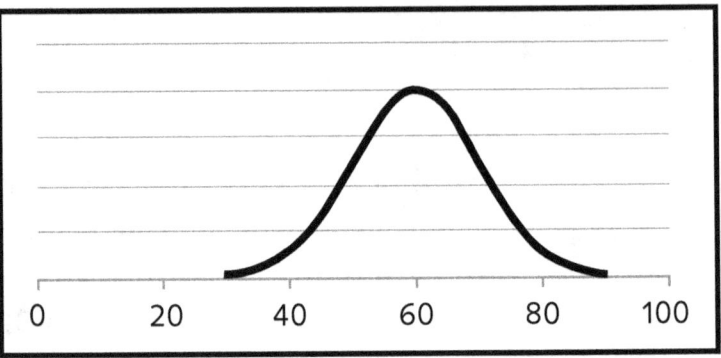

| Rule | Standard Deviation | Standard Error of the Mean |
|---|---|---|
| 68% | +/- 1 | Approximately, 68% of students will get a mark between 50–70 |
| 95% | +/- 2 | Approximately, 95% of students will get a mark between 40–80 |
| 99% | +/- 3 | Approximately, 99% of students will get a mark between 30–90 |

**TIP:** Sampling error (which is estimated from unbiased estimates) and sampling bias are quite different. Sampling error is random, whereas sampling bias is systematic. Thus, in sampling error, the sample estimates will always be equally spread between the high and low estimates.

# SAMPLING BIAS

Sampling Bias is a systematic error which prejudices your findings. It occurs when your study is badly designed and an unrepresentative sample is selected for your study and/or selected participants choose not to participate.

## What Causes Sampling Bias?

An overarching goal in most scholarly research is to strive to collect data which is both accurate and representative of the population of interest. This requires that the researcher devotes sufficient time and financial resources to properly design his/her study so that sampling bias is reduced. Sampling bias occurs when a researcher utilizes a sample selection methodology which excludes certain members of the population from participating in the study. Consequently, non-response from important segments of the population is not captured, and/or the responses from those surveyed may be quite different from those who were not surveyed. Non-response may also be an issue of concern when those who are in the sample choose not to participate in the study either through choice, death, or another reason. Low response rates can create serious sample biases.

Sampling bias may not be an issue of concern for certain types of research (e.g., a class exercise where students are learning about research methodology), however, for any serious research it is of paramount concern. Sampling bias is particularly prevalent when non-probability samples (e.g., convenience samples, volunteer samples) are used since many demographic profiles and elements are excluded when these types of methodologies are used. However, it can also be a source of concern when probability samples are used. For example, if a researcher was conducting research on adolescent drug use in a particular country and wanted to use probability sampling, the most logical sampling frame would be the enrolment list of students at each high school in the country. However, certain groups of adolescents would still be excluded from the research (e.g., those who have dropped out of the school system or those who are homeschooled).

A probability sampling methodology will also be biased if either over or under representation occurs. This might occur as a result of sheer bad luck or genuine lack of knowledge about sampling procedures or the population in question. It can also be a reflection of the reality (i.e., it is virtually impossible to obtain a perfect sample without prohibitive costs). Finally, although unethical, it may be done deliberately in an attempt to skew results to influence some decision.

Generally, sample selection biases can be reduced and controlled in a probability sample by simply using a larger sample. However, note that even when the entire population is used (e.g., a census) bias may still be prevalent since some participants may not take the questionnaire seriously.

## How to Determine if your Sample is Biased

You can determine if your sample is biased by simply comparing your sample characteristics to your population characteristics. For example, sex is almost always an important variable in research. Thus, if you were conducting a study using university students where the sex distribution is 2:1 (female: male) then your sample should reflect this ratio. If this is not done and you end up with more males than females, your results are going to be quite biased. In such a scenario, a stratified random sample might be more appropriate compared to a simple random sample. Failure to consider proportion issues that might be prevalent in your population of interest will affect the manner in which you will be able to report your results.

## Problems Caused by Sampling Bias

Sample biases are likely to occur in most, if not all, studies. Biases will cause problems with data accuracy and reporting. If the misrepresentation is minor, the researcher will still be able to make reasonable inferences from the sample to the population of interest. However, if the misrepresentation is pronounced, the study could be discredited.

## Ways to Reduce Sampling Bias

- Invest time to carefully design your study.
- Use a probability sampling methodology.
- Understand the characteristics of your target population to determine if you need to use a stratified random sample.
- Make your sample as large as is realistically feasible taking into account budgetary constraints and the sample size required for certain statistical tests.
- Review your sampling frame to ensure that it is not dated and members are not duplicated, and so on.

- Try to prevent non-response from the actual sample. A pilot test may help to identify issues that may prevent some members from not responding. Also, use of incentives and/or follow up may help to motivate persons to participate.

Sampling bias can seriously affect your ability to make inferences from your sample to your population. Therefore, invest time and effort upfront to think through the process and come up with a good study design so that sample bias can be controlled and your study can be credible.

# NON-PROBABILITY SAMPLING

Non-probability Sampling refers to a sampling methodology where members in the population of interest/sampling frame do not have an equal chance of selection. This methodology is non-scientific in nature and is based on the researcher's judgment of whom to include in the sample. Findings therefore cannot be generalized since the sample is not a true representation of the population under study.

## When to Use a Non-Probability Sample

Non-probability samples are useful when: (1) cost and time are critical constraints; (2) no sampling frame exists for the population under study; (3) accuracy/rigour are not important factors in the research endeavour; and (4) generalizations of findings is not an important aspect of the research being conducted. Non-probability sampling is also useful in situations where it may not be practical and/or sensible, and may also be morally questionable (e.g., medical trials) to use a probability sampling approach.

## Non-Probability Sampling Methodologies

Similar to probability sampling methods, researchers have a number of non-probability sampling options at their disposal. Non-probability sampling methodologies are used for many types of exploratory research. However, these methodologies have limited use since they lack scientific rigour.

## Convenience Sampling

Convenience sampling is the most common non-probability sampling approach utilized. This method which chooses items arbitrarily is also commonly referred to as haphazard, accidental, opportunity, or grab sampling. As the name suggests, ease of access/availability of the participants is the primary reason for use of this technique. Additionally, this technique allows for quick data collection at an economical cost. An example of convenience sampling would be if a researcher stood at a central location on a university campus and asked each student passing the location if s/he is willing to participate in a study on university student stress. Although the sample would not be representative of the total student body, it will allow the researcher to gather some data for an exploratory or pilot study.

## Purposive Sampling

Purposive sampling which is also referred to as judgmental sampling is used when the researcher relies on his or her own subjective judgment to select participants for a study. Essentially, the researcher selects participants for the study who have special knowledge about or experience with the phenomenon or research topic. Careful selection of the participants facilitates better understanding on the topic. For instance, a researcher interested in learning about ethical practices in the accounting profession would purposefully select accountants for his/her study.

## Snowball Sampling

The snowball sampling technique is generally used for hard to access populations with no available listing, which will be extremely difficult to compile (e.g., gangs, commercial sex workers, illegal marijuana farmers). This methodology relies on previously identified members of a group to recruit and/or identify other persons for the researcher to question/interview. The sample is essentially obtained from each participant who identifies another participant. This type of sampling process appears to grow like a moving snowball.

## Quota Sampling

Quota sampling is a methodology that uses a strategy similar to stratified random sampling whereby the population of interest is first separated into mutually exclusive groups. The researcher then uses judgment to select a proportion from each group. For example, a researcher interested in measuring student stress may select the first 20 females and the first 20 males students in the age group less than 25 and the first 20 female students and the first 20 males students in the age group over 25 from each degree programme in each department at a university to compose a sample for measuring student stress at the university.

## Non-Probability Sample Selection Process

Non-probability samples can also use a variety of strategies for selection of the sample. Convenience sampling techniques tend to use any location where researchers believe that they would get a quick sample that would be appropriate for their research. For example, research on food purchases could be conducted in a supermarket, research on shopping trends could be done in a shopping mall, and public opinion on a trending issue could be done on the street. In snowball sampling, the research will most likely be done in the area where the group of interest operates.

> Non-probability sampling methodologies are cost-effective but lack scientific rigour. Consequently, research from such studies while informative, may be difficult to publish in many disciplines.

# RESPONSE RATE

**Response Rate refers to the percentage/proportion of the target sample who successfully participates in a study.**

## Response Rate Across Disciplines

The response rates across different disciplines can differ substantially. Notwithstanding, regardless of discipline, researchers all hope for a high response rate since non-response can create serious biases in data. No golden standard exists for any discipline. The response rate in any discipline can be influenced by a number of factors, the two most common being distribution mode and whether or not incentives are provided.

Generally, face-to-face questionnaires tend to receive a much higher response rate compared to email questionnaires, mail questionnaires, or telephone questionnaires. Internal questionnaires also tend to receive higher responses compared to external questionnaires. Questionnaires that provide some sort of incentive also tend to attract a higher response rate.

## How to Improve Response Rates

Researchers employ a number of strategies to improve response rates. However, all strategies come with a price tag. For email and mail questionnaires, researchers can send out follow up reminders to encourage participants to complete the questionnaire. However, the success of this strategy is largely dependent on whether participants are interested in participating, but simply have not gotten around to filling out the questionnaire. If the respondent has no interest whatsoever, one or more reminders will not make any difference. They will simply be thrown into the trash. For telephone questionnaires, follow up calls may be tried at different times with the hope that participants may be available. Of course, with caller identification, many persons may opt not to answer their phones.

Some researchers also believe in the use of incentives since research has shown that incentives generally improve response rates. More on this will be discussed later in the chapter. Properly designed and attractive questionnaires that are of a reasonable length and do not require more than ten to 15 minutes to complete may also encourage higher response rates. Finally, researchers can also over-sample to cater for possible non-response.

## Possible Reasons for Non-Response

There are a number of reasons why a researcher may not get a response to his/her questionnaire. Some common reasons are noted below:

*Lack of Interest*: Respondent does not have an interest in the particular research.

*Lack of Time:* Respondent is genuinely interested and/or is not averse to the research but cannot find time to complete the questionnaire.

*Incorrect Address/Telephone Number:* Respondent's email, residential address, or telephone number has changed.

*Unsuitable Distribution Method:* Method of distribution is unsuitable. For example, some older persons may have an email account but do not actually use the account themselves.

*Respondent may be Deceased*: Participants may have died but their names may still be appearing in the sampling frame.

*Sensitivity of the Topic*: The topic may be very sensitive. It may probe into very private issues and/or can be emotionally disturbing to some participants (e.g., discussing sexual abuse, or number of sexual partners).

*Questionnaire Length*: The questionnaire has too many questions and acts as a deterrent to respondents.

*Questionnaire Design:* The questionnaire is unattractive and badly designed in more than one respect. For example, Likert scales are not carried forward to the next page and the respondent has to keep turning back to the first page to review the scale for rating purposes or the font size used is too small for older respondents to read. Additionally, the questionnaire may have been printed on a machine where the ink is poor so that some parts of the survey are faded and/or some lines have smudges because the printer used for printing needed servicing.

No golden rule exists for questionnaire response rates. Check your discipline to see what is an acceptable rate.

In social science research, researchers generally strive for at least a 70 per cent response rate.

# PILOT STUDY

**A Pilot Study is a trial run of your instruments and/or procedures aimed at discovering problems and taking corrective action prior to the actual study.**

## Importance of a Pilot Study

Pilot studies are a normal component of good research design. They enable the researcher to try out new instruments and/or procedures prior to a major research study to determine if the instruments and/or procedures are well designed to collect accurate, reliable, and valid information. Pilot studies can also be used to gain some preliminary insight into an exploratory study so as to convince funders that the research is worthy of investment.

Pilot studies can save both time and money since potential problems can be identified and corrected before the actual research is executed. Pilot studies can be used in both quantitative and qualitative studies and multiple pilots can be conducted depending on the nature of the research (e.g., focus group to determine issues that should be addressed, pilot of actual instrument). Pilot studies should follow the same administrative procedure that you plan to use in your actual study. At a minimum, a pilot study should be used for checking the following:

- Clarity of instructions (e.g., Should respondents circle or shade responses?)
- Clarity of questions (e.g., Are all questions clear? Are there any ambiguous questions?)
- Is the time allocated for completion of the survey adequate?
- Potential logistical problems such as adequacy of the distribution process (e.g., assuming that all respondents have access to either a computer or email).
- Do respondents of the pilot have any suggestions that can improve the survey (e.g., Is the font too small? Is the survey too long?)

## Participants for a Pilot Study

To improve internal validity, a pilot study should be executed using participants who are very similar to the targeted population. Thus, if the sample population is undergraduate female university students, the pilot should also use undergraduate female university students. No gold standard or benchmark exists for the number that should be used in a pilot study. However, a good rule of thumb is at least ten persons. Any participants used in a pilot study should not be included in your actual sample since their inclusion will taint your data.

## Evaluation of the Pilot Study

Following completion of the pilot, the researcher must carefully review the questionnaires as well as the comments provided on the comments sheet regarding clarity of instructions, completion time etcetera. Corrective action should be taken to remedy any problems. For example, if most of the participants reported that the font was too small, and respondents further reported that they answered only a few questions because of the font size, the researcher would be wise to heed this concern and use a larger font, or many participants from the actual sample may choose not to do the questionnaire. Additionally, critical review of the actual responses on the questionnaire may necessitate that certain questions be reworded since the answers may show misinterpretation of the questions.

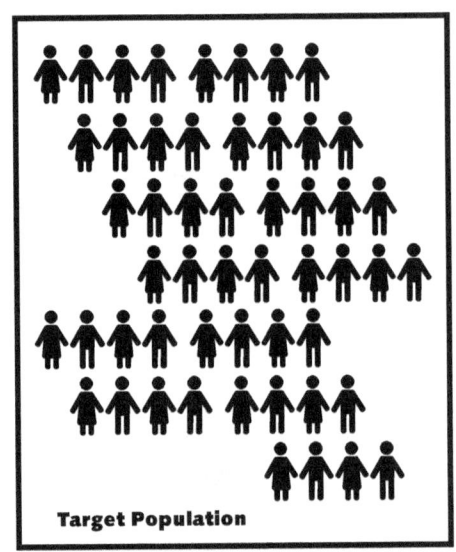

**Target Population**

**Pilot Sample (Use similar participants)**

**TIP**

Pilot studies are useful since they identify problems which can be corrected before an instrument and/or procedure is carried out using the actual sample.

Pilot studies can save time and money and lead to higher quality data collection.

# INCENTIVES

**Incentives are benefits offered to participants to motivate them/ peak their interest to participate in the research.**

## Should Incentives be Used in Research?

Researchers use incentives based on the situation, their personal value systems, and the benefits that can be obtained from use of an incentive. When using an incentive, keep in mind that sampling biases are likely to increase even when probability samples are used, since some participants will do the questionnaire simply to get the incentive and may not necessarily pay attention and/or be honest when completing the questionnaire. Notwithstanding, incentives can actually be effective in certain types of situations (e.g., trying to encourage non-responders to complete your questionnaire, when your questionnaire is long, when your questionnaire has a lot of open-ended questions).

## Types of Incentives

Incentives can be either monetary or non-monetary. Monetary incentives can take a variety of forms (e.g., actual cash, gift cards, coupons). In contrast, non-monetary incentives include some sort of gift (e.g., pens, iPads, headphones). Another type of incentive is where the researcher promises that some monetary amount will be donated to a particular charity for each participant who takes the questionnaire. In general, cash incentives are most effective in boosting response rates.

## Cost of Incentives

An important consideration when using incentives is your budget. Incentives can be expensive. In order for an incentive to motivate a targeted participant, it must be sufficiently attractive. Since cost is a major factor in the use of incentives, a researcher will need to determine if it would be better to offer a single expensive incentive such a television which all participants will have a chance to win in a raffle/sweepstakes manner or whether individual incentives would be more motivating. The web abounds with information on use of incentives, so you might want to do a search prior to considering an incentive to see what other researchers have used in similar types of research to encourage participation.

## Issues to Keep in Mind when Using Incentives

- No gold standard exists regarding use of incentives.
- Incentives can take a variety of forms.
- Incentives increase costs of your research.
- Is there a way to deliver the incentive that would not track the respondents who participated? This is especially important for questionnaires which require disclosure of intimate/sensitive issues.
- How can you ensure quality control? For example, you may need to put some mechanism in place to prevent participants from completing an electronic questionnaire several times. Additionally, you

may need to specify some qualifying criteria for eligibility to participate. For example, if you are evaluating the usefulness of a presentation on ways to reduce workplace stress, you could specify upfront that if a staff member did not attend and stay for the entire duration of the presentation, then s/he should not participate in the survey. Here you may have to rely on the participant's honesty unless you kept a register of attendance and tracked when each participant arrived and left.

- Incentives are a practical way to increase response rates; however, incentives could also lead to demographic biases since certain groups may be more likely to participate in the research (e.g., low income socio-economic groups). Incentives can also result in data quality issues. For example, you can have a situation where some respondents do not answer many of the questions (item non-response) and/or provide inconclusive answers (e.g., the respondents choose the 'Neutral' or 'Don't Know' category for most answers) simply because they want the incentive but do not really want to take the time to answer the questions.

- Choose an incentive that would have universal appeal to a wide demographic group if your research involves the entire population. For instance, offering something as specific as a coupon for $10 worth of beauty products will shift your demographic group primarily to females, while a coupon for baby food will shift your demographic primarily to mothers.

- If your questionnaire is lengthy, an incentive may serve as a good motivator.

- Exercise diligent care with your communication regarding incentives. For example, if you are using a lottery or raffle and only one television can be won, ensure that your communication clearly states that there will be only one prize.

Likewise, when you promise an incentive to only a specified number of respondents, bear in mind that this needs to be clearly communicated. For example, the first 1,000 participants will receive a gift voucher for $10 which can be redeemed at XYZ Store.

Ambiguous communication and/or unclear communication may lead to legal action on the part of the respondent.

- Check with your institutional review board to see if the use of incentives is permitted.

- Finally, in addition to using an incentive, provide a compelling reason to encourage respondents to participate in the study. For instance, indicate on your survey that your research will be used to improve customer service in the hospitality industry and that without the participant's valued feedback this goal cannot be realized.

**TIP**

Incentives can be a practical way to improve response rates.

However, note that incentives are costly and may reduce data quality unless proper thought is put into the process to guard against deteriorations in data quality.

# 6 Ethics and Data Collection

- International Research Protocol and Institutional Review Boards (IRB)
- Ethics in Data Collection
- Data Retention and Data Security
- Preparing for Interview Fieldwork
- Conduct in the Field
- Interviewing Skills
- Coding Quantitative Data
- Coding Qualitative Data

## INTERNATIONAL RESEARCH PROTOCOL AND IRB

**International Research Protocol** refers to the global body of standards and guidelines of best practice in research.

An **Institutional Review Board (IRB)** is a committee set up by an institution to approve and monitor research in the institution. Its primary mission is to ensure that human subjects are protected from harm.

### Necessity for International Research Protocol

Most professions are governed by guidelines that outline how members should conduct themselves. Such guidelines are intended to provide guidance to those within the profession on various practices. Although cultural beliefs and value systems can be different across the globe, there are some fundamental issues that must be interpreted in a like manner. International standards and best practices help to promote effective practices globally and establish minimum standards for a profession.

The web abounds with numerous guidelines for conducting ethical research. However, the principal protocol that governs global research is the Belmont Report of 1979. This report

was commissioned in response to the unethical, dangerous, and harmful abuses which were imposed on thousands of human subjects over the last century without their knowledge and/or consent. Some of the most horrific abuses included the German physicians' medical experiments on thousands of prisoners which resulted in permanent disability and premature deaths for many, severe birth defects in newborns as a result of the experimental testing of the drug thalidomide on pregnant women in the United States (US), radiation experiments in the US during the Second World War, and the Tuskegee syphilis study conducted by the US Public Health Service which involved 600 African Americans with syphilis infections who were never told that they had the syphilis virus or even given treatment for the virus.

The Belmont Report built on previous ethical initiatives such as the Nuremberg Code (1948), the Declaration of Helsinki (1964), and the National Research Act (1974). Today, the Belmont Report provides the overarching framework for global research involving human subjects and is a critical reference for IRBs. It highlights three ethical principles that all researchers must follow to ensure protection of human subjects, namely, respect for persons (autonomy and courtesy), beneficence (do no harm), and justice (fair and equitable treatment).

In addition to the Belmont Report, different disciplines usually have their own personalized guidelines which should be followed by researchers in the discipline (e.g., medicine – Declaration of Helsinki; sociology – American Sociological Association Code of Ethics). For those involved in social science research, the guidelines provided by the American Psychological Association 'Ethical Principles of Psychologists and Code of Conduct' should be consulted. These guidelines explain the principles outlined in the Belmont Report and also discuss issues such as competence, human relations, ethical dilemmas, privacy, and confidentiality.

## Institutional Review Boards

Similar to the Belmont Report, the establishment of IRBs was mandated because of the callous disrespect for humans exhibited by unethical researchers and the unprecedented horrors that human subjects experienced supposedly in the interest of scientific research. Today, IRBs are located in most universities, professional associations, and public and private entities that are involved in research activities. Additionally, a number of independent commercial IRBs are now in existence. These independent IRBs are governed by the same regulations as institutional IRBs.

An IRB is essentially a committee that is set up and empowered to review and approve all research pertaining to use of human subjects. A fundamental mandate of any IRB is to ensure that human subjects are not harmed. Depending on the institution, IRBs may be referred to by another names such as research ethics board (REB), independent ethics committee (IEC), human subjects institutional review board (HSIRB), or ethics review board (ERB). Regardless of name, the general mandate and role of the board will be essentially the same.

## Organizational Policy on Research

Regardless of whether you are a student or a professional researcher, it is important that you know your organization's policy pertaining to research so that you do not violate your institution's research protocol. Research involving human subjects generally require IRB approval, although one exception to the rule pertains to the use of secondary data which is publicly available. Additionally, most academic institutions globally also stipulate that students writing theses/dissertations receive IRB approval. Such approval should be sought early since it can take a few weeks.

Failure to obtain IRB approval for your research can result in dire consequences for researchers (students, academics, and other professionals). For instance, if you are a student and IRB approval was not obtained, the University may not award your degree, particularly if your research involved human subjects. In other cases, your work may be discredited, funding may be withheld, and journals may not publish your work. If you are unsure about whether your research requires IRB approval, you should check with your institution's IRB Office.

All persons seeking IRB approval must complete an online course on ethics prior to the submission of their IRB application. The link for this training will usually be located on your organization's IRB website. Applications which do not have documented proof that the training has been completed are not reviewed.

When vetting an application, IRB checks to see that your research complies with general global research ethical best practices, including a clear and sound research design that shows that your study will not cause any harm to participants. In many cases, your institution's IRB may request one or more revisions before approval is finally granted. Once approval is granted, researchers cannot make any modifications to either their research instruments or methodology without IRB re-approval.

## Research Misconduct

Research misconduct is a very serious offence. It involves issues such as faking data (e.g., making up data), data manipulation (e.g., changing results), making changes without IRB re-approval, releasing confidential information without permission, engaging in plagiarism, failling to maintain adequate documentation (e.g., no code book, not retaining your original surveys or interview transcripts), and conflict of interest issues. Although some researchers may be tempted to engage in such behaviours, researchers should desist from such unethical practices since they can ruin their professional careers and reputation.

## Why Researchers Need to Adhere to International Best Practices for Research

Most researchers publish their work. Therefore, it is important that they adhere to international best practices since failure to do so may result in their work not being published. Scholarly peer-reviewed journals have very strict guidelines about research ethics. The methodology of any published work must detail how the research was conducted. Additionally, some journals specify that they will only publish research which has received IRB approval.

IRB approval is required for most professional research and student theses and dissertations. Remember to check your organization's policy on research and follow their guidelines.

# ETHICS IN DATA COLLECTION

 Ethics in Data Collection embody the fundamental ethical principles that are universally acceptable for conducting research of any nature.

## Best Practices for Data Collection

Data collection is a normal and natural part of all research and numerous ethical guidelines are available to help researchers conduct their research in an appropriate manner. Notwithstanding, researchers still need to use sound professional judgment since guidelines cannot possibly cover every scenario. Moreover, some guidelines may be either too broad or too vague which means that they may be interpreted differently.

Regardless of interpretation, there are a few global best practices that all researchers should follow to ensure that their data is collected in an ethical manner. Fundamental ethical principles include the right to autonomy (which embodies informed consent/implied consent/right to withdraw), the right to anonymity and confidentiality, and use of properly worded questions on interview or survey instruments.

*Right to Autonomy:* Autonomy is a general moral principle and is perhaps the most important ethical principle that should be addressed in research. It basically refers to participants' rights to take part in the research without coercion, and have full detailed knowledge and honest and clear information (i.e., informed consent) of the research, particularly in situations where there are adverse and/or harmful consequences. Prior to the Nuremberg Code (1948), autonomy was not accorded to many participants since they were often not informed of the dangers associated with the research.

Informed consent can be contrasted with implied consent where actions and/or behaviours indicate consent (e.g., if you kiss someone without being forced). Implied consent may also be assumed by the nature of the situation (e.g., when you visit your doctor and your doctor conducts a physical examination, implied consent is assumed).

In general, informed consent is usually obtained from the participants themselves. However, autonomy cannot be obtained from certain groups (e.g., children, mentally incapacitated, differently disabled). Instead, permission for such groups to participate in research must be obtained from the parent, guardian, caretaker, or legally authorized representative.

Today, the rights embodied in autonomy are usually addressed in a cover letter to participants and generally require a signature especially in research that may be adverse and/or harmful. This letter should give full disclosure of the purpose of the research and why participants are being invited to participate in the research. The letter should also indicate that participation is entirely voluntary and that any participant can withdraw from the research at anytime without prejudice. In the case of survey research, participants should be informed that they are free to discontinue the survey at any time if they feel uncomfortable. Additionally, participants should also be informed that they are free to skip any questions which they do not wish to answer. Such a statement should be included as routine best practice even if the research does not include personal or sensitive questions.

Respect for autonomy may, however, need to be violated in situations where individuals pose a danger either to themselves or to others. Another situation in which the ethical and moral principles of autonomy are essentially violated pertains to covert research. Covert research is used when participants are likely to change their behaviour because they are under study. Such research presents a number of legal and ethical challenges and is not recommended without IRB approval. When covert research is undertaken, researchers still have to employ due diligence and care to ensure that participants are not harmed. The British Educational Research Association recommends that if covert research is used that participants be *debriefed* after the study and that consent be obtained post-study.

***Right to Anonymity and Confidentiality***: Regardless of the data collection methodology utilized, anonymity and confidentiality must be preserved for all information collected. This means that no identifying information should be revealed such as participants' names and titles and verbatim quotes should be avoided if such quotes could identify the participant. Similar to autonomy, prospective participants should be assured in the cover letter that anonymity and confidentiality will be preserved by the researcher reporting only aggregate statistics with no identifiers. Although in many cases researchers will know who has filled out a particular survey, all researchers have a professional duty to ensure that due diligence and care is employed so that confidentiality is not violated.

Confidentiality can also be violated in other ways apart from participant identification. For example, someone may overhear a conversation and make it public or the research assistants involved in data entry may discuss some of the data with persons who are not involved in the research. Confidentiality can also be breached if hackers hack into databases or if data is left lying around in an unsecured manner. Breach of confidentiality of any data, especially data of a sensitive or personal nature is a serious offence since it can injure participants emotionally or otherwise.

***Properly Worded Questions:*** Researchers have an ethical responsibility to ensure that survey or interview questions are properly written so that they are not construed as ambiguous, biased, misleading, and/or opinionated. Several approaches can be used to ensure that questions are well constructed such as a pilot study (see chapter 5) or review of the research instrument by one or more colleagues.

## Respect for Intellectual Property

All researchers have a moral duty to respect intellectual property. This means that researchers should never engage in plagiarism. Researchers should review the citation style for their discipline to gain insight into what would be considered as intellectual property violations. The citation style for your discipline will usually indicate when permission needs to be sought for use of copyright or published works and how works should be cited, and so on.

## Ownership and Use of Data

A critical question that needs to be addressed when data is collected pertains to data ownership. In situations where funding is provided for the research and/or when a researcher is working on behalf of an institution, this question needs to be addressed in a formal contract prior to the start of the investigation.

## Other Ethical Best Practices in Research

In addition to the aforementioned, researchers have a professional responsibility to adhere to some other global ethical best practices so that their research is not criticized. For instance, researchers should ensure that they uphold high integrity standards and that they are honest with colleagues, sponsors, and the public. They should avoid biases and discrimination and exhibit due care and diligence at all stages of the research process. They should also conform to global best practices for reporting. This means that both positive and negative results should be reported. Finally, if funding was obtained for the research, this should be declared in the publication.

**TIP:** The ethical principle pertaining to confidentiality may need to be relaxed when dangerous criminal, illegal, and/or terrorist activity is suspected. If you are unsure, have a confidential discussion with a superior or colleague and/or consult the ethics board of your professional association.

# DATA RETENTION AND DATA SECURITY

**Data Retention** refers to the time period data should be retained.

**Data Security** refers to the process for storage, retrieval, and access.

## Importance of Data Retention

Researchers collect data for a variety of reasons and most research eventually ends up getting published in one form or another. However, despite diligent efforts, research may still contain statistical or analytical errors. Such errors may be detected either during the review process (if published in a peer reviewed journal/book) or subsequent to publication.

Thus, it is important for a researcher to retain the original data in its raw form for a certain period of time so that the data can be validated if a concern is raised about data analysis. Another critical reason for data retention is to safeguard against possible allegations of research misconduct. Finally, national and institutional policies and/or funders may stipulate that the data be retained for a specified period of time. Data retention should therefore be considered as routine best practice in all research.

## Time Period for Data Retention

No golden standard exists on the number of years that data must be retained. However, it is universally accepted that data which is collected should be retained for a certain period of time. Institutions involved in data collection generally have their own organizational guidelines that detail a policy for data retention. These policies are developed and aligned with global practices/policies/standards for the type of research being undertaken. The time period for data retention may also be governed by a country's national data retention policy or the funder/sponsor of the research.

Most institutions generally retain data for about three to five years. However, a shorter time frame may be acceptable for data that is likely to become obsolete quickly (e.g., research conducted on a particular cell phone brand). In contrast, research in the medical field generally requires a much longer retention period. For instance, the Australian Code for Responsible Conduct of Research mandates 15 years for clinical trials and permanent retention in research involving gene therapy.

Academics and students should follow their institutions' guidelines for data retention. They may even need to agree to their organization's policy for data retention on their IRB application. Your discipline and/or the nature of your research may also dictate the time frame for data retention. A good rule of thumb for anyone who publishes work would be six years from the publication date. Any critique of your work and/or allegations of scientific misconduct will most likely occur within the first five years of publication. If you do not have the original data, questions could be raised about whether your research was fabricated or not. Such a situation could lead to all or part of your published work being retracted.

## Who is Responsible for Data Storage?

Even if an organization has a data storage facility, the principal investigator is ultimately responsible for getting the data to the facility. For instance, if an entity has a special room for data storage for all research emanating in the institution, each principal investigator must take the data to the storage facility and hand over the data to the appropriate personnel, so that the data can be properly stored and secured. If your organization does not have a data storage facility, the principal investigator must personally secure the data.

## Importance of Data Security and Protection

Many types of research contain very sensitive and personal data. Researchers promise participants that their identities will be protected. Thus, researchers are obligated to exercise care and diligence to ensure that all collected data is properly stored, secured, and protected. Given the recent 'Wannacry' ransomware hack of many huge enterprises around the world, it is imperative that you try to ensure that your computers and digital backups have the latest/best anti-virus, anti-malware, and system updates. Note, however, that despite your best efforts, your electronic records may still be hacked.

Physical data such as paper based surveys should be placed in a locked cabinet or storage room with restricted access. Data in computerized databases may need to have restricted access and may also need to be encrypted to protect against hackers.

Many developed countries have national policies on data security and protection (e.g., United Kingdom's Data Protection Act 1998; European Union General Data Protection Regulation 2016).

## Cost of Data Security

Data storage and security obviously come at a price. Data that is tangible (e.g., paper, samples) requires a physical storage space. Computerized data is becoming cheaper to maintain; however, costs may be incurred for offsite back-up, firewalls, intrusion detection software and constant software upgrades to prevent hacking and unauthorized access. In addition, if the data was collected using paper based surveys (e.g., census data), these paper based surveys will also need to be retained for a certain period of time. This means that costs will be incurred for storage of both the physical and electronic data.

## Disposal of Data

Once the time period for data retention is over, it is important that due care and diligence be exercised for the disposal of the data. Paper records should be shredded or burnt, not tossed into the trash. Electronic records should be deleted from storage using commercial software such as Eraser or CyberScrub. Tapes, compact discs, and other types of storage media should also be properly destroyed. This may entail unravelling the tapes, cutting the tape into pieces, or incineration. Finally, data in the form of objects/specimens/samples should also be destroyed via incineration.

**TIP**

If your project is not sponsored and/or your organization does not have an official policy on data retention, storage, and security, check your discipline and/or the journal you have published in to see if they provide any guidance on the length of time that your data should be retained.

Good research practices dictate that all data collected be securely stored.

Many organizations incorporate restricted access for different personnel.

# PREPARING FOR INTERVIEW FIELDWORK

Preparation for Interview Fieldwork requires creating a checklist of what needs to be done and engaging in strategic planning prior to actual fieldwork to ensure that the fieldwork is successful and uneventful.

## Strategic Planning for Successful Fieldwork

Your ultimate goal in any interview is to collect good quality and informative data. You will therefore need to engage in some strategic planning to ensure success whilst in the field. A successful strategy will focus on a number of critical issues such as interviewer training, interview location, scheduling of the interview(s), determining who should be present during the interview, and sequencing of the questions.

## Interviewer Training

Training of interviewers is an important activity that should be conducted prior to fieldwork. Success of the interview process depends on the professionalism of the interviewers, the thoroughness of the interview, flexibility of the interview guide, and the actual time allocated for the interview. It makes good sense to spend some substantial time in planning, training and preparation since substantial payoffs will occur during actual fieldwork.

It is good practice to conduct training especially when several persons will be responsible for data collection. Training ensures that there is consistency in the interview process. The type of training provided will be dependent on the nature and sensitivity of the interview. Training should at a minimum involve going through the interview guide to ensure that all interviewers understand the guide.

Training should use demonstrations to teach interviewers how to conduct a professional interview. Depending on the sensitivity of the interview, the training may also involve presenting various scenarios to show interviewers how to deal with different situations. For example, if an interviewer is conducting an interview with a survivor (e.g., a victim of domestic abuse), and the interviewee breaks down and starts to cry, the interviewer should be sufficiently trained to make a decision on whether the interview should be stopped, or whether a short or lengthy pause would be adequate to allow the interviewee sufficient time to recompose and resume the conversation. Another scenario might demonstrate how an interviewer can develop rapport and trust with an interviewee who is either emotional or reluctant to talk.

## Choosing an Appropriate Interview Location

Interview locations should be carefully chosen for two reasons. The first pertains to interviewer safety. Some types of research may place interviewers at risk if the research is conducted in certain areas such as known drug dens. The second reason pertains to interviewee comfort, safety concerns, and potential for distraction. You need your respondent to feel comfortable and secure. Some interviewees may be concerned about safety issues and may feel uncomfortable with an interview taking place in their home. In the case of domestic abuse or rape victims, they may not want to use their homes because the perpetrator may still inhabit the home. Finally, certain environments may provide distractions. For instance, a mother who is at home may be constantly distracted by her children.

The location selected should be comfortable and agreeable to both parties. If interviewer safety is not a concern, the interviewer should chat with the interviewee to find out where s/he would prefer to have the interview. Possible public venues might include a restaurant, coffee shop, park, office, or school. When choosing a venue, consider privacy, as well as distractions such as noise, lights, and the potential for other interruptions.

## Scheduling the Interview

You should always try to accommodate the interviewee's schedule rather than your own. When scheduling, bear in mind that if you insist on a date and time that are not convenient to the interviewee, the interviewee may cut the interview short and/or be distracted. You may, therefore, end up with little or no data or the data may be of a poor quality.

When scheduling interviews (especially in foreign countries) take account of national holidays (e.g., Good Friday and Easter Monday are public holidays in many parts of the world) and major cultural events (e.g., carnival in Brazil). Also, keep in mind the time of the year. For example, if your research involves interviews with public servants, be cognizant that many public servants may take their vacation during July–August and late December to facilitate family vacations. Therefore, time of the year may be an important factor for some types of interviews.

## Who Should be Present During the Interview?

Many persons do not like to be alone when they are being interviewed by a stranger. In other cases, research ethics dictate that a guardian or custodian be present for some groups (e.g., children, differently disabled). If you are interviewing a rape or domestic abuse survivor, the interviewee may need support from a close friend, family member, or someone such as a social worker. Otherwise, the interviewer, interviewee, and a research assistant should be sufficient for the interview.

## Type and Sequence of Questions

Prior to the interview, the interviewer should develop a protocol guide for use in the field. This is particularly important if multiple interviewers will be collecting data for the study. This guide should detail the types of questions that will be asked. The order in which questions should be asked may also be important. Some researchers believe that sensitive questions should come at the end of an interview rather than at the beginning of the interview.

A combination of question types may be necessary in a given interview (see Chapter 4 Closed-Ended and Open-Ended Questions and Interview Schedule Design). Free narrative allows the interviewee to speak uninterrupted about his/her particular incident, opened-ended questions allow responses to specific questions from the interviewer, and closed-ended questions permit responses using predetermined categories (e.g., Likert scale responses or yes/no responses).

It is also important for your interview guide to have some flexibility so that it can quickly be adapted if necessary. Keep the following guidelines in mind when developing your interview guide. Ensure that you sequence your questions so that you get solid facts before feelings. Capture facts on the present, and then work back to the past, and into the future. If you have an interview guide with only predetermined questions, put an open-ended question as your final question to give the interviewee an opportunity to provide information which might be insightful and important but was not captured. For instance, your last question could be '*Is there anything else that you would like to add that was not discussed today?*'

Finally, keep your questions clear and neutral (do not construct questions to influence answers), ensure that they are not ambiguous or double/triple-barrelled (i.e., touching two or three issues, but only allowing a response for one issue), and be cognizant that certain terminology might require definitions since they may be interpreted differently by each respondent (e.g., younger, older).

Invest time and effort to prepare adequately for your interview fieldwork since it can make the difference between quality data collection versus sloppy data collection.

# CONDUCT IN THE FIELD

Conduct in the Field refers to all the attitudes and behaviours that should be exhibited by the interviewer to make the interview process successful and uneventful.

Dress appropriately → Arrive on time → Meet, greet, and develop rapport → Use suitable etiquette → Seek permission to record

## Dress

Interviewers must dress in an appropriate manner conducive to the setting in which the interview will take place. For instance, if you are conducting a study among inmates in a local prison, it is recommended that women dress modestly so as not to attract unwanted attention and produce distractions during the research. Similarly, if you are entering an affluent neighbourhood, it is important that you are well groomed and attired.

In certain cultures, dressing in local cultural dress may also be important so that you can blend in with the local community and make your interviewees feel more comfortable. For instance, a westerner conducting an interview with women in certain Muslin communities in the East would stand out if dressed in western attire, and the interview will probably not be as effective compared to if the interviewer was dressed in the local attire.

## Punctuality

Globally, various norms exist regarding punctuality. In some parts of the world, punctuality standards are clearly defined (e.g., Germany, Japan, New Zealand, Sweden, and Switzerland). In other parts of the globe, the norms pertaining to punctuality may be quite imprecise and idiosyncratic (e.g., the Caribbean, India, Panama, and Nigeria). Notwithstanding, all interviewers should strive to be punctual regardless of the culture and social norms of the country in which the data is being collected since it is the interviewer who needs to collect information. One of your interviewees might just happen to have grown up in a country where punctuality is valued and may be quite annoyed if you arrive late even though the country in which the interview is taking place may place low priority on punctuality.

Being late is considered impolite and rude in many cultures and may leave a really bad impression regarding your professionalism and trustworthiness. Therefore, if you are in an unfamiliar setting, you should strategize to get to your destination early since there is always the possibility that you could get lost or perhaps run into horrendous traffic. If you suspect that you are going to be unavoidably late due to events beyond your control, telephone or send a text message to the person you are meeting (if possible) so that s/he is aware that you are going to be delayed.

## Pre-Interview Rapport

Greet your interviewee with a handshake, introduce yourself, thank your interviewee for agreeing to facilitate the interview, and explain the purpose of the research. Give an approximate time for the completion of the interview. Explain how the interview will be conducted and how the data will be used.

Ensure that you adhere to high ethical principles whilst conducting the interview. International best practice suggests that you should inform respondents that they have the right to stop the interview if they feel uncomfortable or distressed, that they can skip questions which make them embarrassed and/or uncomfortable, that data will be aggregated for reporting purposes, that no identifying information will be revealed, and that data will remain confidential. Note, however, that the confidentiality agreement may need to be broken in certain cases (e.g., if there is a perceived risk of harm to the interviewee or clear evidence of illegal or terrorist activity).

Finally, ask interviewees if they have any questions and concerns and take sufficient time and interest to address concerns prior to commencement of the interview so that the interviewee can feel comfortable and be well informed. Also, give the interviewee your contact information so that s/he can contact you with later questions or concerns pertaining to the research.

## Etiquette, Mannerisms, and Language Sophistication

Interviewers need to adapt their etiquette, gestures, speech, and body language to the local culture and environment in which they are working so as to avoid any cultural faux pas. Many mannerisms that are acceptable and respectful in one culture may be considered as quite rude and disrespectful in other cultures. For example, a 'thumbs up' is generally used to signify a job well done in Western cultures, however, this gesture may be considered as quite rude in other parts of the world like the Middle East. Likewise, pointing with an index finger at someone is considered offensive in many Asian countries.

Eye contact and personal space are other important issues that need to be observed. In some cultures, prolonged eye contact can make someone feel quite uncomfortable, whereas in other cultures it may appear as though you are disinterested in what the respondent is saying if you do not maintain regular eye contact. Different cultures also have boundaries regarding the amount of personal space that should be observed between two parties.

The best advice is to do your homework before arriving in an international setting so that you do not unintentionally offend the persons who will be providing the data. Peruse the web and carefully research the culture and environment that you will be working in so that you can conduct yourself in a manner which will not be construed as disrespectful, rude, offensive, and/or vulgar since inappropriate mannerisms may limit or completely curtail data collection efforts.

Interviewers also need to use language appropriate to the interview setting and context. For instance, if you are interviewing persons with little or no formal education, you will need to be flexible and adjust your vocabulary to suit. Sometimes, it may be necessary for you to resort to slangs and the local dialect so that you can engage in a meaningful conversation that puts the respondent at ease and does not make you stand out as an outsider. In contrast, if you are dealing with an educated populace, you should avoid use of slangs and dialect. Also, keep in mind that you may need to limit the use of technical jargon unless the persons being interviewed are acquainted with discipline-specific jargon.

## Recording

Many persons tend to speak more openly when they are not recorded. However, sometimes it may be difficult to conduct the interview and record accurately (in handwriting) at the same time. If you plan on recording, you must get permission from the interviewee and this permission acknowledgement should be recorded as part of the interview recording. If permission is granted to record, the interviewer may still need to use professional judgment and sensitivity and pause the recording for certain portions of the conversation. The interviewer should alert the interviewee whenever the recording is paused since this may encourage and facilitate a freer and more candid conversation.

If you plan on recording the interview and your interview is likely to be lengthy, you should purchase a digital recorder since changing cassette tapes may provide an unnecessary distraction which can break the interviewee's train of thought. Modern digital recorders provide hours of recording and can easily be transferred to your computer since most of them carry a USB port.

TIP: Your conduct in the field can have a major impact on the quality and richness of data that is collected.

## INTERVIEWING SKILLS

Interviewing Skills in research refer to the essential toolkit of skills necessary for successful data collection.

## Social Skills

Interviewers need to have good social skills so that they can effectively communicate and interact with their interviewees or they will not be very successful in collecting high quality data. Interviewers need to be friendly, sensitive, and genuinely interested in their participants. In many types of interviews, a pleasant tone of voice may also be instrumental in encouraging continued dialogue with an interviewee. Interviewers should not come across as being aggressive or arrogant since such characteristics can be detrimental to the success of the interview.

When assigning interviewers for face-to-face interviews, keep in mind that in addition to good social skills, it may be important to match interviewers and interviewees on demographics such as sex, age, and ethnicity since matching may facilitate better rapport and more candid conversation, as well as gain interviewee cooperation and trust, especially for research topics that are sensitive in nature (e.g., domestic violence, racial discrimination). For instance, a mature female interviewer of the same ethnicity as a rape victim will be more appropriate than a young male interviewer of a different ethnicity. Likewise, a male may be better suited as an interviewer for interviews with dangerous groups (e.g., criminals). In some situations it may even be wise to have two or more interviewers conducting the same interview, particularly if safety is a concern.

## Impartiality, Respect, Professionalism

Interviewers need to remain impartial and non-judgmental at all times. They also need to respect respondents and exhibit high professionalism so that respondents can feel comfortable. If respondents do not feel respected and if they perceive that the interviewer is insincere and judgmental, they will most likely not be forthcoming or candid with responses. They may even decide not to take part in the interview.

In cases involving survivors, interviewers need to listen with composure, avoid temptations to interject personal stories, and allow the interviewee to tell his/her story uninterrupted. Interviewers should also help survivors assess their risk, should tell them about available resources which may be of assistance, provide them with actual contact information for the various resources, and help them to think through safety options. Patience, empathy, and a calming tone of voice are important personality traits for such interviews. Thus, interviewers who do not possess such traits should not be used in situations where the interview could be emotionally upsetting for the interviewee.

## Effective Listener, Active Observer

Effective listening is a crucial skill that all interviewers need. Effective listening involves more than simply hearing and recording verbatim what was said. An effective listener should be an active observer so that s/he can make sense of what is said and communicated from tone of voice, body language, and facial expression of the interviewee. What is left unsaid may be just as significant as what is actually said by an interviewee.

In the same manner that an interviewer can observe body language, an interviewee will also similarly observe the body language of the interviewer. Interviewers thus need to guard against perceptions that they are disinterested in what their respondents are saying. An interviewer should use both body language (e.g., nods) and voice sounds (e.g., uhmm) to communicate active listening and to encourage the interviewee to continue the conversation. Paraphrases should be used to sum up the accuracy of a point, and can also be effective as a transition to another question. During an interview, an interviewer may also need to use some probes (i.e., follow up questions) to better understand a response and/or to get the full story. For example, an interviewer can ask 'How did you do this?' 'When was that done?' 'What did you do?'

**Are you an active listener?**

YOU ARE IF...
- You listen to replies after you speak.
- You do not interrupt when others speak.
- You try to understand what they say.
- You clarify what you hear.
- You rephrase replies to avoid misinterpretation.

## Building Rapport with the Interviewee

Depending on the nature of the interview, it may be quite easy to develop trust and build rapport with an interviewee. However, in other situations (e.g., domestic abuse, rape), developing trust and building rapport may be extremely difficult since the survivor will most likely be in an emotional state of mind and may even break down (e.g., cry) during the conversation.

In such cases, interviewers need to be sensitive and allow the interviewee to dictate the pace of the interview. The interviewer may need to chat on a totally unrelated topic for a while (e.g., a recent media story) so that the interviewee can become recomposed to continue the interview. During the interview, the interviewer may also need to pause on multiple occasions and demonstrate empathy by allowing sufficient silence so that the respondent can recompose himself/herself before continuing the conversation.

## Sensitive Questions

Many types of interviews involve sensitive and personal questions which can make respondents embarrassed, uncomfortable, and/or emotional. Interviewers conducting sensitive interviews need to be properly trained so that they can recognize verbal and non-verbal cues that the respondent is uncomfortable and see if they can remedy the situation and put the respondent at ease. Properly trained interviewers should also avoid reactions and expressions of heightened emotion (e.g., verbal exclamations of shock, disgust, or uncontrollable bursts of laughter).

The sequencing of questions in an interview is entirely at the discretion of the researcher. Some researchers prefer to start with questions which are not sensitive and gradually move on to more sensitive questions. It is believed that this helps to develop trust and build rapport and helps to make the interviewee more comfortable. When researchers put sensitive questions at the end of an interview, the respondent may become tired and the quality of the answers may be diminished if the interview is lengthy. In some types of interviews such as those involving child abuse, all types of questions may be sensitive except for demographic characteristics. Therefore, the researcher really has no choice for question sequencing but should approach the interview with sufficient care and thoughtfulness.

When sequencing questions, ensure that the questions are placed in an order that allows the respondent to make a logical transition from the previous question. When dealing with sensitive questions, you should brief the respondent during the pre-interview pleasantries about the types of questions that will be asked so that the respondent is not shocked when the questions are asked. Discussing the sensitivity of the questions at this phase will also give the respondent an opportunity to decline the interview if s/he feels that it would be too invasive. To encourage the respondent to continue with the interview, the interviewer could suggest that the respondent start the interview with the option of discontinuing if s/he feels too uncomfortable or emotional.

## Retaining Control of the Interview

Interviewers need to be in control of an interview or an interviewee may veer off topic or continue indefinitely on a certain topic. An effective way to regain control is to interrupt politely and provide a transition to another question. For example, the interviewer can say something such as *'What you are saying is really interesting, however, we really must move on to Question 2.'* Interviewers should also only ask one question at a time so that the respondent can focus on each specific question.

**TIP:** Interviewers need to be carefully matched to interviewees so that they can engage interviewees in candid conversations.

Important characteristics of a good interviewer include:
- Professionalism
- Good Social Skills
- Pleasant Demeanour and Personality
- Sensitivity and Empathy
- Effective Listener, Active Observer
- Ability to Maintain Neutrality

# CODING QUANTITATIVE DATA

Coding Quantitative Data is a process used to transform data into an understandable format for statistical software programs. When coding, the coder must adhere to program specific restrictions and limitations embedded in the particular software.

## Quantitative Research

Researchers can use an abundance of research methodologies to collect their data. Notwithstanding, a researcher needs to keep in mind two primary issues when deciding on choice of a methodology, namely, which methodology would best be suited to the particular study and what the researcher is trying to learn versus the cost of the methodology.

When in-depth learning of experiences is not the object of the research, researchers generally use a quantitative research methodology. Quantitative research allows the researcher to generate numerical data, perform statistical analyses, and make generalizations. Its primary advantage over qualitative research is simplicity since this method is quite structured which makes data coding relatively simple and cost effective. Quantitative research is therefore preferred when large samples or data sources are involved.

## Why Code Quantitative Data?

Researchers collect enormous amounts of quantitative data, most commonly via surveys, which need to be analysed. Coding provides a means for the researcher to reduce large volumes of data and to make the data more manageable. More importantly, however, coding transforms data into an understandable format that can be interpreted by specially designed statistical processing software programs such as the statistical package for social sciences (SPSS), comprehensive statistical package (SAS), and Stata.

Depending on the research goals and objectives, even data that is collected at an individual level (e.g., actual age) may later be coded into age categories (e.g., < 25 years, 25–35 years, etc.). Income is another variable which may be collected at an individual level but may be coded into income categories for reporting purposes. Some types of data may not require any coding. For instance, if the unique identification number system for your surveys is one to 1,000, this information will not need to be coded.

## Preparation of the Code Book

Preparation of the code book for a quantitative study is a critical function that should be done carefully. Essentially, a code book or template is created in a software program such as SPSS that provides instructions to the program so that it can interpret the various properties of the data. All statistical analysis software carry unique instructions that must be followed for data entry, storage, and retrieval. The code book must, therefore, reflect the program's unique restrictions or nonsensical output will be generated during the analysis phase. All survey data collected is entered directly into the created code book.

Prior to preparation of the code book, the researcher must determine how variables will be defined and what numerical code will be assigned to each possible response. Researchers have considerable flexibility in creating their code books. There is no right and wrong way to do this, although some best practice standards exist. For instance, many researchers prefer to code variables with binary response categories (e.g., sex) with 0 and 1. Thus 0 is often used as the code for males, while one is used as the code for females. However, it would not make a difference if females = 0 and males = 1 or even if males = 1 and females = 2. Similarly, it makes no difference if No = 0, Yes = 1 or vice versa.

## Navigating the SPSS Variable View Worksheet

SPSS is a common software used for statistical analysis. Like any other statistical analysis software, SPSS requires that the code book for the data entry be properly prepared so the program can generate sensible output. In other words, if garbage is entered, garbage will be generated (GIGO). This discussion will focus on SPSS (Version 22).

SPSS has two screen views (tabs). The first tab, data view, is used for actual data entry. The second tab, variable view, is used to establish the actual properties of the variable. The variable view worksheet must be prepared first. Once this worksheet is prepared, data can then be entered in the data view worksheet. An SPSS worksheet in the variable view mode looks like this; it has 11 columns and an infinite number of rows:

|   | Name | Type | Width | Decimals | Label | Values | Missing | Columns | Align | Measure | Role |
|---|------|------|-------|----------|-------|--------|---------|---------|-------|---------|------|
| 1 |      |      |       |          |       |        |         |         |       |         |      |
| 2 |      |      |       |          |       |        |         |         |       |         |      |

*Name:* A unique variable name must be created for each question or item on your survey. A unique identification number must also be created for each survey. Therefore, if your survey has 20 questions (five demographic questions and 15 general questions) you will need to create 21 unique names in the 'name' column – a name to identify all survey numbers (eg., *Survey No.*), 5 demographic names (eg. you can use *Age* to represent age), and 15 general question names.

Some researchers prefer to omit identification numbers from the actual survey since this tends to unnerve some respondents who feel that their identities are being tracked. If your surveys do not carry identification numbers, you will need to number them in consecutive order prior to the data entry process into the code book. For example, if 1,000 surveys were executed, number them 1 to 1,000. The order in which the surveys are numbered does not matter. That is, you do not need to batch surveys by any specific demographic such as age or religion to facilitate the numbering process. The reason for assigning a unique identification number to each survey is to assist with fast retrieval of a survey in the event that you needed to verify information from the survey. For instance, suppose on question 1 of Survey 100 (see example 6.1), the respondent chose 8. You decide that for question 1 that you prefer to enter the raw numbers selected by the respondents directly into SPSS, rather than creating a coding system for this question which would require that you select the participant's choice from a drop down menu. If you entered 89 in error but did not notice this error until data entry is complete, it will be quite easy to locate the original survey (because it has a unique identification number 100) and correct your mistake. However, if an identification number was not assigned to each survey, you will spend considerable time to locate the original survey.

To create a unique variable name, keep in mind the following rules: (1) each variable must be unique, (2) variable names can only begin with a letter, and (3) variable names can include only certain punctuation marks or symbols (e.g., period, underscore).

Although new versions of SPSS allow users to use longer variable names than was allowed on older versions of SPSS, it is recommended that variable names be kept short (up to eight characters). Possible unique variable names for Question 1 shown in example 6.1 might be 'semstres' 'q1stress' or simply 'q1'. Note, however, that these names are not very descriptive. The *Label* property should, therefore, be used to provide a better description of the variable name.

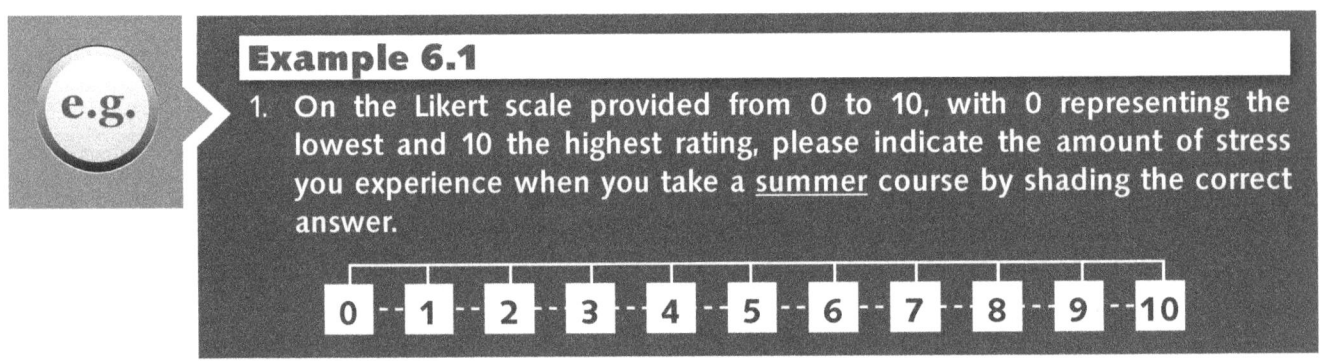

**Example 6.1**
1. On the Likert scale provided from 0 to 10, with 0 representing the lowest and 10 the highest rating, please indicate the amount of stress you experience when you take a summer course by shading the correct answer.

0 -- 1 -- 2 -- 3 -- 4 -- 5 -- 6 -- 7 -- 8 -- 9 -- 10

When creating variable names, use a method that makes sense and be consistent. For instance, if you decide to use q1 for question 1, use q2 for question 2, q3 for question 3, and so on.

As soon as you type in a variable name in the 'name' column, default information for the remaining properties will automatically appear in nine of the remaining columns. The only column that will not get default information is your 'label' column. You can change any of the default values that are automatically inserted. This is what the SPSS variable view worksheet will look like when we enter our first variable name 'id' in column 1, row 1.

|   | Name | Type | Width | Decimals | Label | Values | Missing | Columns | Align | Measure | Role |
|---|------|------|-------|----------|-------|--------|---------|---------|-------|---------|------|
| 1 | id | Numeric | 8 | 2 |  | None | None | 8 | Right | Scale | Input |
| 2 |  |  |  |  |  |  |  |  |  |  |  |

**Type:** SPSS allows you to define your data as either *numeric* (numbers) or *string* (combination of letters/numbers/characters). Choosing the correct type is critically important. The *numeric* property accommodates only numerical responses and will allow numeric operations. In contrast, a string property accommodates textual and non-numerical responses and will not permit any numeric operations. Therefore, basic descriptive statistics such as the mean and standard deviation will not be possible if *string* is selected. Note that SPSS automatically defaults to *numeric*. If you want to change to *string*, click on the three dots next to *numeric* and the *Variable Type* menu will open. You can then select the *string* option and select OK.

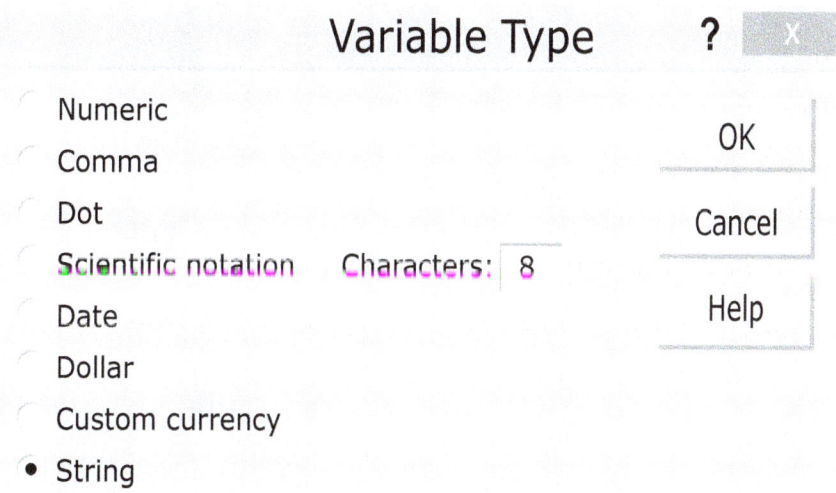

**Width:** Width is essentially the number of characters required for data display. The default width in SPSS for numeric variables is eight digits. For string variables, the default is eight characters. If you need more width, simply enter a larger number.

**Decimals:** The number displayed in this column shows the number of decimal places that will be displayed after the point. The default for decimals in SPSS is two. Zero decimal places may be preferred for some variables.

**Label:** Labels provide a proper description of your variable which really helps since the *Name* may not make much sense. You can therefore enter your question verbatim from the survey. For instance, the label for question 1, in example 6.1, could be 'Indicate the amount of stress you experience when you take a semester course and rate your stress from Low (0) to High (10).'

**Values:** The values column/tool is quite important. Since most of our data may be categorical in nature, we need to use some sort of numbering system to represent the various categories in each question. Sometimes the numbering system may be quite simple since the categories may already carry a number on the survey. For example, question 1 used a scale of 0–10. Therefore, value labels would be created using the existing numbers 0–10. Suppose respondent 1 chose 8. We could either manually enter 8 in the values cell for q1 in the data view mode or we could create 11 labels for q1 (corresponding to 0–10) in the variable view worksheet and then select 8 from the drop down menu. Similarly Likert scales may already carry a number on your survey. For instance, a Likert scale to gauge satisfaction may be presented as follows: Very Satisfied = 5, Satisfied = 4, Neutral = 3, Dissatisfied = 2, and Very Dissatisfied = 1. This would be very easy to code since the existing numbers can be used.

The variable 'Age' will now be used to demonstrate how value labels are created. Suppose your variable 'age' carried the following categories: ≤ 20 years, 21–25 years, 26–30 years, 31–35 years, 36–40 years, and > 40 years. We would create the value labels as follows. Go to the row containing the word 'age' and click in the value cell to open the *Value Labels* box. In the value field, enter 1, then go to the value label field and type ≤ *20 years*. Click add. Repeat the process until you have added the remaining age groups. Use 2 to represent 21–25 years; 3 to represent 26–30 years; 4 to represent 31–35 years; 5 to represent 36–40 years; and 6 to represent > 40 years. Click the OK button to save. This is how your Value Labels box would appear as the information is being entered.

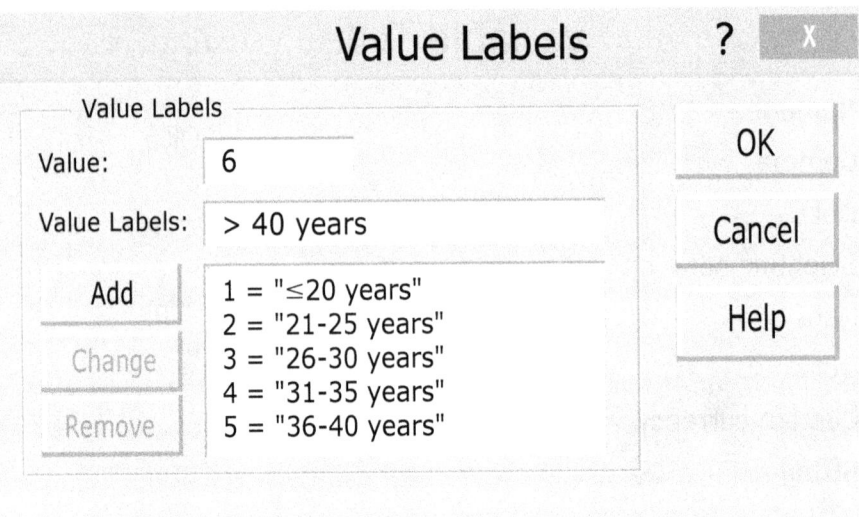

***Missing***: SPSS is programmed to recognize two types of missing values, namely, system-missing (used when a numerical cell is left blank) and user-missing (used when the researcher wants to record a reason why data is missing such as a non-response on a particular question or when the respondent gives two responses to the same question when only one should have been selected).

Suppose you want to signal to SPSS that whenever a cell is blank (i.e., because of non-response), an arbitrary value such as '999' should appear in the blank cell. To do this, go to the Variable View, select the Missing Values column next to the variable that has the missing value and select the Missing Values box. A new menu will appear. Select discrete missing value and enter 999 into the first box. Click OK. The number 999 will appear in the blank cell. Set your decimal places to zero.

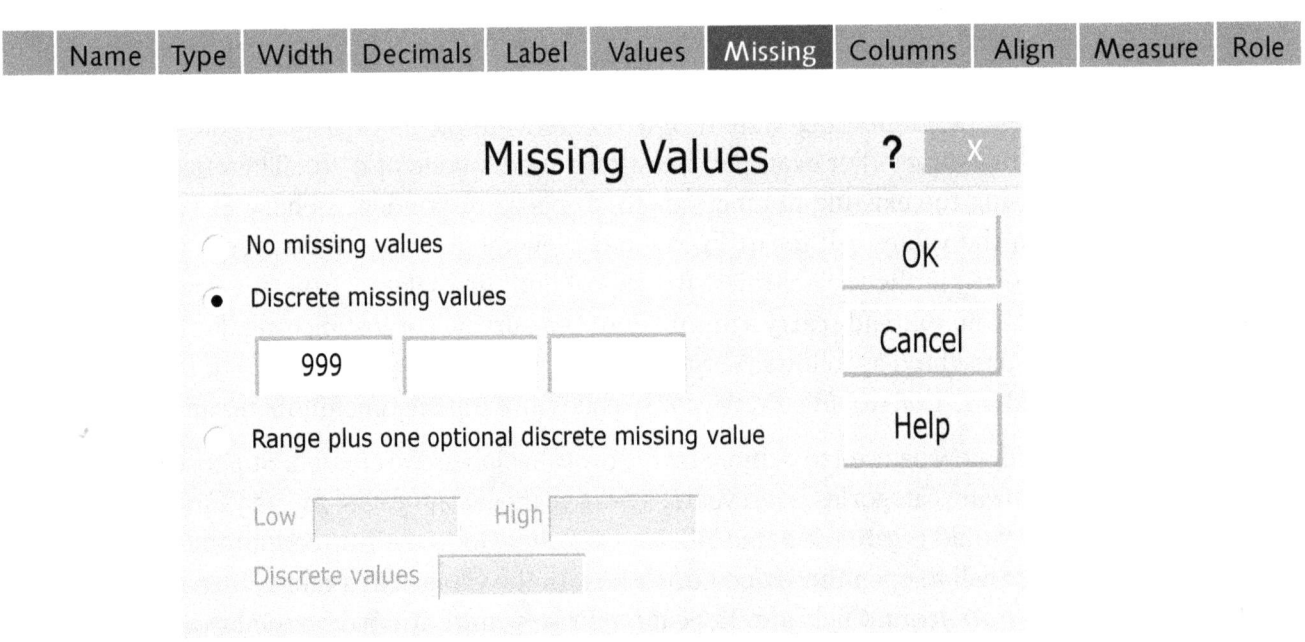

Note that it is critical that you tell SPSS the number that you will use to represent a missing value (e.g., 999). If you simply enter 999 in the cell without specifying in the Missing Values menu that 999 represents a missing value, then SPSS will use this number as a normal data point and your data will be skewed.

***Columns***: This property essentially determines the column width that will be displayed in the Data View mode in SPSS. The default is generally set to 8 and can be increased or decreased. Keep in mind that if the column is too narrow, you can simply expand the column width by dragging the column line to the right.

***Align:*** The Align property is similar to the align feature in most software programs such as Microsoft Word and Microsoft Excel. It simply facilitates how the data will be displayed (i.e., left-justified, right-justified, centred) in the data view template.

***Measure***: This property allows you to choose your level of measurement. Levels of measurement were discussed in chapter 4. SPSS offers three options for measurement: nominal, ordinal, and scale. The scale option is used to represent both interval and ratio measurements.

***Role:*** This property is new to SPSS (version 22) and essentially assigns roles to the research variables. Many have argued that users should ignore this feature when defining variables. However, if you use this property, note that *input* is selected for independent variables since these are predictor variables and *target* is selected for dependent variables since these are outcome variables.

## Training for Personnel Involved with Data Entry

When several individuals are involved with data entry for the same study, it is important that the principal investigator conduct some training prior to the data entry so that all persons can become thoroughly acquainted with the code book. The purpose of this training is to ensure that data from each survey is entered in a similar manner. Thus, if three research assistants were to enter data from the same survey during a training session, all three assistants should enter the data in an identical manner.

If data is interpreted differently by each research assistant, this will distort the data and inaccurate results will be reported when the data is subsequently analysed. Detailed instructions should therefore be provided so that all research assistants understand the properties in the variable view worksheet (the code book) so that they can select the correct properties when entering data in the data view worksheet.

**Invest time to create a proper codebook and to train all research assistants since this will reduce data entry errors.**

**The time invested in this effort will pay off when large volumes of data have to be entered.**

# CODING QUALITATIVE DATA

Coding Qualitative Data essentially refers to the process used to organize your qualitative transcript data into a manageable format that makes sense using some sort of indexing system to organize your data into themes.

## Data Type

Some researchers prefer to collect purely quantitative data. Others may find that a qualitative approach is better suited to the nature of their research. Many researchers also find it useful to utilize a mixed methods approach, that is, a hybrid of quantitative and qualitative approaches (see chapter 3). Using a qualitative approach can yield rich in-depth information not possible with a purely quantitative approach. However, analysis of qualitative data requires a systematic process for sorting, coding, and organizing your data to reduce a huge amount of verbatim data into a manageable format that makes sense and tells a story.

## Developing a Storyline for your Qualitative Data

A helpful approach to facilitate your sorting, coding, and organization process is to figure out what you are really trying to learn from your data. Once this is ascertained, you need to figure out the best way to communicate your information. In other words, your coding system needs to be developed in the context of your storyline so that it can have coherence and structure.

## The Code Book and the Coding Process

Similar to quantitative research, the code book is also the most important document in qualitative research. However, unlike quantitative research, the qualitative code book is quite complex to develop since similar responses need to be extracted from transcripts and grouped into categories or themes. Qualitative coding is a way for you to organize your data in a way that makes sense. Think about a manual filing system. You do not just throw papers into any file. You use some sort of system to group papers so that papers in a specific file are related in some way. The coding process for qualitative data is based on similar logic. Since qualitative data is verbatim information, qualitative research assistants will require considerably more training compared to quantitative research assistants since the extraction of themes requires considerably more skill.

There is no global best practice for coding qualitative data. However, the process must have consistency. Do not use numbers for some codes and phrases for other codes. Note also that numbers and symbols by themselves may be quite confusing and should be avoided especially when you have many codes since it will be impossible to remember what each code represents without constantly referring to your code book. A better approach would be to use phrases and code into categories or themes. For instance, if you were conducting a study on university students' stress, you could create themes such as *work-related issues, balancing family life with studies,* and *insufficient time for studies.*

When creating codes, keep in mind that you want a manageable set of data so that you can do proper analysis. If you create a code for every new item in your transcript, you may find that your coding system may become useless. You may end up with dozens of codes and most of them may contain only one to two items under each code. Too many codes may also result in numerous data entry errors.

# Ethics and Data Collection

Note also that the coding process for qualitative data must be flexible. You may start out with some code names which may be revised later. Some codes may need to be completely deleted because they may have only one or two responses. New codes may be added as new themes emerge. It may even be necessary to collapse some codes to make your data analysis more meaningful and sensible.

Your coding system can basically be developed in two ways. Similar to quantitative research, you can use sound judgment and insights from the literature review to come up with some categories in advance of the actual research so that you can ask questions on predetermined topics. The second approach is to allow respondents to speak freely, and then read through your transcripts and try to formulate a storyline to assist with the development of your themes.

## Cross-Referencing and Creation of Themes

Like quantitative research, you need some sort of identification system so that you can corroborate information in your code book if necessary. A simple method would be to number your transcripts in sequential order and assign page numbers. Two transcript examples are now used to illustrate the emergence of themes. Transcript 1 shows three main themes while Transcript 2 adds three additional themes. To cross-reference our themes to each transcript, the letter 'T' will be used to refer to transcript, and the letter 'P' will be use to refer to the page.

### Code 1 – Work-related Issues
- Stressful and demanding job with long hours          T1, P1
- Self-employed, work seven days a week, long days    T2, P3

### Code 2 – Balancing Family Life with Studies
- Cannot spend sufficient time with family – family annoyed    T1, P1
- Just got married. Cannot spend enough time with wife         T2, P3

### Code 3 – Insufficient Time for Studies
- Do not have sufficient time to devote to studies    T1, P1
- Full-time student status, heavy workload            T2, P3

---

**Transcript No: 1**

**Question:** *What are some of the issues that cause stress?*

**Response: My job is stressful and demanding. I have long hours of work.** ❶ I also have a family and I am finding it **difficult to spend quality time with my family** ❷ now that I enrolled in a graduate programme. My wife is getting really annoyed and I had to cancel several outings with my children, and they were not happy. I really need to get my MSc in Project Management because it will provide an opportunity for upward mobility. However, I am lagging behind in my studies. I find that I cannot meet the deadlines for my assignments and my assignments are not up to graduate level standards, but I simply **do not have sufficient time to devote to my studies.** ❸

⇐ Work related issues ①

⇐ Balancing family life with studies ②

⇐ Insufficient time for studies ③

p1

## Code 4 – Other Commitments
- Supervising building of personal home  T2, P3

## Code 5 – Group Projects are a Nightmare
- Often have to miss group meetings; group members make unkind remarks about my commitment to project  T2, P3

## Code 6 – Out of School for a While
- Mature student, left school 20 years ago, finding difficulty getting back into study mode.  T2, P3

---

**Transcript No: 2**

**Question:** *What are some of the issues that cause stress?*

**Response: Long hours of work. I am self-employed.** I have my own construction firm which means that **I basically work seven days a week.** Some days I am at work from **7:00 a.m. to 7:00 p.m.** ❶ Now I have to leave the office every weekday at 4:00 p.m. to make class daily at 5:00 p.m. and then go back to work after class. I am also **building my home** ❹ which I am supervising myself. I just got **married** and my **wife has been complaining that she hardly sees me.** ❷ I am on **full-time student status, the work load is demanding, and I don't have sufficient time for my studies.** ❸ All courses carry group projects. I understand why group work is important in this discipline. A project manger must work with a team with very differing personalities. However, I find that **group projects are really stressful.** ❺ The group members are not very accommodating when I miss group meetings due to work commitments and sometimes are quite unkind in their remarks. Some group members are quite immature. A lot of time is wasted in group meetings. I am the oldest student in class and I **completed my BSc 20 years ago.** ❻ I cannot seem to grasp concepts as easily as the younger students. Maybe I need to switch to part-time status because currently I am not performing well.

p3

*Codes for Themes 1, 2, and 3 have already been created when Transcript 1 was analysed.*

⇐ Other committments ④

⇐ Group projects are a nightmare ⑤

⇐ Out of school for a while ⑥

---

**TIP:** Use themes that can help develop your storyline. Collapse themes when the number of responses under a particular theme are few.

# 7 Quantitative Data Analysis

- Descriptive Statistics
- Measures of Central Tendency
- Measures of Dispersion
- Frequency Analysis and Crosstabulations
- Inferential Statistics
- Comparative Inferential Statistics
- Associational Inferential Statistics
- Effect Sizes

## DESCRIPTIVE STATISTICS

**Descriptive Statistics represent a general category of quantitative statistics aimed at providing descriptive or preliminary analyses of data derived from a sample.**

## Nature of Statistics

Statistics represent a set of mathematical operations and techniques that are employed to present, analyse, and interpret quantitative data. Two general categories of statistics exist: descriptive statistics and inferential statistics. Descriptive statistics are the subject of this chapter. Recall that descriptive research questions represent one of three categories of quantitative research questions (alongside associational and comparative research questions). Descriptive statistics are typically used to address descriptive research questions in quantitative research.

## Types of Descriptive Statistics

Descriptive statistics are the most basic or preliminary forms of statistical tools which are used to describe, graph, and present data in a sample of cases or observations. A case or observation represents a participant or a response in the dataset. In particular, descriptive statistics provide quantitative summaries of various features or characteristics of data or variables. Recall variables can either be categorical or quantitative/continuous in nature. The type of descriptive statistical technique employed depends on the type of variable in question. Hence, we have descriptive statistics exclusively for categorical variables and descriptive statistics exclusively for quantitative/continuous variables.

Descriptive statistics (like inferential statistics) can be classified into univariate, bivariate, and multivariate statistics.

- **Univariate Statistics** describe a single variable at a time across a sample of observations.
- **Bivariate Statistics** describe simple relationships between a pair of variables.
- **Multivariate statistics** describe more than two variables in tandem.

Table 7.1 presents a sample of popular univariate, bivariate, and multivariate statistical applications within the descriptive statistics family.

**Table 7.1: Univariate, Bivariate, and Multivariate Statistical Applications**

|  | Categorical | Quantitative/Continuous |
|---|---|---|
| **Univariate** | • Frequency<br>• Percentages | • Measures of central tendency (mean, median) |
| **Bivariate** | • Two-way crosstabulations<br>• Contingency table analysis | • Graphical scatterplots |
| **Multivariate** | • Multi-way crosstabulations<br>• Contingency table analysis | • Descriptions of conditional continuous distributions and scores |

## Key Considerations for Employing Descriptive Statistics

A number of considerations should be taken into account by researchers seeking to utilize descriptive statistics to address their data needs:

- Consider the types of research questions you are seeking to address. Recall that descriptive research questions invite the application of descriptive statistics.
- All quantitative data require some form of descriptive statistics to provide descriptions of key sample characteristics such as participants' sex, age, income, occupation, etc.
- Descriptive statistics depend on the types of variables being examined. Categorical and quantitative variables require different types of descriptive tools.
- Descriptive statistics are almost always depicted using tabular or graphical presentations that illustrate the descriptive nature of the analyses (e.g., table of means, pie chart, line graph).

Descriptive statistics are applied to provide descriptions of key data characteristics, allowing researchers and analysts to better understand their data.

Even if your research questions do not call for descriptive statistics, it is normal practice to precede your main analyses with descriptive analyses of key data characteristics and variables.

# MEASURES OF CENTRAL TENDENCY

Measures of Central Tendency are a category of descriptive statistics which describes a quantitative dataset using a single typical or central value.

## Nature of Measures of Central Tendency

Measures of central tendency are popular descriptive statistical approaches used to summarize a set of data values based on a single value depicting a central position. There are three measures of central tendency namely, the mean, median, and mode. All three statistical measures provide useful summary assessments of different datasets under different conditions.

## The Mean

The mean (or the arithmetic average) is the most typical of the three measures of central tendency. It is equal to the sum of all data values in a set divided by the number of values in the same set.

**Mean**

$$\bar{x} = \frac{\sum x}{n}$$

where

$\bar{x}$ = the mean
$\sum$ = sum of
$x$ = each data value in set
$n$ = sample size

**Interpretation: The sample average or typical value in a data set.**

Let us assume that the values in example 7.1 indicate the number of days a sample of nurses in the maternity ward at a hospital in the USA were absent from work during the period October–December 2018. According to our calculations, the mean in example 7.1 is 1.62 days. This indicates that a typical nurse in the maternity ward at that particular hospital was absent from work for 1.62 days during the period October–December 2018.

**Example 7.1:** Mean (Original Data Set)
Absentee Days Maternity Nurses (October–December 2018)

| Participant | 1 | 2 | 3 | 4 | 5 | 6 | 7 | 8 | 9 | 10 | 11 | 12 | 13 |
|---|---|---|---|---|---|---|---|---|---|---|---|---|---|
| Days | 4 | 0 | 0 | 2 | 3 | 0 | 4 | 2 | 5 | 0 | 0 | 1 | 0 |

$$\bar{x} = \frac{\sum x}{n}$$

= (4 + 0 + 0 + 2 + 3 + 0 + 4 + 2 + 5 + 0 + 0 + 1 + 0) / 13

= 1.62 days

The mean acts as a prime statistical representative of a quantitative dataset and cannot be used to describe categorical variables. Specifically, there is no such thing as the mean sex or racial background of a participant. Hence, the mean is reserved only for summarizing quantitative variables or datasets.

The key problem with the mean is that it is overly sensitive to extreme values (called outliers) in a given dataset. Suppose participant number 13 had reported 60 days instead of 0 days (see example 7.2). Considering the values in the data set, this value '60' is clearly an extreme number (an outlier). Recomputation of the mean now shows that the mean is 6.23 days. This extreme value '60' pushes up the mean statistic and essentially distorts and skews our data. As a result, the mean no longer represents a typical data value in the dataset. Can we say the average nurse in this dataset is absent for 6.23 days? Not at all! We have to be careful when using the mean with data that contain outliers because it is poorly representative in such conditions.

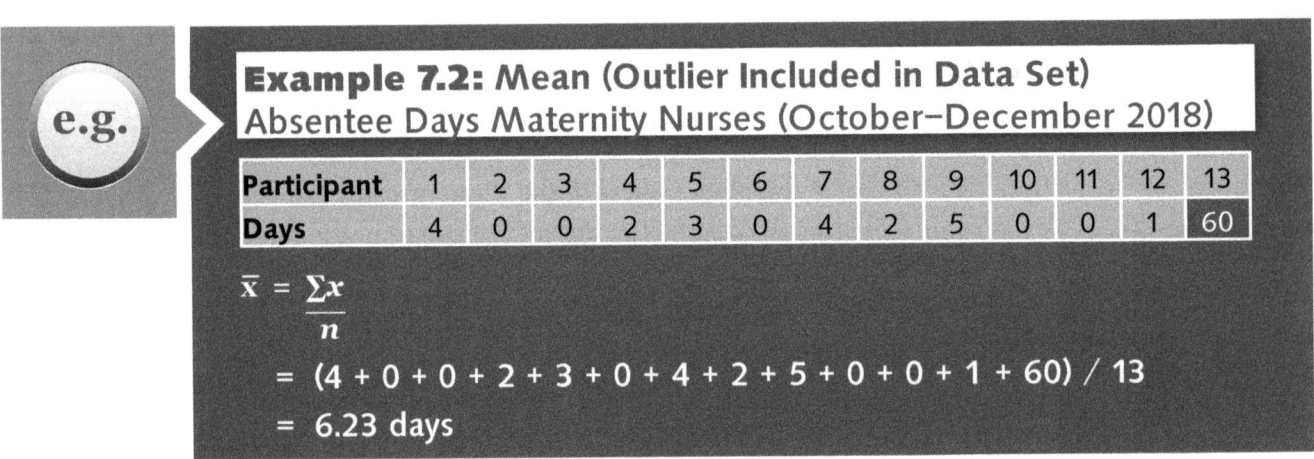

**Example 7.2:** Mean (Outlier Included in Data Set)
Absentee Days Maternity Nurses (October–December 2018)

| Participant | 1 | 2 | 3 | 4 | 5 | 6 | 7 | 8 | 9 | 10 | 11 | 12 | 13 |
|---|---|---|---|---|---|---|---|---|---|---|---|---|---|
| Days | 4 | 0 | 0 | 2 | 3 | 0 | 4 | 2 | 5 | 0 | 0 | 1 | 60 |

$$\bar{x} = \frac{\sum x}{n}$$
$$= (4 + 0 + 0 + 2 + 3 + 0 + 4 + 2 + 5 + 0 + 0 + 1 + 60) / 13$$
$$= 6.23 \text{ days}$$

When dealing with an outlier, researchers have a few options. First and foremost, the researcher needs to investigate the outlier to see if it is possible that a data entry error occurred with the information for participant number 13. For example, participant 13 may have reported either '0' or '6', but the research assistant may have entered '60' in error. Alternatively, a data recording error may have occurred which could be due to either the researcher or the participant not paying attention during an observational study. When dealing with an outlier, note the following:

1. If it is clearly obvious that a data entry error or data recording error has occurred, the researcher can omit the outlier completely. However, if you do this, it should be highlighted in your paper/report. For instance, if we completely exclude participant number 13, then the mean becomes 1.75 days.

2. If the outlier will affect your results, you have a few options.

    i. Take the median value (discussed shortly) in the data set and substitute this value for the outlier so that the mean is more representative of the overall sample. If this is done, you should report the value of the outlier, the value that was substituted, and what the mean would be with the outlier versus the substituted value.

    ii. Use the sample *mode* (discussed shortly) and substitute the mode for the outlier. If this is done, you should report the value of the outlier, the value that was substituted, and what the mean would be with the outlier versus the substituted value.

iii. Keep the outlier in your computation but ensure that it is flagged as an outlier when you report your results. You can also include in your reporting the mean using either option (i) or (ii) so that a more representative average is provided.

## The Median

The median is the middle score in a quantitative dataset that is arranged in ascending order. Compared with the mean, it is less affected by outliers.

**Median**

$$\text{Median} = \frac{n+1}{2}$$ where $n$ = number of observations or elements in the data set

**Interpretation:** The value that falls in the exact middle position in a sample dataset.

Using the original data from example 7.1, the median is 1 (see example 7.3).

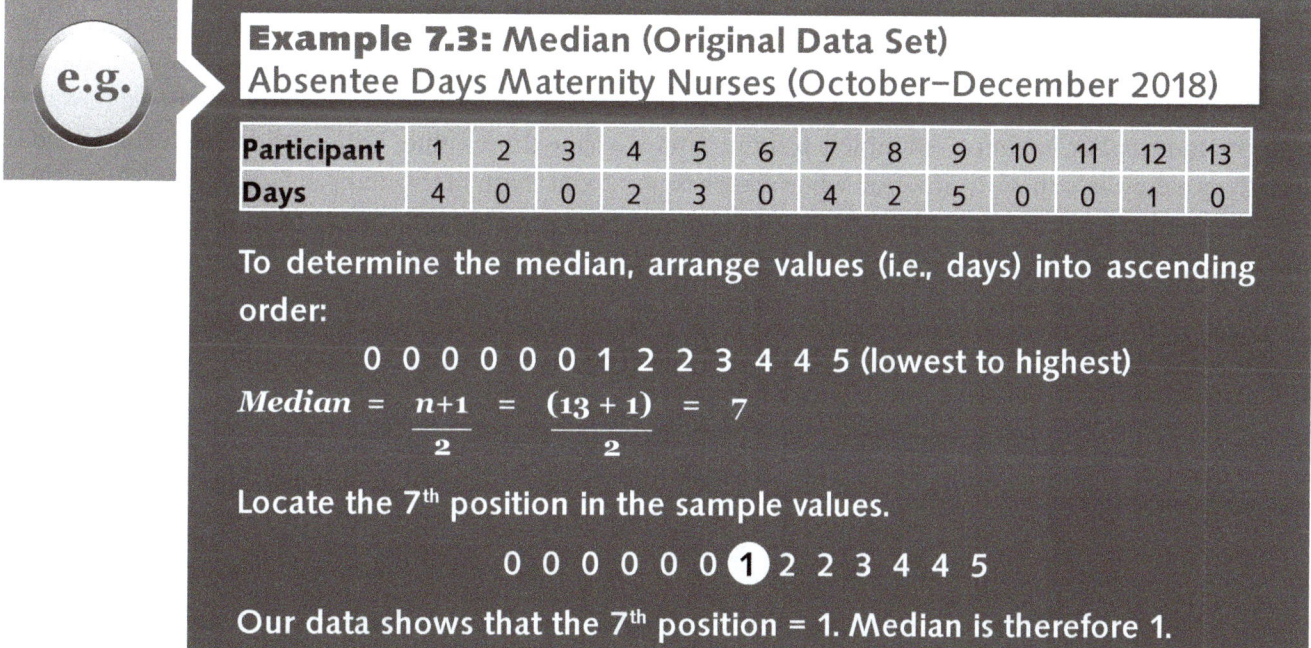

**Example 7.3:** Median (Original Data Set)
Absentee Days Maternity Nurses (October–December 2018)

| Participant | 1 | 2 | 3 | 4 | 5 | 6 | 7 | 8 | 9 | 10 | 11 | 12 | 13 |
|---|---|---|---|---|---|---|---|---|---|---|---|---|---|
| Days | 4 | 0 | 0 | 2 | 3 | 0 | 4 | 2 | 5 | 0 | 0 | 1 | 0 |

To determine the median, arrange values (i.e., days) into ascending order:

0 0 0 0 0 0 1 2 2 3 4 4 5 (lowest to highest)

$$\text{Median} = \frac{n+1}{2} = \frac{(13+1)}{2} = 7$$

Locate the 7$^{th}$ position in the sample values.

0 0 0 0 0 0 ①  2 2 3 4 4 5

Our data shows that the 7$^{th}$ position = 1. Median is therefore 1.

Now consider example 7.4 that includes our outlier of 60 in the data set. The inclusion of our outlier changes the median value to 2, thus illustrating the superiority of the median over the mean when data are skewed by outliers. Essentially, it is important to present the median (sometimes alongside the mean) when there are extreme values (big or small) in datasets.

> **Example 7.4:** Median (Outlier Included in Data Set)
> Absentee Days Maternity Nurses (October–December 2018)
>
> | Participant | 1 | 2 | 3 | 4 | 5 | 6 | 7 | 8 | 9 | 10 | 11 | 12 | 13 |
> |---|---|---|---|---|---|---|---|---|---|---|---|---|---|
> | Days | 4 | 0 | 0 | 2 | 3 | 0 | 4 | 2 | 5 | 0 | 0 | 1 | 60 |
>
> To determine the median, arrange values (i.e., days) into ascending order:
>
> 0 0 0 0 0 1 2 2 3 4 4 5 60
>
> Locate the 7th position in the sample values.
>
> 0 0 0 0 0 1 ②  2 3 4 4 5 60
>
> Our data shows that the 7th position = 2. Median is therefore 2.

## The Mode

The mode is the most frequent value in a given dataset. Unlike the mean and median, the mode can be used for categorical and continuous data. Imagine you have a dataset of 100 males and 40 females where males are coded as 1 and females are coded as 2. The modal score is 1, given there is a higher number of males than females in the dataset.

Continuing with our original quantitative data in example 7.1, the mode is equal to '0' as this value has the highest frequency in the dataset (see example 7.5). It is also possible to get a situation where we have two or more modes. For instance, example 7.6 shows that we have three values with 0 and three values with 2. Finally, we may even have a situation where there is no modal score in this dataset (see example 7.7). Note that the mode is problematic when the most common score or value is far away from the other values; it presents an unrepresentative measure of central tendency in these cases.

> **Example 7.5:** Mode (Original Data Set)
> Absentee Days Maternity Nurses (October–December 2018)
>
> | Participant | 1 | 2 | 3 | 4 | 5 | 6 | 7 | 8 | 9 | 10 | 11 | 12 | 13 |
> |---|---|---|---|---|---|---|---|---|---|---|---|---|---|
> | Days | 4 | 0 | 0 | 2 | 3 | 0 | 4 | 2 | 5 | 0 | 0 | 1 | 0 |
>
> Mode is the value with the highest frequency. The mode is therefore 0.

> **Example 7.6:** Scenario Illustrating Two Modes
> Absentee Days Maternity Nurses (October–December 2018)
>
> | Participant | 1 | 2 | 3 | 4 | 5 | 6 | 7 | 8 | 9 | 10 | 11 | 12 | 13 |
> |---|---|---|---|---|---|---|---|---|---|---|---|---|---|
> | Days | 2 | 0 | 0 | 2 | 2 | 0 | 4 | 3 | 5 | 1 | 6 | 8 | 7 |
>
> Mode is the value with the highest frequency.
> We have three values with 0 and three values with 2. Therefore, we have two modes: 0 and 2.

**Example 7.7:** Scenario Illustrating no Mode
Absentee Days Maternity Nurses (October–December 2018)

| Participant | 1 | 2 | 3 | 4 | 5 | 6 | 7 | 8 | 9 | 10 | 11 | 12 | 13 |
|---|---|---|---|---|---|---|---|---|---|---|---|---|---|
| Days | 2 | 0 | 9 | 10 | 11 | 15 | 4 | 3 | 5 | 1 | 6 | 8 | 7 |

Mode is the value with the highest frequency.
In this example, each value has only one frequency. Therefore, there is no modal value in this dataset.

## The Relationship between the Mean, Median, and Mode

When the mean, median, and mode are equal in size, the data values are said to approximate a distribution known as a normal distribution. A normal distribution is a symmetrical frequency distribution of values in which most of the values fall in the centre or middle of the distribution. Specifically, it is usually depicted as a bell-shaped curved graph and the rest of the values taper off into the tails of the curved graph (see figure 7.1).

**Figure 7.1: Normal Distribution**

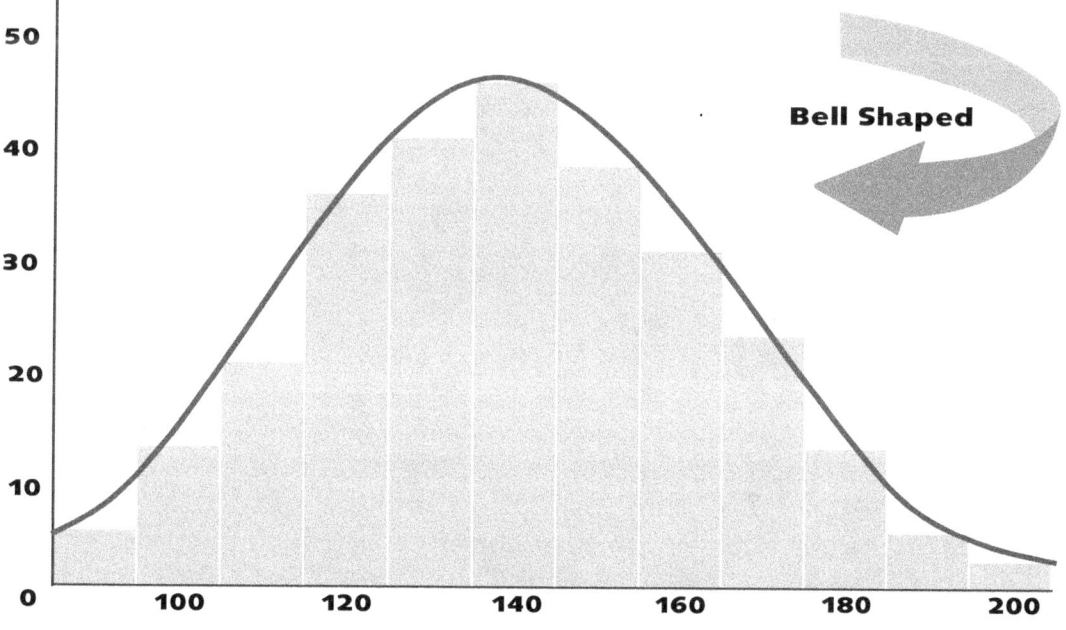

Measures of central tendency are popular measures in descriptive statistics.
Although the mean is the most popular of the three, it is important to assess your data to determine if you have significant outliers before presenting it as your main summary measure for quantitative datasets.

# MEASURES OF DISPERSION

Measures of Dispersion are a category of descriptive statistics which examine the extent to which values of a quantitative dataset deviate from each other or from a measure of central tendency.

## Nature of Measures of Dispersion

Measures of dispersion capture the extent to which data or a set of values in a distribution are skewed or deviates from a measure of central tendency. Three common values used to measure dispersion are the range, variance, and standard deviation.

## Range

The simplest measure of dispersion is the range which is the mathematical difference between the highest and lowest values in a quantitative (continuous) dataset. Using our original data in example 7.1, the difference between our highest value and our lowest value gives us a range of 5 (see example 7.8). A low range statistic of 5 tells us that the data values tend to be close to each other, whereas a high range statistic such as 60 (see example 7.9) tells us that the data values are widely spread out. A major criticism against the range statistic is that it does not adequately capture the overall variability in the data as it only takes into account two values – the highest and lowest.

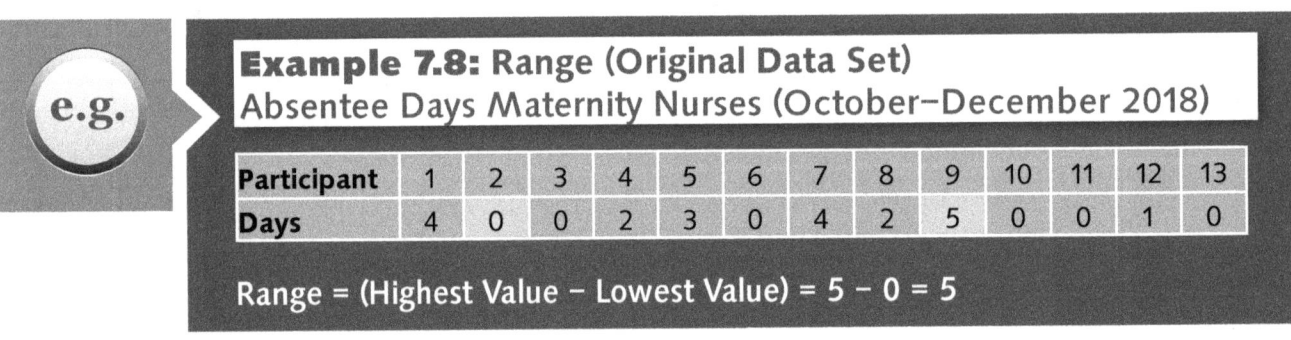

**Example 7.8:** Range (Original Data Set)
Absentee Days Maternity Nurses (October–December 2018)

| Participant | 1 | 2 | 3 | 4 | 5 | 6 | 7 | 8 | 9 | 10 | 11 | 12 | 13 |
|---|---|---|---|---|---|---|---|---|---|---|---|---|---|
| Days | 4 | 0 | 0 | 2 | 3 | 0 | 4 | 2 | 5 | 0 | 0 | 1 | 0 |

Range = (Highest Value – Lowest Value) = 5 – 0 = 5

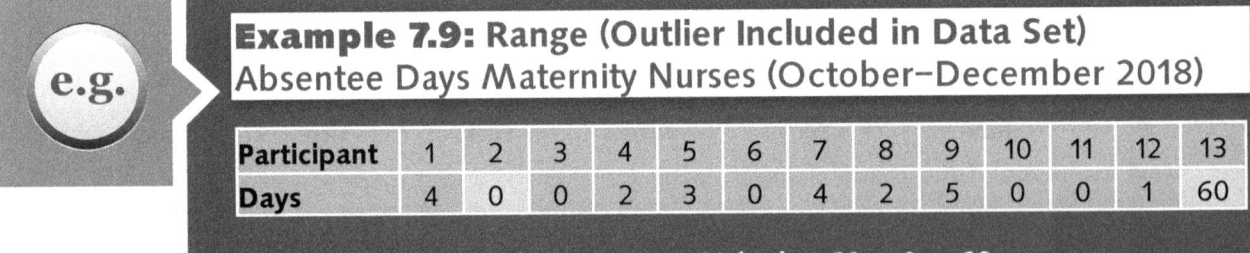

**Example 7.9:** Range (Outlier Included in Data Set)
Absentee Days Maternity Nurses (October–December 2018)

| Participant | 1 | 2 | 3 | 4 | 5 | 6 | 7 | 8 | 9 | 10 | 11 | 12 | 13 |
|---|---|---|---|---|---|---|---|---|---|---|---|---|---|
| Days | 4 | 0 | 0 | 2 | 3 | 0 | 4 | 2 | 5 | 0 | 0 | 1 | 60 |

Range = (Highest Value – Lowest Value) = 60 – 0 = 60

# Quantitative Data Analysis

## Variance

A more popular measure of dispersion is the variance. The variance takes into account the average variation of the data values with respect to their overall mean in squared units.

**Variance**

$$S^2 = \frac{\sum(x-\bar{x})^2}{n-1}$$

where

- $S^2$ = sample variance
- $\sum$ = sum of
- $x$ = each value in data set
- $\bar{x}$ = sample mean
- $^2$ = squared
- $n$ = sample size

**Interpretation:** The results suggest that the data values are $S^2$ (i.e., your answer) units squared from mean. Due to the squared format of the variance, it is not practically useful or interpretable.

Using the data from example 7.1, we will now calculate the variance (see example 7.10). Recall that our mean was 1.62 days. According to our calculations, the variance is 3.42.

### Example 7.10: Variance
**Absentee Days Maternity Nurses (October–December 2018)**

| Participant | 1 | 2 | 3 | 4 | 5 | 6 | 7 | 8 | 9 | 10 | 11 | 12 | 13 |
|---|---|---|---|---|---|---|---|---|---|---|---|---|---|
| Days | 4 | 0 | 0 | 2 | 3 | 0 | 4 | 2 | 5 | 0 | 0 | 1 | 0 |

| x | (x - x̄) | (x - x̄)² |
|---|---|---|
| 4 | 4 − 1.62 = 2.38 | 5.66 |
| 0 | 0 − 1.62 = −1.62 | 2.62 |
| 0 | 0 − 1.62 = −1.62 | 2.62 |
| 2 | 2 − 1.62 = 0.38 | 0.14 |
| 3 | 3 − 1.62 = 1.38 | 1.90 |
| 0 | 0 − 1.62 = −1.62 | 2.62 |
| 4 | 4 − 1.62 = 2.38 | 5.66 |
| 2 | 2 − 1.62 = 0.38 | 0.14 |
| 5 | 5 − 1.62 = 3.38 | 11.42 |
| 0 | 0 − 1.62 = −1.62 | 2.62 |
| 0 | 0 − 1.62 = −1.62 | 2.62 |
| 1 | 1 − 1.62 = −0.62 | 0.38 |
| 0 | 0 − 1.62 = −1.62 | 2.62 |
|   |   | ∑41.02 |

$$S^2 = \frac{\sum(x-\bar{x})^2}{n-1}$$

$$= \frac{41.02}{13-1}$$

$$= 3.42$$

## Standard Deviation

The most popular measure of dispersion is the standard deviation which is simply *the square root of the variance*. Like the variance, it takes into account the average deviation of the data values with respect to their overall mean. However, it presents this average deviation in the same units (e.g., days) as the original data values. The formula for the standard deviation is:

**Standard Deviation**

$$S = \sqrt{\frac{\sum(x-\bar{x})^2}{n-1}}$$

where

$S$ = sample standard deviation
$\sum$ = sum of
$x$ = each value in data set
$\bar{x}$ = sample mean
$^2$ = squared
$n$ = sample size

**Interpretation: The result suggests the data values vary around the mean, on average, by $S$ (i.e., your answer) units.**

Example 7.11 indicates that the standard deviation is 1.85. This suggests the data values vary around the mean, on average, by 1.85 days. The standard deviation is the best method of dispersion for summarizing quantitative data. The standard deviation provides an assessment of how representative the mean is of the data. A larger standard deviation suggests the mean is a poor representative of the data, whereas a smaller standard deviation indicates a more representative or accurate mean statistic.

**Example 7.11: Standard Deviation**

$$S = \sqrt{\frac{\sum(\bar{x}-x)^2}{n-1}} \quad = \sqrt{3.42} \quad = 1.85 \text{ days}$$

**TIP**

When reporting the mean statistic, you should always include the standard deviation. The two are inseparable. For example:

Our analysis indicates that a typical nurse in the maternity ward at XYZ hospital in the USA was absent from work during the period October–December 2018 for 1.62 days (SD = 1.85).

# FREQUENCY ANALYSIS AND CROSSTABULATIONS

Frequency Analysis and Crosstabulations are special types of descriptive statistics aimed at providing descriptive and preliminary analyses for categorical variables.

## Overview

Frequencies and crosstabulations are popular methods of descriptive statistics used to summarize categorical variables. A frequency is a count of observations on a particular response option; it is a univariate statistic focused on a single categorical variable. In contrast, a crosstabulation is used to summarize two or more categorical variables in a contingency table. Crosstabulations can be bivariate (i.e., two variables) or multivariate (i.e., multiple variables) descriptive statistics.

## Frequency Analysis

Frequency analysis is useful when a single categorical variable is the target of the analysis. This type of analysis provides a graphical or tabular display of observations and related counts for various responses to a given variable. For example, suppose we ask a sample of 95 hotel workers to identify their most desirable reward for enhancing motivation within the hotel sector. We provide employees a single question which asks them to choose the most attractive reward using a categorical response choice with five possible choices.

Example 7.12 provides the frequency distribution of the responses of the 95 hotel workers. As can be seen in example 7.12, the frequency distribution analysis also provides the analyst with percentage values which are more informative than frequencies as they offer relative weights for assessment. According to our frequency distribution, the largest percentage of the participants (42 per cent) chose 'money' as the most attractive reward for employee motivation, whereas the least percentage of the participants (five per cent) chose 'training opportunities'. Hence, frequency analyses allow for a comparison of the most and least popular responses based on a sample of participants or observations.

**Example 7.12:** Frequency Analysis of Employee Rewards

| Category | Frequency | Per Cent |
|---|---|---|
| Management Support | 10 | 11 |
| Money | 40 | 42 |
| Promotion | 25 | 26 |
| Recognition | 15 | 16 |
| Training Opportunities | 5 | 5 |
| **Total** | **95** | **100** |

## Crosstabulations

As aforementioned, crosstabulations are popular descriptive statistical methods for summarizing two or more categorical variables within a contingency table. A crosstabulation allows for responses of two or more categorical variables to be directly compared and a descriptive relationship explored. The crosstabulation shown in example 7.13 explores the relationship between two categorical variables, sex of respondent and home ownership. It resembles two frequency distributions which are cross-referenced. According to our crosstabulation, 20 per cent of males (i.e., 20 out of 100 males) own a home, compared with 83 per cent of females (75 out of 90 females).

When interpreting a crosstabulation, it is important to make comparisons using percentages and not frequencies. Hence, you will not say 20 males own a home compared with 75 females. Note also that it is common to present the group comparison variable (i.e., sex), in the column section of the table, and the other variable (i.e., home ownership) in the row section. However, it would not make a difference if home ownership was placed in the column section and sex in the row section. Example 7.13 is referred to as a 2 x 2 crosstabulation because there are two variables with two categories each in the table.

**Example 7.13:** Crosstabulation – Respondent Sex and Home Ownership

| Home Ownership | Males | | Females | | Total |
|---|---|---|---|---|---|
| | n | % | n | % | n |
| Owns a Home | 20 | 20 | 75 | 83 | 95 |
| Does not Own a Home | 80 | 80 | 15 | 17 | 95 |
| **Total** | **100** | **100** | **90** | **100** | **190** |

You can use larger crosstabulation tables in your analysis to add greater detail.

For example, if you want to compare whether Barbadians, Grenadians, and Vincentians are equally likely to own their own homes, you will have a 3 x 2 table. Nationality will be the group comparison variable or column variable, and home ownership will be the row variable.

# INFERENTIAL STATISTICS

 Inferential Statistics are a special category of quantitative statistics used to infer from statistical results of sample data to the general population based on probability rules.

## Overview

Inferential statistics, also known as tests of significance, represent a more sophisticated category of statistics used to make inferences from results of a sample to the population of interest. Descriptive statistics apply only to the sample but inferential statistics apply to the population of interest. Inferential statistics rely on probability rules to help analysts determine the likelihood that a set of sample results generally reflect the state of a targeted population.

For example, in the previous section we analysed a crosstabulation of sex and home ownership and found that females were more likely to own their own home compared with males. However, this result applies only to our sample dataset. *How do we know whether these results are also systematic in the larger population and with what degree of error?* Inferential statistics can help us answer this question based on a concept known as statistical significance. Two popular forms of inferential statistics are (1) associational inferential statistics and (2) comparative inferential statistics. Discussions on both follow this section.

## Important Concepts/Issues in Inferential Statistics

Researchers need to be familiar with a number of terms common to inferential statistics. These include:

### *Statistical Significance*

Statistical significance concerns the probability that an acquired set of results are likely to be caused by some factor other than random chance or sampling error. A result that is statistically significant is one that is highly unlikely to be a function of sampling error, that is, it is more reflective of a genuine effect in the population.

In traditional hypothesis testing in research, null and alternative hypotheses are posed, data are collected, and the hypotheses are assessed or tested using inferential statistics. Recall from chapter 1 that a null hypothesis is a statement that two variables are not related or that there is no genuine effect of one variable on another variable, whereas an alternative hypothesis is a statement that that there is a genuine effect or relationship between variables.

Based on the results, evidence of statistical significance normally leads to the rejection of a null hypothesis in favour of the alternative hypothesis, whereas a non-significant result leads to the non-rejection of the null hypothesis. Contemporary hypothesis testing which simply involves the advancement of a research hypothesis guided by an existing body of empirical work or some theory is subject to statistical significance testing in the same way.

### *The P-Value*

The probability value or the p-value assesses whether a finding generated from an inferential statistical procedure is statistically significant. A p-value ranges from 0 to 1. Based on conventions, a p-value of

0.05 (or five per cent) or less indicates that an inferential statistical result is statistically significant; however, a p-value greater than 0.05 indicates a non-significant result. Although the five per cent level is a typical convention, others have recommended different levels (e.g., 0.1 or .01) depending on the context or discipline particularly in the social sciences.

> **p-value ≤ .05 indicates a statistically significant result**

> **p-value > .05 indicates that the result is not statistically significant**

## Statistical Significance vs Practical Significance

A result that is statistically significant does not automatically indicate that the same result is practically important or useful. For instance, you might find that there is a statistically significant difference between men and women in relation to job satisfaction in a particular hotel, but the size of this difference might be too small to attract any meaningful, practical attention. In contrast, practical significance examines whether statistical relationships or differences are large enough to be considered practically important or worthwhile. Practical significance can be assessed by effect sizes (discussed later in this chapter) and confidence limits which are also generated in inferential testing procedures.

**TIP:** When using inferential statistical tests, do not focus solely on statistical significance as a criterion of importance. Practical significance should also be assessed and established.

# ASSOCIATIONAL INFERENTIAL STATISTICS

Associational Inferential Statistics are a special category of inferential statistics aimed at directly examining relationships or associations between two or more variables.

## Nature of Associational Inferential Statistics

Associational inferential statistics are used to examine direct relationships or associations between two or more variables. A number of statistical tests fall into this category:

- Pearson Chi-Square
- Pearson Product Moment Correlation
- Linear Regression
- Logistic Regression
- Factor Analysis

These tests examine whether the relationship between variables is statistically significant based on the p-value statistic discussed in the previous section. The first three tests will be discussed in this section. However, logistic regression and factor analysis which are more advanced statistical tests are outside the scope of this text. A number of software packages can be used to generate inferential statistics such as SPSS and Stata. In this text, we will use SPSS to analyse our inferential statistics since SPSS is one of the most popular software packages available to statisticians.

## Pearson Chi-Square

### Overview

This inferential test is used when we want to examine whether a relationship exists between two *categorical variables*. Consider the research question in example 7.14.

**Example 7.14:** Research Question

Is there a relationship between *nationality* and *revisit intentions* among tourists in Barbados?

This associational research question consists of two categorical variables.

1. **Nationality,** that is, the groups surveyed. In this example, it comprises two categories: US and Canadian tourists.
2. **Revisit intentions** is based on responses to the question.

    *Would you return to Barbados for a holiday visit?*

    Yes     No     Don't Know

Both categorical variables will warrant the application of the Chi-Square test to statistically examine their relationship. Suppose we surveyed 115 US and Canadian tourists and entered our data into SPSS. We can run a Chi-Square test in SPSS to explore the relationship between nationality and revisit intentions to Barbados. It is important to identify the independent variable (i.e., nationality) and the dependent variable (i.e., revisit intentions) for the analysis.

**Instructions for Running a Chi-Square Test in SPSS**

- Select the Analyse tab
- Click on Descriptive Statistics
- Select Crosstabs
- Select *Nationality* (the group comparison variable) and use the arrow to move Nationality into the Column box
- Select *Response* 'Would you return to Barbados for a holiday' and use the arrow to move this variable into the Row box.
- Click on the Cells button
- Select Percentages in the column box (where the independent variable is located)
- Click continue
- Select the Statistics button
- Choose Chi-Square
- Select Phi or Cramer's V to see the effect size (to be discussed later)
- Click on Continue and then OK

**Analysis of Chi-Square Results Generated by SPSS**

SPSS will generate two output tables. The first table will provide your crosstabulations which is referred to as 'Crosstab' on the SPSS output generated (see table 7.2) and the second table will show the actual Chi-Square test results (see table 7.3). Let us examine the crosstabulation table. Recall that we would like to compare US and Canadian tourists on their likelihood of returning (revisit intentions) to Barbados. The goal here is to determine whether participants in one nationality group will be more likely than the other to state that they will return (by comparing their 'Yes' response) thus implying some possible relationship between the two variables. If we compare the percentage of US tourists with the percentage of Canadian tourists who said they will return to Barbados for a holiday visit (see table 7.2), we can see that 65.5 per cent of US tourists said they will return to Barbados for a holiday compared to 36.8 per cent of Canadian tourists.

## Table 7.2: Crosstabulation of Nationality and Return Visits to Barbados

**Crosstab**

|  |  |  | Nationality | | Total |
|---|---|---|---|---|---|
|  |  |  | US | Canadian |  |
| Would you return to Barbados for a holiday? | Yes | Count | 38 | 21 | 59 |
|  |  | % within Nationality | 65.5% | 36.8% | 51.3% |
|  | No | Count | 20 | 19 | 39 |
|  |  | % within Nationality | 34.5% | 33.3% | 33.9% |
|  | Don't Know | Count | 0 | 17 | 17 |
|  |  | % within Nationality | .0% | 29.8% | 14.8% |
| Total |  | Count | 58 | 57 | 115 |
|  |  | % within Nationality | 100.0% | 100.0% | 100.0% |

As previously explained, a crosstabulation is simply a descriptive test of our sample of 115 respondents. It does not allow an inference to our targeted population. The Chi-Square test shown in table 7.3 is an inferential test which allows the researcher to go beyond the descriptive assessment of the sample data to explore whether the results observed in the crosstabulation is statistically significant. We would like to know if we can infer from our sample to the general population (i.e., all US and Canadian tourists who have visited Barbados). We therefore need to examine our Chi-Square test to ascertain if a statistically significant relationship exists in order to make this inference.

To interpret the Chi-Square test in table 7.3, focus on the first line with the narrative *Pearson Chi-Square*. According to the data provided in this line, our Chi-Square Value = 21.917, df (or degrees of freedom) = 2, and the p-value = 0.000. The p-value of 0.000 suggests that the result is indeed statistically significant as it is well below the 0.05 criterion. Note that SPSS reports up to three decimal places but a p-value *cannot* be zero (.000). Therefore, p = 0.000 should be reported as p < .001.

## Table 7.3: Chi-Square Tests of Nationality and Return Visits to Barbados

**Chi-Square Tests**

|  | Value | df | Asymp. Sig (2-sided) |
|---|---|---|---|
| Pearson Chi-Square | 21.917[a] | 2 | .000 |
| Likelihood Ratio | 28.552 | 2 | .000 |
| Linear-by-Linear Association | 18.489 | 1 | .000 |
| N of Valid Cases | 115 |  |  |

a. 0 cells (.0%) have expected count less than 5. the minimum expected count is 8.43

## Interpretative Write-up of Chi-Square Test Results

Now that we have analysed our results, the final step is to provide an interpretative write-up or narrative (see example 7.15) of the Chi-Square test. The narrative should comprise:

1. Identification of the test and its purpose.
2. The results along with an interpretation in relation to the overall research question or research hypothesis posed.

> **Example 7.15:** Narrative of Chi-Square Test Results
>
> A Pearson Chi-Square test was used to examine whether a relationship exists between nationality and revisit intentions among tourists visiting Barbados. The results revealed that there was a statistically significant relationship between these variables (Chi-Square value = 21.917, df = 2, p < .001). US tourists (65.5%) were more likely to report that they would revisit the destination than did Canadian tourists (36.8%).

## Pearson Product Moment Correlation

### Overview

This inferential test is used when we want to examine whether a statistically significant relationship exists between two *quantitative (continuous) variables*. This relationship is described by a correlation coefficient, $r$ which is a statistical measure that estimates the *strength* and *direction* of the relationship.

The correlation coefficient ranges from -1 (perfect negative correlation) to +1 (perfect positive correlation), with the value of 0 indicating no relationship or correlation. In terms of direction, a positive $r$ indicates a positive correlation or relationship between two variables where higher values on one variable correspond to higher values on the other variable. In contrast, a negative $r$ indicates a negative correlation or relationship between variables where higher values on one variable correspond to lower values on the other variable.

In terms of strength, $r$ values closer to either +1 or -1 indicate stronger relationships. Based on conventions in social sciences, values between .10 and .30 indicate weak relationships, values between .30 and .50 indicate modest relationships, and values greater than .50 indicate strong relationships. In other disciplines, different conventions may apply.

Suppose we want to examine a relationship between overall satisfaction with prices in a destination – a composite score ranging from 1 (low satisfaction) to 5 (high satisfaction) and shopping expenditure, that is, average money spent at the destination. We can run a Pearson Correlation test to examine whether a statistically significant relationship exists between these two quantitative variables.

### Instructions for Running a Pearson Correlation Test in SPSS

- Select the Analyse tab
- Click on Correlation
- Select Bivariate
- Select the variable *Overall Satisfaction With Prices* and move it into the Variables box using the arrow
- Select the variable *Shopping Expenditure* and move it into the Variables box using the arrow
- Note that Pearson Correlation is already ticked as your default choice
- Select OK

## Analysis of Pearson Correlation Results Generated by SPSS

Table 7.4 shows that the Pearson Correlation $r$ value is 0.169 indicating a positive and weak correlation between satisfaction with prices and shopping expenditure. In this example, satisfaction is the independent variable and shopping expenditure is the dependent variable, as one's satisfaction is likely to influence one's spending. Hence, the higher the level of satisfaction with prices, the higher the expenditure. However, we need to determine whether this relationship is statistically significant. Our p-value titled Sig. (2 tailed) is 0.025. This indicates a statistically significant correlation. Hence, we can conclude that there is a statistically significant and positive relationship between the variables.

### Table 7.4: Pearson Correlation Tests of Satisfaction with Prices and Shopping Expenditure

**Correlations**

|  |  | Satisfaction with Prices in Destination | Shopping Expenditure per person per night |
|---|---|---|---|
| Satisfaction with Prices in Destination | Pearson Correlation | 1 | .169* |
|  | Sig. (2-tailed) |  | .025 |
|  | N | 332 | 176 |
| Shopping Expenditure per person per night | Pearson Correlation | .169* | 1 |
|  | Sig. (2-tailed) | .025 |  |
|  | N | 176 | 176 |

*Correlation is significant at the 0.05 level (2-tailed).

### Interpretative Write-up of Pearson Correlation Test Results

Producing an interpretative write-up or narrative (see example 7.16) of the Pearson Correlation test should comprise:

1. Identification of the test and its purpose.
2. The results along with an interpretation in relation to the overall research question or research hypothesis posed.

**Example 7.16:** Narrative of Pearson Correlation Test Results

A Pearson Correlation test was used to examine whether a relationship exists between tourists' satisfaction with prices and shopping expenditure among tourists visiting Barbados. The results revealed that there was a statistically significant relationship between these variables (r = 0.169, n = 176, p = .025). The correlation was positive and weak, suggesting that tourists who were more satisfied with prices in Barbados spent more money shopping in the destination.

## Linear Regression

### Overview

This inferential test is used to examine whether one or more independent variables (known as predictors) impact or predict a single quantitative dependent variable. Independent variables can be either quantitative or dichotomous in nature. The most basic form of linear regression is called a simple linear regression which can only accommodate a single independent variable and a single dependent variable. However, the unique aspect of this technique is its ability to examine the effects of multiple independent variables, in tandem, on a single dependent or outcome variable driven by its multiple or multivariate linear regression version. Linear regression is a relative of the Pearson Product Moment Correlation.

Suppose we conducted a survey of clients of a financial firm (e.g., a bank) to determine whether a client's sex, age, and years associated with the firm make a difference or relate to the number of client accounts opened at the same bank. Let us say we have the research question presented in example 7.17.

**Example 7.17** Research Question

What is the effect of clients' sex, age, and years associated with a bank, on the number of client accounts owned?

Sex (coded as male = 1 and female = 2) is dichotomous; age in years (is quantitative), and client years (which is also quantitative) are all independent variables, whereas the dependent variable is the number of client accounts at the bank (quantitative). Assume that all variables fit the assumptions for independent and dependent variables in linear regression (i.e., normality, linearity, and homoscedasticity). We can run a linear regression to examine whether any statistically significant relationships exist.

### Instructions for Running a Linear Regression Test in SPSS

- Select the Analyse tab
- Select Regression
- Choose Linear Regression
- Use the arrow to move your dependent variable (i.e., *number of client accounts at the bank*) into the Dependent Variable box
- Use the arrow to move your independent variables (i.e., *sex, age*, and *client years*) into the Independent Variable box
- Select the Statistics tab
- Tick the boxes marked Estimated, Model Fit, Descriptives, and Collinearity diagnostics
- In the Standardized Residual Plots section, tick Normal probability plot
- Select Continue
- Select OK

## Analysis of Linear Regression Results Generated by SPSS

The first table titled 'Model Summary' provides an assessment of the overall relationship or effect of all three independent variables on the dependent variable measured by the R-Square statistic (see table 7.5). Our focus is on R-Square statistic which is also referred to as the coefficient of determination. The R-Square statistic measures the proportion of variation that the independent variables (referred to as the regression model, or simply, *the model*) explain in the dependent variable.

According to our data, 82.4 per cent of the variation (or change) in the dependent variable (i.e., number of client accounts at the bank) is explained by clients' sex, age and years (i.e., our three independent variables). To get the percentage of 82.4 multiply the value of .824 by 100. The Adjusted R-Square statistic provides a slightly more conservative assessment of this relationship, which explains 82.1 per cent of variation. Note that results can be reported using either the R-Squared statistic or the Adjusted R-Square statistic.

### Table 7.5: Assessment of Overall Effect of Independent Variables on the Dependent Variable

**Model Summary**

| Model | R | R Square | Adjusted R Square | Std Error of the Estimate |
|---|---|---|---|---|
| 1 | .908[a] | .824 | .821 | .496 |

a. Predictors: (Constant), How many years have you been a client of our business?; Sex of client; Age of client.

The second table titled ANOVA provides information to assess whether our results are statistically significant (see table 7.6). The ANOVA results (also known as the F-test results) show that our F value is 280.772 while the p-value (shown under the Sig. column) is .000. Recall that when p = .000 it should be reported as p < .001. This result indicates that the overall combined effect of the three independent variables (captured by the R-Square) on the dependent variable is statistically significant. Note that this test revealed statistical significance for the overall effect (combined effect). However, it does not suggest that each independent variable is making a significant effect on the dependent variable.

The final table titled Coefficients (see table 7.7) shows the unique effects of sex, age, and clients' years associated with the bank on the number of client accounts. Observe that separate p-values (Sig.) are generated for all three of our individual independent variables in the last column. A perusal of table 7.7 shows that *client years* is the only statistically significant predictor or determinant of number of client accounts (p = .000). Note that the relationship between sex of client and number of client accounts was not statistically significant (p = .936). The relationship between age and number of client accounts was also not statistically significant (p = .058). However, some authors would argue that such a close p-value (.058 versus .050) might point to marginal statistical significance.

### Table 7.6: Overall Effect of Regression Model on Dependent Variable

**ANOVA[a]**

| Model | | Sum of Squares | df | Mean Square | F | Sig. |
|---|---|---|---|---|---|---|
| 1 | Regression | 207.104 | 3 | 69.035 | 280.722 | .000[b] |
| | Residual | 44.265 | 180 | .246 | | |
| | Total | 251.370 | 183 | | | |

a. Dependent Variable: How many client accounts do you have at our business?
b. Predictors: (Constant), How many years have you been a client of our business?; Sex of client; Age of client.

## Table 7.7: Effects of Independent Variables on the Dependent Variable

### Coefficients[a]

| Model | | Unstandardized Coefficients | | Standardized Coefficients | t | Sig. |
|---|---|---|---|---|---|---|
| | | B | Std. Error | Beta | | |
| 1 | (Constant) | .736 | .282 | | 2.611 | .010 |
| | Age of client | -.019 | .010 | -.061 | -1.910 | .058 |
| | Sex of client | -.007 | .088 | -.003 | -.081 | .936 |
| | How many years have you been a client of our business? | .934 | .033 | .917 | 28.656 | .000 |

a. Dependent Variable: How many client accounts do you have at our business?

For the variables that are statistically significant, you can describe both the strength and direction of the effects or relationships with the dependent variable using the Standardized Coefficients column or Beta section in table 7.7. Beta coefficients range from -1 to +1 and are interpreted in the same way as correlation coefficients. For example, *client years* is positively and strongly associated with number of client accounts (Beta = .917, p = .000). Specifically, clients with more years at the bank report a higher number of client accounts. If age was considered marginally significant, we can say that older persons report fewer client accounts than do younger persons.

### Interpretative Write-up of Linear Regression Test Results

Producing an interpretative write-up or narrative (see example 7.18) of the linear regression should comprise:

1. Identification of the test and its purpose.
2. The results along with an interpretation in relation to the overall research question or research hypothesis posed.

**Example 7.18:** Narrative of Linear Regression Results

A Multiple Linear Regression was used to examine the effects of clients' age, sex and years at the bank, on the number of client accounts held at the bank. The results revealed that the variables explained 82 per cent of variation in number of client accounts. The overall effect of this regression model was statistically significant (F = 280.722, p <.001). An examination of the individual predictors revealed that clients' years was the only significant predictor of number of client accounts. This effect was both strong and positive, indicating that clients with more years at the bank reported a higher number of client accounts (Beta = .917, p < .001).

## Assumptions in Statistical Tests

All statistical tests make a number of typical assumptions about the data being analysed. For example, linear regression makes assumptions about the data, including normality/linearity/outliers (which can be observed when you peruse your Scatterplot), homogeneity of variances, independence of residuals, non-zero variance, independent errors, and the absence of multicollinearity (where some independent variables are highly correlated with each other, generally $>.8$). It is important for novice researchers to assess these assumptions using the right methods and checklists before applying and interpreting the results of statistical tests.

To better understand these issues, refer to other statistical texts to get further insight so that you can learn about (1) the different assumptions that must be considered in various statistical tests and (2) how to deal with assumptions that are violated.

Remember to always consult similar journal papers in your discipline that have applied similar inferential tests to get ideas on choosing and interpreting inferential tests.
Note also that different disciplines have different formats for presenting statistical results.

# COMPARATIVE INFERENTIAL STATISTICS

Comparative Inferential Statistics are a special category of inferential statistics aimed at examining statistical differences between groups of respondents.

## Nature of Comparative Inferential Statistics

Comparative inferential statistics are used to examine statistical differences between two or more groups of respondents. Statistical tests in this category include:

- Independent Samples T-Test
- Paired Samples T-Test
- One-Way Analysis of Variance (ANOVA)
- Multivariate Analysis of Variance (MANOVA)
- Analysis of Covariance (ANCOVA)
- Multivariate Analysis of Covariance (MANCOVA)

These tests examine whether differences between two or more groups are statistically significant based on the probability value (or p-value). The first three tests will be discussed in this section. However, the latter three tests which are more advanced statistical tests are outside the scope of this book.

## Independent Samples T-Test

### Overview

The independent samples t-test is an inferential statistical technique used to examine whether there is a statistically significant difference between two groups of respondents. The test requires a dichotomous, categorical independent variable and a quantitative dependent variable.

Let us consider a scenario concerning a survey of tourists on their satisfaction with a destination. You want to examine whether there is a difference in satisfaction between European and US tourists. Your independent variable is *nationality* which is a dichotomous, categorical variable and your dependent variable is *satisfaction*, a composite numerical variable (ranging from one to five). Our research question is presented in example 7.19. Using SPSS we will run an independent samples t-test and analyse the results to see if our results are statistically significant.

**Example 7.19: Research Question**

Is there a difference in satisfaction with the destination between European and US tourists?

**Instructions for Running an Independent Sample T-test in SPSS**

- Select the Analyse tab
- Select Compare Means
- Choose Independent Samples T-Test
- Use the arrow to move your dependent variable (i.e., *satisfaction*) into the section Test Variable
- Use the arrow to move your independent variable (i.e., *nationality*) into the secton Grouping Variable
- Click on define groups and type in your codes for nationality in the Group 1 and Group 2 boxes. For example, if you used US = 1, and European = 2, type 1 in the Group 1 box and 2 in the Group 2 box.
- Select Continue
- Select OK

### Analysis of the Independent Samples T-Test Results Generated by SPSS

The results of the independent samples t-test produce two tabular displays. The first table titled Group Statistics (see table 7.8) shows the mean values on overall satisfaction (i.e., our dependent variable using a scale of 1 to 5) for European and US tourists. When examining table 7.8, a preliminary scan of the sample sizes for each group should be done to ensure that the sample size for each group is correct.

Next, we need to examine our mean values. According to our data, US tourists express greater satisfaction with the destination compared with European tourists (M = 4.04, SD = .89 versus M = 3.42, SD = .93). However, we must determine whether this difference is genuinely reflective of the population, that is, whether it is statistically significant.

## Table 7.8: Overall Satisfaction with Destination for European and US Tourists

### Group Statistics

|  | Nationality of Tourist | N | Mean | Std. Deviation | Std. Error Mean |
|---|---|---|---|---|---|
| Overall satisfaction with the destination | European | 78 | 3.42 | .933 | .106 |
|  | US | 184 | 4.04 | .892 | .066 |

An inspection of our second table titled 'Independent Samples Test' shows a number of statistical tests and values embedded (see table 7.9). The first section of the table shows the Levene's test for Equality of Variances results. This test examines a popular assumption of the independent samples t-test, namely, the assumption of equality of variances, that is, whether the variability in scores between the two groups (i.e., Europeans and US) being compared is equal or not.

If equal variances are observed, the equal variances t-test results should be consulted (i.e., the top line in table 7.9 titled *Equal Variances Assumed*). If the equal variances assumption is violated (not assumed), then the unequal variances t-test should be interpreted (i.e., the second line in table 7.9 titled 'Equal Variances Not Assumed'). If the Levene's test is non-significant (i.e., p > .05), then equal variances are assumed and you read the equal variance t-test results. However, if the Levene's test is significant (i.e., p ≤ .05), the assumption is violated and you rely on the unequal variances t-test results.

An examination of table 7.9 shows that the *Equal Variances Assumed* line of results provides a Sig. value of .025. This means that the equal variances assumption is violated (not assumed) because the p-value is less than .05. Therefore, we need to examine and interpret the *Equal Variances Not Assumed* t-test results.

## Table 7.9: Levene's Test for Overall Satisfaction for European and US Tourists with Destination

### Independent Samples Test

|  |  | Levene's Test for Equality of Variances | | t-test Equality of Means | | | | | | |
|---|---|---|---|---|---|---|---|---|---|---|
|  |  | F | Sig. | t | df | sig. (2-tailed) | Mean Difference | Std. Error Difference | 95% Confidence interval of the Difference | |
|  |  |  |  |  |  |  |  |  | Lower | Upper |
| Overall satisfaction with the destination | Equal variances assumed | 5.092 | .025 | -5.077 | 260 | .000 | -.620 | .122 | -.861 | -.380 |
|  | Equal variances not assumed |  |  | -4.985 | 139.433 | .000 | -.620 | .124 | -.866 | -.374 |

Now that we have ascertained which Levene's test will be reported, we will now focus in on the section titled *Levene's Test for Equality of Variances* in table 7.9. The values of interest are: (1) t-statistic (i.e., *t*) of -4.985, (2) degrees of freedom (i.e., *df*) of 139.433, and (3) p-value of .000 (i.e., *Sig. 2-tailed*) which is reported as p < .001. It is the p-value of .000 that is associated with the t-test that confirms that the difference we sought in table 7.8 was indeed statistically significant. Hence, we can conclude that there is a statistically significant difference between the two nationality groups with respect to their overall satisfaction with the destination.

### Interpretative Write-up of the Independent Samples T-test Results

Producing an interpretative write-up or narrative (see example 7.20) of the independent samples t-test should comprise:

1. Identification of the test and its purpose.
2. The results along with an interpretation in relation to the overall research question or research hypothesis posed.

> **Example 7.20:** Narrative of Independent Samples T-Test Results
>
> An independent samples t-test was conducted to examine whether there was a difference between European and US visitors in relation to their overall satisfaction with the destination. The test revealed a statistically significant difference between European and US visitors (t = -4.99, df = 139.43, p < .001). US visitors (M = 4.04, SD = .89) reported significantly higher levels of satisfaction with the overall destination experience than did European visitors (M = 3.42, SD= .93).

## Paired Samples T-test

### Overview

The paired samples t-test (also known as the repeated measures t-test) is an inferential statistical technique used to examine whether there is a statistically significant difference between two sets of scores for a single sample of respondents. Whereas the independent samples t-test examines separate groups, the paired samples t-test examines the same group on two occasions (e.g. pretest versus posttest) or based on two sets of scores on a numerical variable (e.g., tourist satisfaction in 2017 versus tourist satisfaction in 2018, or participants' self-esteem measured in 2017 and 2018) among the same group of participants. A dichotomous, categorical related group variable is the independent variable in the test, while the dependent variable is a quantitative variable.

Let us consider a scenario concerning a survey of employees whose mental health status was measured using a quantitative health index (using a self-reported instrument) capturing overall mental health ranging from one (poor mental health) to four (excellent mental health). Let us say you want to introduce a therapeutic counselling intervention for improving mental health and employees are expected to attend this intervention for six months. You decide to measure employees' mental health before the intervention and repeat the measurement after the intervention.

Your independent variable here is the intervention itself which consists of two related groups: before counselling (pretest) and after counselling (posttest), and mental health status which is a composite numerical variable (ranging from one to four) represents the dependent variable. This design is a pretest and posttest experimental design (see discussion on experimental designs in chapter 3). However, note that the paired samples-test can also be used with non-experimental designs. Using SPSS, let us answer the research question presented in example 7.21 using the paired samples t-test.

### Example 7.21: Research Question
Is there a difference in employees' mental health before and after counselling?

### Instructions for Running a Paired Samples T-test in SPSS

**SPSS**

- Select the Analyse tab
- Select Compare Means
- Choose Paired Samples T-Test
- Select the two variables that you want to compare (i.e., *health before counselling and health after counselling*) and use the arrow to move them into the box labelled Paired Variables
- Select OK

### Analysis of the Paired Samples T-Test Results Generated by SPSS

The first table (titled Paired Samples Statistics) compares the mean scores on mental health (on the one to four scale) for the pretest and posttest groups (see table 7.10). We can see that employees' mental health after counselling (M= 3.74) is much higher (better) than their mental health before counselling (M = 1.35). However, we need to determine whether this difference is statistically significant.

### Table 7.10: Pretest-Posttest Mean Scores on Employee Mental Health

**Paired Samples Statistics**

|  |  | Mean | N | Std. Deviation | Std. Error Mean |
|---|---|---|---|---|---|
| Pair 1 | Health before Counselling | 1.3450 | 322 | .47896 | .02669 |
|  | Health after Counselling | 3.7422 | 322 | .81574 | .04546 |

The second table provides the results of the paired samples test (see table 7.11). The focus in this table is on: (1) the t-statistic (i.e., $t$) of -48.131, (2) degrees of freedom (i.e., $df$) of 321, and (3) the p-value (i.e., *Sig 2-tailed*) of .000 (reported as $p < .001$). Since our criterion p-value is generally set at .05, these results suggest that there is a statistically significant difference between the two related groups. Specifically, after counselling, employees' mental health status was much higher than their mental health status before counselling.

## Table 7.11: Pretest-Posttest Results on Employee Mental Health

### Paired Samples Test

| | | Paired Differences | | | | | t | df | Sig. (2-tailed) |
|---|---|---|---|---|---|---|---|---|---|
| | | Mean | Std. Deviation | Std. Error Mean | 95% Confidence interval of the Difference | | | | |
| | | | | | Lower | Upper | | | |
| Pair 1 | Health before Counselling – Health after Counselling | -2.38820 | .89037 | .04962 | -2.48582 | -2.29058 | -48.131 | 321 | .000 |

### Interpretative Write-Up of the Paired Samples T-Test Results

Producing an interpretative write-up or narrative (see example 7.22) of the paired samples t-test should comprise:

1. Identification of the test and its purpose.
2. The results along with an interpretation in relation to the overall research question or research hypothesis posed.

**Example 7.22:** Narrative of Independent Samples T-Test Results

A paired samples t-test was conducted to examine whether there was a difference in mental health status of employees before and after a counselling intervention at work. The results revealed that there was a statistically significant difference (t = -48.131, df = 321, p < .001). After counselling, employees' mental health status (M= 3.74, SD = .82) was much higher than their mental health status before counselling (M= 1.35, SD = .48).

## One Way ANOVA

### Overview

The one-way ANOVA is an inferential statistical test that examines the differences among three or more groups of respondents with respect to a quantitative dependent variable. It is a generalized version of the independent samples t-test as it caters to a categorical independent variable with more than two groups, but the dependent variable remains quantitative in nature.

The one-way ANOVA allows for the assessment of differences of various groups at a time in relation to a single quantitative variable. Let us examine the scenario concerning whether tourists in four different age groups are equally satisfied (or not) with an overall tourist destination. Here, age is a categorical variable with four groups. An independent samples t-test cannot be done because we are comparing more than two groups. Overall satisfaction with the destination is a quantitative dependent variable ranging from one to five. Using SPSS, let us answer the research question presented in example 7.23 using the one-way ANOVA.

# Quantitative Data Analysis

**Example 7.23:** Research Question

Are there significant differences in overall satisfaction among tourists in different age groups?

### Instructions for Running a One Way ANOVA Test in SPSS

**SPSS**

- Select the Analyse tab
- Select Compare Means
- Choose One-Way ANOVA
- Use the arrow to move your dependent variable (i.e., *satisfaction*) into the *Dependent List* box
- Use the arrow to move your independent variable (i.e., *age*) into the *Factor* box
- Click on the Options button and select Descriptives and Homogeneity of Variance
- Select Continue
- Select the Post Hoc button and tick Scheffe (equal variances assumed) and Games-Howell (equal vaiance not assumed).
- Select Continue
- Select OK

## Analysis of One-Way ANOVA Test Results Generated by SPSS

The first table titled 'Descriptives' provides the mean scores of overall satisfaction for the four age groups (see table 7.12). An examination of the means shows that all groups report different mean scores, with the *highest* satisfaction being reported by those in the age group 26–40 and the *lowest* satisfaction being reported by those in the age group over 60. At this stage, although there are revealed differences among the age groups, we need robust evidence that these differences are statistically significant before making any definitive conclusions.

### Table 7.12: Descriptives on Overall Satisfaction with Destination by Age Group

**Descriptives**

Overall satisfaction with the destination

| | N | Mean | Std. Deviation | Std. Error | 95% Confidence interval for Mean | | Minimum | Maximum |
|---|---|---|---|---|---|---|---|---|
| | | | | | Lower Bound | Upper Bound | | |
| 18 – 25 | 14 | 3.86 | 1.167 | .312 | 3.18 | 4.53 | 2 | 5 |
| 26 – 40 | 95 | 4.03 | .818 | .084 | 3.86 | 4.20 | 1 | 5 |
| 41 – 60 | 134 | 3.84 | .949 | .082 | 3.68 | 4.01 | 1 | 5 |
| Over 60 | 19 | 3.11 | 1.049 | .241 | 2.60 | 3.61 | 1 | 5 |
| Total | 262 | 3.86 | .964 | .058 | 3.74 | 3.97 | 1 | 5 |

The second table (Test of Homogeneity of Variances) provides the results on the Levene's test of equality of variances. The one-way ANOVA assumes equal variances. If there is a violation, you should request and report the results of two alternative tests, namely, the Welch Test and the Brown-Forsythe Test. These inferential tests provide evidence of statistical significance for the ANOVA when violations of equal variances occur. To ascertain if any violation has occurred, you need to zoom in on the Sig. or p-value to see if this number is greater than .05. According to table 7.13, the p-value is .175 which indicates that equal variances are observed. We can therefore move on to the ANOVA test results.

### Table 7.13: Levene's Test of Homogeneity of Variances

**Test of Homogeneity of Variances**

Overall satisfaction with the destination

| Levene Statistic | df1 | df2 | Sig. |
|---|---|---|---|
| 1.664 | 3 | 258 | .175 |

The third table titled 'ANOVA' (see table 7.14) provides direct evidence as to whether the differences revealed in the Descriptives table (which compared the age groups on overall destination satisfaction) are statistically significant. The focus in this table is on the last column (Sig.). If the p-value here is ≤ .05, then there is a statistically significant difference among the mean scores. An examination of table 7.14 shows that the p-value = .001 which indicates a statistically significant result. However, we have a dilemma. *Does this mean that all age groups are significantly different from each other?* The answer is a solid NO! The p-value for the ANOVA test only indicates that there is at least one age group comparison that is statistically significant but does not indicate which one. We need another set of tests to help us locate these significant age group comparisons on satisfaction.

### Table 7.14: ANOVA Results for Overall Satisfaction with Destination by Age Group

**ANOVA**

Overall satisfaction with the destination

| | Sum of Squares | df | Mean Square | F | Sig. |
|---|---|---|---|---|---|
| Between Groups | 13.657 | 3 | 4.552 | 5.336 | .001 |
| Within Groups | 220.118 | 258 | .853 | | |
| Total | 233.775 | 261 | | | |

The final table titled "Multiple Comparisons" is the Post-Hoc Test results (see table 7.15). This table provides special tests (referred to as post-hoc tests) that examine every possible pair of group comparisons in relation to the dependent variable (e.g., 18–25 versus 26–40 versus 41–60 versus over 60) with respect to overall satisfaction. The goal is to locate which pairwise comparison (i.e., pairs of groups) is statistically significant as was revealed by the prior ANOVA test table.

Note that there are two categories of post-hoc tests: equal variances post-hoc tests (which assume equal variances) and unequal variances post-hoc tests (which do not assume equal variances). Recall that when we ran our SPSS ANOVA command, we selected two post-hoc tests, one under the equal variances assumed section (i.e., Scheffe) and the other under equal variances not assumed (i.e., Games-Howell). Both Scheffe and the Games-Howell were selected due to their popularity in the statistical literature. Since our Levene's test in table 7.13 revealed that equal variances can be assumed, we should focus on the equal variances assumed post-hoc test (i.e., the Scheffe test). The results of this test are displayed in the top half of table 7.15. We will completely ignore the results of the Games-Howell test in light of the assumption of equal variances.

### Table 7.15: Post Hoc Tests for Overall Satisfaction with Destination by Age Group
### Multiple Comparisons

Dependent Variable: Overall satisfaction with the destination

|  | (I) Age | (J) Age | Mean Difference (I-J) | Std. Error | Sig. | 95% Confidence interval Lower Bound | 95% Confidence interval Upper Bound |
|---|---|---|---|---|---|---|---|
| Scheffe | 18 – 25 | 26 – 40 | -.174 | .264 | .933 | -.92 | .57 |
|  |  | 41 – 60 | .014 | .259 | 1.000 | -.72 | .74 |
|  |  | Over 60 | .752 | .325 | .151 | -.16 | 1.67 |
|  | 26 – 40 | 18 – 25 | .174 | .264 | .933 | -.57 | .92 |
|  |  | 41 – 60 | .188 | .124 | .512 | -.16 | .54 |
|  |  | Over 60 | .926* | .232 | .001 | .27 | 1.58 |
|  | 41 – 60 | 18 – 25 | -.014 | .259 | 1.000 | -.74 | .72 |
|  |  | 26 – 40 | -.188 | .124 | .512 | -.54 | .16 |
|  |  | Over 60 | -.738* | .226 | .015 | .10 | 1.38 |
|  | Over 60 | 18 – 25 | -.752 | .325 | .151 | -1.67 | .16 |
|  |  | 26 – 40 | -.926* | .232 | .001 | -1.58 | -.27 |
|  |  | Over 60 | -.738* | .226 | .015 | -1.38 | -.10 |
| Games-Howell | 18 – 25 | 26 – 40 | -.174 | .323 | .948 | -1.11 | .76 |
|  |  | 41 – 60 | .014 | .323 | 1.000 | -.92 | .94 |
|  |  | Over 60 | .752 | .394 | .249 | -.33 | 1.83 |
|  | 26 – 40 | 18 – 25 | .174 | .323 | .948 | -.76 | 1.11 |
|  |  | 41 – 60 | -.188 | .117 | .378 | -.12 | .49 |
|  |  | Over 60 | .926* | .255 | .007 | .22 | 1.63 |
|  | 41 – 60 | 18 – 25 | -.014 | .323 | 1.000 | -.94 | .92 |
|  |  | 26 – 40 | -.188 | .117 | .378 | -.49 | .12 |
|  |  | Over 60 | .738* | .254 | .038 | .03 | 1.44 |
|  | Over 60 | 18 – 25 | -.752 | .394 | .249 | -1.83 | .33 |
|  |  | 26 – 40 | -.926* | .255 | .007 | -1.63 | -.22 |
|  |  | Over 60 | -.738* | .254 | .038 | -1.44 | -.03 |

*The mean difference is significant at the 0.05 level.

On examining the Scheffe tests and associated p-values on the various group comparisons we can see that (1) a statistically significant difference exists between tourists in the 26–40 age group and those in the over 60 age group (p = 0.001), and (2) a statistically significant difference exists between tourists in the 41–60 age group and those in the over 60 age group (p = 0.015). No other significant differences are observed under the Scheffe test output.

Post hoc tests are appropriate for ANOVA scenarios when the goal is to simply compare each of the various groups on the independent variable of a dependent variable. However, if the analyst is interested in comparing only specific groups, planned comparisons (or contrasts) can be used. Planned comparisons allow you to compare specific groups (neglecting others) on a given dependent variable. In such situations, we are not concerned about comparing all possible combinations of groups. For example, if we wanted to compare only the youngest and oldest age groups on overall satisfaction, we can request planned comparisons instead of post-hoc tests in SPSS.

### Interpretative Write-Up of the One-Way ANOVA Test Results

Producing an interpretative write-up or narrative (see example 7.24) of the one-way ANOVA should comprise:

1. Identification of the test and its purpose.
2. The results along with an interpretation in relation to the overall research question or research hypothesis posed.

**Example 7.24:** Narrative of One-Way ANOVA Test Results

A one-way ANOVA was conducted to examine whether there were differences among tourists in different age groups in relation to their overall satisfaction with the destination. The results revealed statistically significant differences among the age groups (F = 5.34, p = .001). Post-hoc comparisons using the Scheffe tests revealed that tourists in the 26–40 age group (M = 4.03, SD= .82) and 41–60 age group (M = 3.84, SD = 0.95) reported significantly higher overall satisfaction with the destination compared with tourists over 60 years (M =3.11, SD = 1.05). No other significant differences were observed between the other age groups.

The associational and comparative statistics discussed in this text are referred to as parametric tests (with the exception of Chi-Square tests) which have stringent assumptions about the data that they assess. When these assumptions are broken, researchers would normally refer to non-parametric tests.

# EFFECT SIZES

Effect Sizes are special quantitative measures used to quantify the relationships or magnitude of group differences.

## Nature of Effect Sizes

An effect size is a statistical measure of the size of a relationship between variables or the magnitude of a difference between groups. It is a useful indicator of practical significance. The larger the effect size measure, the stronger the effect. Effect sizes can be computed for both associational and comparative inferential tests.

## Effect Sizes for Associational Tests

### Pearson Chi-Square Test

The Pearson Chi-Square test carries a number of effect sizes. The Phi coefficient is an effect size measure that captures the strength of a relationship between two dichotomous categorical variables in a contingency table. The computation for the Phi coefficient and interpretation is as follows:

**Phi Coefficient**

$$\varphi = \sqrt{\frac{x^2}{n}}$$

where  $x^2$ = Chi-Square test statistic
       $n$ = Sample size

| Interpretation: | Phi Coefficient Effect Size | Small | = .10 |
| --- | --- | --- | --- |
| | Phi Coefficient Effect Size | Medium | = .30 |
| | Phi Coefficient Effect Size | Large | = .50 |

The Cramer's V is a more popular effect size measure for the Chi-Square test used in larger contingency tables (tables larger than 2 x 2). The interpretation of the Cramer's V varies according to the size of the contingency table. The degrees of freedom of a Chi-Square are directly related to the number of columns and rows of a contingency table as the degrees of freedom (df) = (rows -1) x (columns -1). The Cramer's V is interpreted based on the degrees of freedoms in a Chi-Square test. The computation for Cramer's V and interpretation are as follows:

### Cramer's V

$$V = \sqrt{\frac{x^2}{n - df^*}}$$

where
- $x^2$ = Chi-Square test statistic
- $n$ = Sample size
- $df^*$ = Degrees of freedom

| Interpretation: | | | |
|---|---|---|---|
| df = 1 | (Small = .10 | Medium = .30 | Large = .50) |
| df = 2 | (Small = .07 | Medium = .21 | Large = .35) |
| df = 3 | (Small = .06 | Medium = .17 | Large = .29) |
| df = 4 | (Small = .05 | Medium = .15 | Large = .25) |
| df = 5 | (Small = .05 | Medium = .13 | Large = .22) |

## Pearson Correlation and Linear Regression

The correlation coefficient, $r$, of the Pearson Product Moment Correlation is its own effect size of a linear relationship between two variables. For a simple linear regression, the $R$-squared value or coefficient of determination ($R^2$) can be used in the same manner. For multivariate linear regression, the preference is the Cohen's $f^2$ effect size which is based on the following calculation:

### Cohen's $f^2$

$$f^2 = \sqrt{\frac{R^2}{1 - R^2}}$$

where
- $R^2$ = Coefficient of determination
- $1 - R^2$ = Coefficient of alienation

| Interpretation: | | | |
|---|---|---|---|
| Cohen's $f^2$ Effect Size | Small | = | .02 |
| Cohen's $f^2$ Effect Size | Medium | = | .15 |
| Cohen's $f^2$ Effect Size | Large | = | .35 |

## Effect Sizes for Comparative Tests

### Independent Samples T-Test

The independent t-test relies on the Eta-Squared effect size or the Cohen's $d$ effect size. The computation for the Eta-Squared effect size and interpretation are as follows:

### Eta-Squared

$$\eta^2 = \frac{t^2}{t^2 + (N_1 + N_2 - 2)}$$

where
- $t^2$ = Squared t-statistic
- $N_1$ = Sample size of group 1
- $N_2$ = Sample size of group 2

| Interpretation: | | | |
|---|---|---|---|
| Eta-Squared Effect Size | Small | = | .01 |
| Eta-Squared Effect Size | Moderate | = | .06 |
| Eta-Squared Effect Size | Large | = | .14 |

Example 7.25 provides the Eta-Squared calculation for the independent t-test results generated by SPSS and shown in tables 7.8 and 7.9. According to our calculations, our Eta-Squared value is .09. Expressed as a percentage, this converts to nine per cent which means that only nine per cent of the variance with overall satisfaction with destination is explained by nationality.

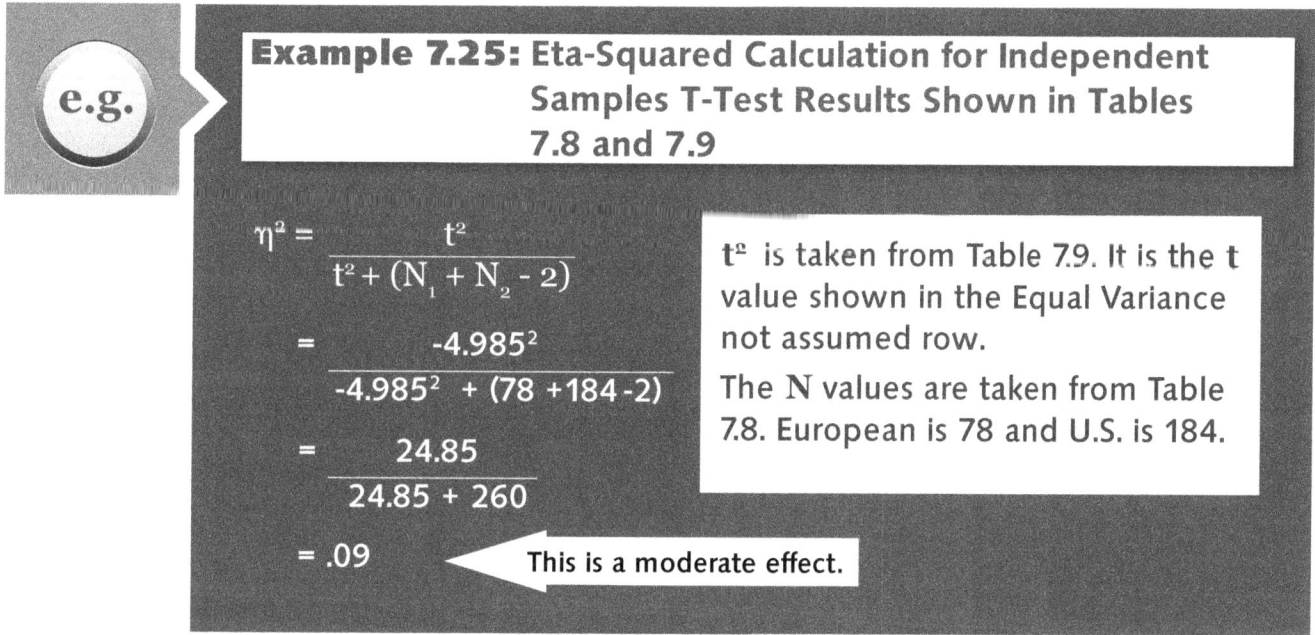

**Example 7.25:** Eta-Squared Calculation for Independent Samples T-Test Results Shown in Tables 7.8 and 7.9

$$\eta^2 = \frac{t^2}{t^2 + (N_1 + N_2 - 2)}$$

$$= \frac{-4.985^2}{-4.985^2 + (78 + 184 - 2)}$$

$$= \frac{24.85}{24.85 + 260}$$

$$= .09$$

This is a moderate effect.

$t^2$ is taken from Table 7.9. It is the t value shown in the Equal Variance not assumed row.

The N values are taken from Table 7.8. European is 78 and U.S. is 184.

The Cohen's *d*-statistic is an alternative effect size measure for the independent samples t-test. The computation for the Cohen's *d*, the pooled standard deviation and interpretation are as follows:

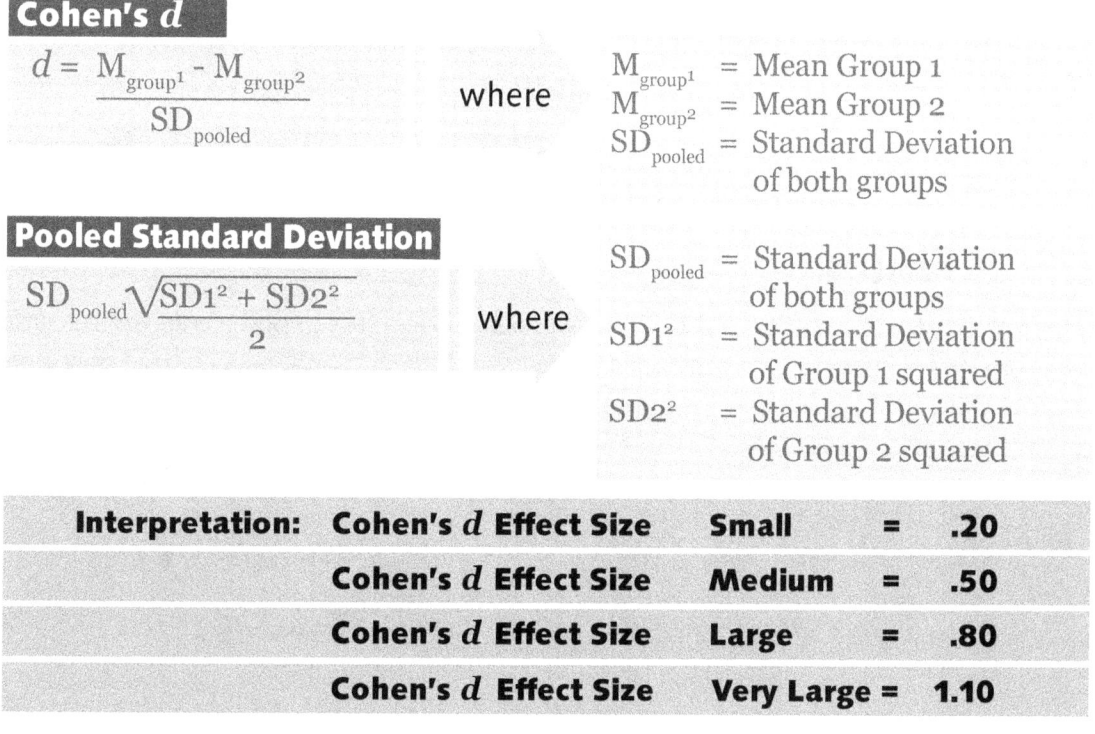

### Cohen's *d*

$$d = \frac{M_{group1} - M_{group2}}{SD_{pooled}}$$

where  $M_{group1}$ = Mean Group 1
$M_{group2}$ = Mean Group 2
$SD_{pooled}$ = Standard Deviation of both groups

### Pooled Standard Deviation

$$SD_{pooled} = \sqrt{\frac{SD1^2 + SD2^2}{2}}$$

where  $SD_{pooled}$ = Standard Deviation of both groups
$SD1^2$ = Standard Deviation of Group 1 squared
$SD2^2$ = Standard Deviation of Group 2 squared

| Interpretation: | Cohen's *d* Effect Size | Small | = | .20 |
|---|---|---|---|---|
| | Cohen's *d* Effect Size | Medium | = | .50 |
| | Cohen's *d* Effect Size | Large | = | .80 |
| | Cohen's *d* Effect Size | Very Large | = | 1.10 |

## Paired Samples T-test

Similar to the independent samples t-test, the same eta-squared effect size measure is used for the paired samples t-test but follows a different computation. The computation and interpretation are as follows:

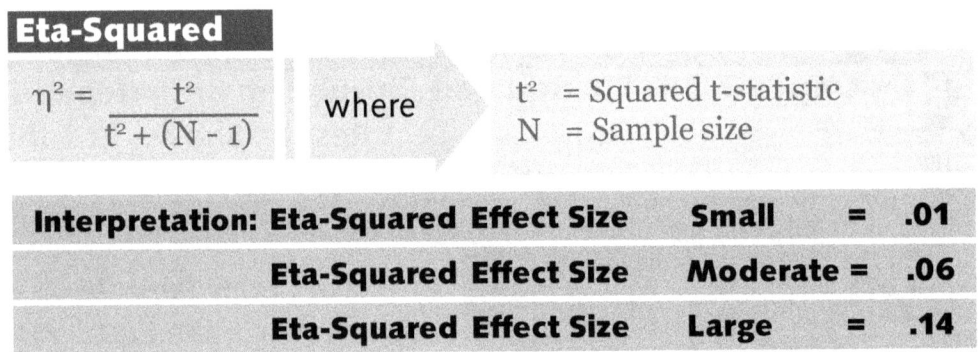

## One-Way ANOVA

The one-way ANOVA also relies on the same eta-square effect size measure based on a different computation. The computation and interpretation are as follows:

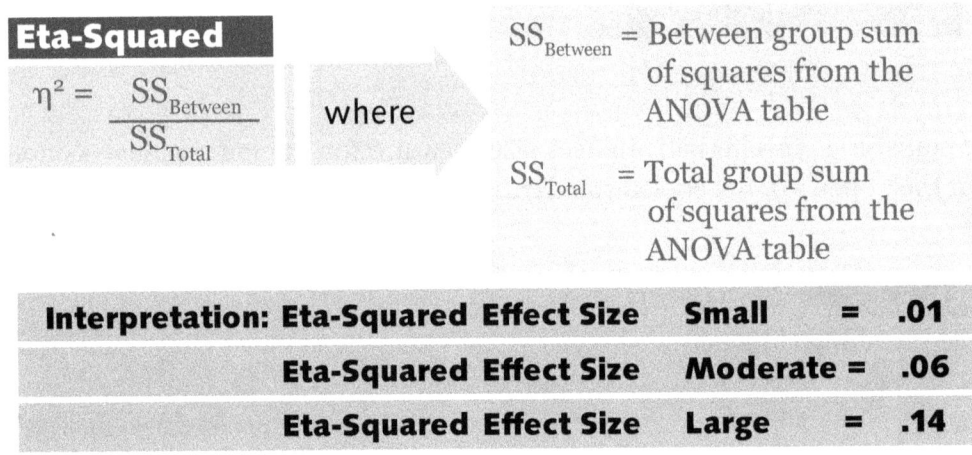

## Final Note on Effect Size

The power of a statistical test concerns the capacity of a statistical test to find a true genuine effect. Effect sizes can be computed using many software packages such as SPSS and other specialized online calculators. However, some effect sizes have to be computed through manual operations.

# Quantitative Data Analysis

> **Effect size measures are critical to calculating the power of statistical tests.**
>
> **The power of a test is affected by the statistical significance, the effect size, and the sample size.**
>
> **An effect size is a useful indicator of practical significance.**

Note that some referencing systems such as APA require that analysts report and interpret effect sizes alongside their inferential statistical test results. For example, recall that our calculated eta-squared statistic for the independent samples t-test which was computed using the SPSS results shown in tables 7.8 and 7.9 was .09 (see example 7.25). If we include this result in our narrative, this is how our write-up of our Independent Samples T-Test results would appear (see example 7.26).

**Example 7.26:** Narrative of Independent Samples T-test

An independent samples t-test was conducted to examine whether there was a difference between European and US visitors in relation to their overall satisfaction with the destination. The test revealed a statistically significant difference between European and US visitors (t = -4.99, df = 139.43, $p < .001$). US visitors (M = 4.04, SD = .89) reported significantly higher levels of satisfaction with the overall destination experience than did European visitors (M = 3.42, SD= .93). The magnitude of the differences in the means was moderate (eta-squared = .09).

A good understanding on the value of power of analysis in statistical testing and the role of the effect size measures is fundamental to good research.

To enhance your understanding of this topic, do further reading in other statistical texts.

# 8 Qualitative Data Analysis

- Qualitative Data
- Thematic Analysis
- Discourse Analysis
- Interpretative Phenomenological Analysis
- Narrative Analysis
- Conversation Analysis
- Grounded Theory Analysis

## QUALITATIVE DATA

**Qualitative Data is textual, non-numerical data derived from open-ended questions or other textual (documentary) sources.**

### Qualitative Data Sources

Qualitative data is naturally non-numerical in nature and can be derived from a number of sources including the following:

**In-depth Interviews**

Focus groups (see chapter 3) and individual (face-to-face) interviews (see chapter 3) normally gather general and in-depth views and perspectives from participants. Such sources offer opportunities for study participants to provide detailed, unrestricted responses to a wide cross section of questions (see example 8.1). Interview data can be derived from semi-structured and unstructured interviews which might manifest in the form of digital recordings that can be transcribed before analysis.

## Qualitative Data Analysis

**Example 8.1:** In-depth Interview Questions

What are your views on employees with mental illness?

How do you normally interact with female employees in the workplace?

Why do you think discrimination against persons with disabilities is a concern in Barbados?

In what ways do you contribute to the well-being of your employees.

What work challenges do you face as an employee with HIV/Aids?

### Observations

Ethnographic or ethology research and other research designs that seek to directly observe study participants in naturalistic or controlled environments (see chapter 3) gather data in a variety of ways that are consistent with qualitative formats, including audio, video, textual, visual/pictorial, and other non-numerical formats.

### Written/Documentary Sources

Existing documentary sources are popular sources used by qualitative researchers who engage in non-reactive research in which the emphasis is on assessing written (textual) narratives and materials. These sources may include newspapers, magazines, books, websites, online posts/blogs, transcripts of conversations or interviews, annual reports, letters/memos, and other documentary formats worthy of investigation (see further discussion under document review and analysis in chapter 3).

## Issues to Consider when Using Qualitative Research

Qualitative data normally represents types and categories of information that cannot be measured numerically or analysed statistically. Hence, the data is typically abstract, descriptive, and subjective in nature. In order to determine whether qualitative data is appropriate for a given research study, a number of considerations have to be taken into account in the early planning and design stages:

### Type and Nature of Research Questions

Your research questions should be qualitative in nature. Remember research questions serve to direct the types and nature of data you can obtain. Qualitative research questions are addressed by qualitative research data, whereas quantitative research questions are addressed by quantitative research data.

### Research Design and Methods of Data-Collection

The type of research design depends on the type and nature of your research questions. Qualitative research questions can use a number of different qualitative research designs for a given study. Your choice of research design in qualitative research will automatically influence how you gather qualitative data as well as the types of qualitative data you gather. For example, an ethnographic research design which relies on participant observations will gather different types of qualitative data (observational notes, drawings or photographs), whereas a case study design might involve the collection of written (textual) narratives from a variety of primary and secondary sources.

## Types of Data Sources

Data sources including transcripts, newspapers/magazines, observational texts and notes, photographs, and audio-visual materials/formats are common qualitative data sources. The more varied our data sources are in a given study, the more varied our qualitative data and analyses for the study. Different data sources can serve to support or complement each other in a given study to improve the validity of the data-gathering experience.

## Types of Data Analyses

Different types of qualitative data require different types of analytical tools and techniques. Content analysis, thematic analysis, interpretative phenomenological analysis, and discourse analyses are typical qualitative techniques. However, each technique has different assumptions and data requirements.

# Strengths and Limitations of Qualitative Research

Researchers who rely on qualitative data have to be thorough, flexible, and analytical in their gathering and analytical activities in order to enhance the utility of the qualitative data to answer their various research questions. Table 8.1 highlights some key strengths and limitations of qualitative research.

Overall, researchers must ensure that various sources of qualitative data gathered should be properly assessed to ascertain the extent to which they are credible and accurate.

### Table 8.1: Strengths and Limitations of Qualitative Research

| STRENGTHS | LIMITATIONS |
|---|---|
| ▪ Provides unique and subjective experiences from diverse perspectives. | ▪ Derived from smaller, unrepresentative samples or sources. |
| ▪ Provides much richer and in-depth assessments of attitudes, behaviours, and situations than does quantitative research alone. | ▪ Data analysis can be highly subjective due to the unstructured nature of the analytical techniques in qualitative research. |
| ▪ Can be supportive and complementary to quantitative statistical research and data. | ▪ Organizing and analysing qualitative data is a relatively tedious and time consuming process. |

> Qualitative data is different from quantitative data and, as such, requires different analytical (non-statistical) techniques and tools. Qualitative data can be used by itself or it can be used alongside quantitative data using a mixed methods approach.
>
> Different qualitative techniques carry different assumptions and data requirements that must be assessed beforehand.

# THEMATIC ANALYSIS

Thematic Analysis is a form of qualitative data analysis which focuses on the extraction and assessment of core thematic categories.

## Phases in Thematic Analysis

Thematic analysis is a popular form of qualitative data analysis in which researchers assess qualitative responses to extract underlying patterns (or themes) within the data. Themes are depicted as core categories that are critical to a study's research questions. As a process, thematic analysis can be performed based on six interrelated stages.

### Phase 1 – Data Familiarization

This phase involves a careful reading and re-reading of the text in order to become familiar with the data. The goal of this phase is to initially search for meanings and patterns and record any important and interesting notes and ideas that are essential to the coding and analytical stages that follow. Essentially, if the data is verbal in nature (e.g., recorded interviews or conversations; audio-visual materials), it is important that this data be transcribed into a written format before conducting thematic analysis.

### Phase 2 – Generating Initial Codes

Once you are familiarized with the data, the second phase concerns producing initial codes from the data. This coding process involves identifying features of the data or segments of text that are particularly interesting to the researcher and the core research question(s). Coding may involve writing short notes or labels on the lines of text under analysis or using coloured pens or highlighters to discriminate between different segments of text (see also coding qualitative data in chapter 6).

The overall goal is to ensure that relevant data are essentially coded and collated where large masses of text are collapsed into smaller chunks of coded categories and segments. Example 8.2 shows a basic scenario in which an interviewer is seeking to identify *key work motivators* from an interviewer. As shown in the illustration, the interviewer highlights core segments or key words that seem to depict those motivators from the rest of the text by highlighting initial codes. The interviewer also makes short notes or labels (depicting the codes) around the key portions of the text.

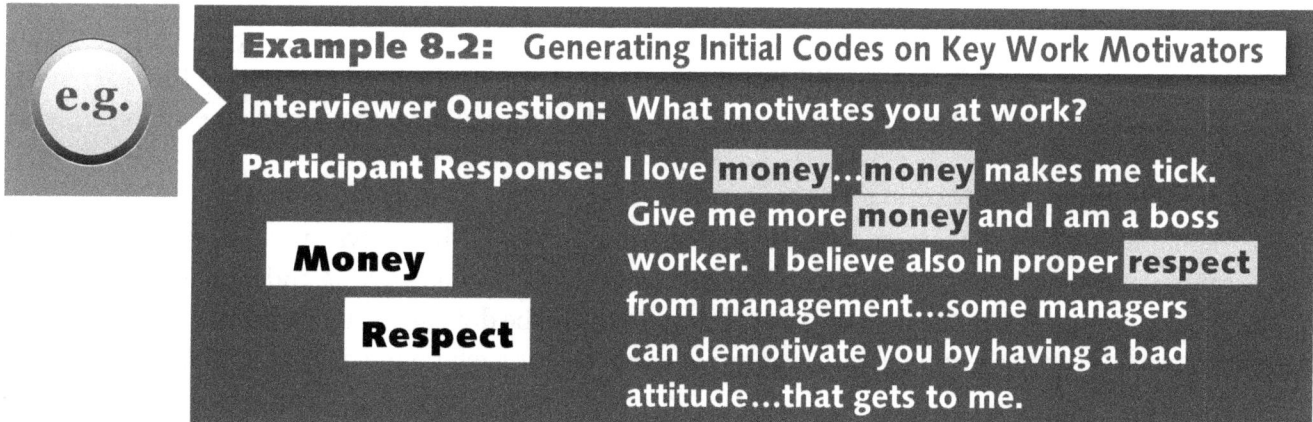

**Example 8.2:** Generating Initial Codes on Key Work Motivators

**Interviewer Question:** What motivates you at work?

**Participant Response:** I love money…money makes me tick. Give me more money and I am a boss worker. I believe also in proper respect from management…some managers can demotivate you by having a bad attitude…that gets to me.

Money

Respect

## Phase 3 – Searching for Themes

Once the coding process is completed, phase 3 involves sorting the derived codes into potential themes, that is, scaling the data from minor categories to much more meaningful, broader categories. Analysing codes carefully can allow analysts to identify which codes 'go together' to form composite thematic categories based on some known commonality or set of interrelated features.

One way to facilitate this is to write down different codes on different slips of paper and organize them into 'thematic piles'. For example, in phase 2 you might have identified the following codes (increased pay, upward mobility, promotion, and financial rewards) derived from the analysis of several responses to the question *What motivates you at work?* At this point you may decide that it makes more sense to report using broader categories. For example, you may decide that financial rewards and increased pay can easily form a thematic category called *Monetary Outcomes,* while upward mobility and promotion can translate to the thematic category of *Advancement Opportunities*.

## Phase 4 – Reviewing Themes

This phase involves a careful assessment of the themes that were extracted in phase 3. Key aspects within this phase concern decisions on whether (1) each theme is fully supported by the data, (2) two or more themes might be combined to form a more meaningful thematic category, (3) certain themes need to be broken down into separate sub-themes, and (4) thematic labels/names are adequately and sufficiently representative of the underlying patterns and codes.

The first level of reviewing normally invites a reassessment of coded data extracts (prior to thematic formation) from phase 2, while the second level concerns the reassessment of the entire dataset to ensure that derived themes are sufficiently valid and representative of meanings evident within the text. At the end of this phase, the analyst should have a finalized set of themes to move forward to the analysis phase.

## Phase 5 – Defining and Naming Themes

Once thematic categories have been formed, reviewed and finalized, the analyst must identify and explain the *essence* of each extracted theme which involves specifying a thematic name and its definition, as well as associating the aspects of the data with each theme (this can be done in a tabular format). The emphasis here is to provide some accompanying descriptive narrative for each theme depicting what is interesting about each and why it is interesting. This narrative provides a detailed assessment of the nature and importance of each theme and how they fit within a broader context in addressing the core research question under study.

## Phase 6 – Producing the Report (Final Narrative)

The write-up of the thematic analysis is the key deliverable for this last phase. The analyst provides a concise, interesting and coherent narrative account of the thematic analysis in relation to how it addresses the core research question(s) and key results that emerged from the analysis. The write-up should include a scholarly interpretative analysis of the themes derived as well as supportive evidence that contributed to the thematic categories being extracted and formed. The use of direct quotations from the text should be used (albeit sparingly) to support the scholarly narrative of each theme.

Thematic analysis provides a rich and in-depth account of an underlying story emanating from the analysis of concrete thematic categories derived from different patterns of responses and data.

# DISCOURSE ANALYSIS

Discourse Analysis is a form of qualitative data analysis which focuses on analysis and interpretation of language and its use in different contexts.

## Overview

Discourse analysis represents an interesting approach to analysing qualitative data expressed in the form of vocal, written, and sign language. This analytical technique provides a comprehensive assessment of the use of language and conversation outside of simple sentences but within more meaningful and broader contexts. Researchers in the discipline of linguistics and languages typically rely on this type of qualitative analysis to achieve a number of key objectives underlying their research.

## Discourse Analysis Criteria

When performing discourse analysis on a set of data, researchers need to think about the following criteria:

*Cohesion*: the extent to which the various parts of texts and sentences go together or relate to each other to form an essential piece of communication for analytical interpretation.

*Coherence*: the manner in which the various parts of text and data flow in ways that provide internal consistency in interpretation.

*Intentionality:* the way in which the intent of the message within the overall text is deliberately conveyed to the analyst and others.

*Acceptability:* the extent to which the audience or consumers of the text approve the message behind the overall text.

*Informativeness:* the degree to which the text under study provides new and interesting information for interpretive assessment or analysis.

*Situationality:* the circumstances and conditions in which the piece of communication was provided.

*Intertextuality:* the degree to which the text or piece of communication references or alludes to external events, conditions or meanings.

## Action Phases in Discourse Analysis

Discourse analysis is a versatile approach to unpacking core meanings and patterns underlying various pieces of communication and language to make sense of its intent and interpretation. Similar to thematic analysis, discourse analysis can be performed using different action phases.

### Understanding and Documenting Context

Prior to a direct assessment of text using discourse analytics, it is critical for the analyst to identify (in writing) where the information came from and how it fits within a wider context or story. Key attributes for consideration should include the formal language in which the piece of communication was first established, the country or place of origin, its source author, and when it was first written or published. It is critical for the analyst to explore the source author's context, his/her institutional and personal background and affiliations before delving into the assessment of the text itself.

### Preparing the Source Materials and Coding Process

The analyst should ensure that all relevant text and affiliated materials for coding and analysis is up to date, accurate, and sufficiently representative of the data s/he requires for final analysis. Coding involves 'tagging' (or assigning labels) certain attributes to portions of the text that depict interesting and meaningful material points. For example, suppose you were assessing a written speech made by a famous politician to identify elements of sexism or racism. The coding process will require you to label sentences or parts of the speech that are indicative of sexist or racist remarks, through the assignment of codes to these units of text.

The analyst should identify a set of coding categories that will be useful in classifying the text relevant to sexism and racism. These categories can be derived from other key sources or relevant literature outside of the primary text. For example, certain words depicting sexist language in particular cultures and within particular time frames can be adopted, especially if the primary text under study also operates within the same parameters of culture and time period. This inventory of codes can be used to scan the primary text under study to determine if it contains any points or references to these codes directly or indirectly. You can make certain markers in the text (coloured text, notes/labels, etc.) to match those portions of text that relate to key coding categories of interest.

### Exploring the Structural Makeup of the Text

Once various portions of the text are coded, it is important to pay attention to structural components of text which relate to (1) the manner in which various aspects of discourse throughout the text are related in some way, (2) what kinds of issues/topics are emanating from the text in general and how these are conveyed throughout the text, and (3) the number and types of messages being conveyed within the piece (and the various types of discourses emerging from the overall text). Generally, the analyst focuses more on the flow and interrelationships of different aspects of meanings, arguments and units of text throughout the analysis.

## Exploring Key Units of Discourse

Once structural components of text are covered, the analyst searches through the text to draw out important features of discourse, including discourse fragments (individual statements with the same underlying code), cultural references (contextual circumstances outside of this text which influence the meanings and contents of the text – e.g., intertextuality), and linguistic and rhetorical elements of the text (vocabulary, parts of speech used, grammar, use of allegories/metaphors, and direct and indirect speech etc.). All of these elements should be documented and classified accordingly throughout the analysis.

## Final Analysis and Interpretation

The most tedious part of the process involves bringing all the aforementioned elements extracted from the assessment together to form a clearly guided analytical narrative. The emphasis here is to provide a written account of the source material in a way that addresses the core research question(s). The narrative account should consider explaining to the reader what the entire discourse is all about, as well as the overall story and message(s) being conveyed, taking into account the other contextual and textual elements that are supportive of this interpretive analysis.

# Other Approaches to the Discourse Analysis Process

Several authors including Potter (2003) have identified other approaches to performing discourse analysis in qualitative research, two types of which are as follows:

1. Micro-textual discourse analysis which focuses the analysis at the level of the social interaction in the text.
2. Macro-textual discourse analysis which focuses the analysis at the broader societal level.

## Micro-textual Discourse Analysis

With respect to micro-textual discourse analysis, a number of stages have been recommended:

**Step 1 – Gathering Materials for Analysis**: Gathering and collating qualitative data from various sources critical to the research questions is an important first step in the discourse analysis process. Source materials may include individual and focus group interview transcripts, naturalistic conversations, newspapers, magazines, online sources and documents, and other related sources involving an interactive, conversational context, or environment.

**Step 2 – Recording and Transcribing**: Discourse analysts are very likely to record and transcribe data from different sources to enhance their analysis and interpretation phases of the process. This also provides the researcher with an opportunity to establish an effective form of communication and analysis with other researchers.

**Step 3 – Generating Hypotheses**: This step does not refer to the typical scientific quantitative hypothesis but concerns the need for the discourse analyst to deliberately develop general ideas, propositions, and perspectives about what is going on in the data that have been gathered and transcribed. This may normally occur at the transcription stage (if not, earlier) and might involve the development of analytic notes to help with the generation of these qualitative hypotheses.

**Step 4 – Coding:** The purpose of coding in discourse analysis is to encourage a line-by-line assessment of the text or data to start the process of building key analytic ideas. Segments of texts are extracted and placed into general categories based on known commonalities that are shared among them.

**Step 5 – The Analysis:** The analyst engages in a thorough, in-depth analysis of the data using both inductive and deductive principles. In the inductive sense, the analyst goes through a particular extract to develop substantive ideas about the processes going on within it. From the deductive angle, the analyst then evaluates and compares these inductive findings against other related extracts from the data. This second component helps the analyst determine whether certain analytical explanations are viable and generalizable. A more detailed analytical framework for discourse analysis would involve the following:

- Identification of patterns in the body of data.
- Assessment of sequencing of interactions within the text patterns or conversations.
- Assessment of deviant cases which communicate different things from the normal patterns.
- Assessment of additional similar materials to compare against the main set of source materials.

**Step 6 – Validation:** The analyst seeks to validate his or her analysis by incorporating a number of procedures and materials including the following:

- *Participants' Orientations* – The analyst validates his or her interpretation in a particular excerpt by assessing whether the interpretation is supported by how another participant in the discourse reacts or responds.
- *Coherence* – The analyst makes an assessment of the extent to which the findings are consistent with those of similar prior studies.
- *Readers' Evaluations* – The analyst incorporates all of the necessary extracts at the end of the document to allow for validation by other researchers and readers.

## Macro-textual Discourse Analysis

Another approach to discourse analysis is referred to as macro-textual discourse analysis or Foucauldian discourse analysis which involves a critical assessment of objects (target area of analysis: e.g., child sexual abuse) and subjects (those actors that share some subjective experience with the object: e.g., child and perpetrator) within a broader (or macro-level) discursive context. The goal of this particular type of discourse analysis is to assess how various texts relate to broader or major aspects of the organization of society.

In discourse analysis, the analyst must be careful not to attribute the analytical elements evident in the text to any underlying motives, personal biases or beliefs about the author of the source material.

Discourse analysis is used in many disciplines including the social sciences, social work, and psychology.

# INTERPRETIVE PHENOMENOLOGICAL ANALYSIS

Interpretive Phenomenological Analysis is a form of qualitative data analysis which focuses on meanings that participants attach to different experiences and contexts.

## Overview

Interpretive phenomenological analysis (IPA) is a popular form of qualitative analysis which provides a detailed exploration of how various participants make sense of, or interpret, various experiences, events, and contexts in a personal or shared way. In IPA, two dimensions are assessed: (a) the participants attempt to make sense of their experience or personal world, and (b) the researcher attempts to make sense of how participants interpret their experience or personal world.

Essentially, the analyst attempts to capture the meanings participants attach to their personal experiences and contexts by exploring and documenting their interpretations. Indeed, this approach emphasizes the relevance of interpretation and sense-making from both participants' and researchers' perspectives and is rooted in facilitating a better understanding of the data.

## Steps in Interpretive Phenomenological Analysis

Interpretive phenomenological analysis involves a number of key steps:

### Formulation of Key Research Questions

In light of the focus of IPA on lived experiences of participants and the meanings assigned, research questions posed must follow an inductive, open-ended format (see example 8.3).

**Example 8.3:** Research Question Types

How do young people in schools interpret the value of technology in the classroom?

How do managers interact with persons with mental illness in the workplace?

How do women with HIV/AIDS deal with stigma and discrimination in the workplace?

How do persons with physical disabilities cope with heavy workloads?

The questions in example 8.3 concern different events or phenomena that participants experience and how they have interpreted the same. IPA requires that research questions focus deeply on extracting subjective, personal experiences, and stories from a diverse range of participants.

## Formulation of Interviews and Data-collection Materials

IPA requires the use of certain research tools and instruments such as semi-structured interview schedules. These types of interviews allow the necessary flexibility to facilitate a rich dialogue between the researcher and participant as well as an adaptive questioning context in which questions can be modified even during the interview stage. The researcher, during this interview, is able to probe clearly and deeply, extracting sufficient details critical to IPA.

IPA also relies on other sources such as diaries and journals that express participants' interpretations of various experiences and events. For example, a diary written by a war veteran about his or her experiences throughout a period of war and conflict between two countries might reveal some interesting headlines and messages about his or her feelings, beliefs, actions, and even personal biases at that time.

## Coding and Analysis

IPA requires a similar strategy to that used by thematic analysis. The IPA process involves:

### *Close and Repeated Reading of the Text and/or Transcript and Note-Taking*

This allows analysts to immerse themselves in the data, acknowledging key aspects of the context in which the interview was done and the general atmosphere in which it occurred. Notes and written observations can be documented by the analyst during this stage to capture key or significant highlights of the interview, including context, content, language, and even interpretive viewpoints of the material.

### *Converting and Translating Written Notes into Emergent Themes*

Here analysts focus more on the notes (as opposed to the text). Hence, it is critical that the notes obtained and documented in the former stage be detailed and comprehensive enough to represent the text. The analyst attempts to classify the notes into more abstract categories or thematic labels, condensing the detailed notes into more manageable units or categorizations.

### *Grouping Emergent Themes or Exploring Relations among Themes*

In this phase, the analyst tries to determine any special connections or associations between the various thematic categories derived. The focus is to group thematic categories, according to similarities, into broader clusters and provide overarching labels describing the overall clusters. Themes that do not share any connections with the overall clusters may be redefined or dropped from the analysis; other thematic categories might be broken down into separate sub-themes or categories. At the end, a compilation of major themes and sub-themes are extracted under different cluster categories.

## Analysis and Write-up

The analyst approaches a narrative account of the IPA process by writing up each theme under the different clusters. This write-up includes a definition and description of each theme, supporting quotations or extracts from the text, and analytical comments of the analyst to provide interpretations and theoretical/conceptual insights into the significance of thematic categories within the broader analytical frame and review of literature.

## Summary of Interpretive Phenomenological Analysis

**TIP:** The IPA process presents the researcher with an opportunity of taking participants' account of various events and experiences together and formulating a more cohesive, flowing narrative account that shows the relationship between the researchers' interpretation and their participants' interpretation of the same.

# NARRATIVE ANALYSIS

Narrative Analysis is a form of qualitative data analysis which focuses on analysis of participants' narrative accounts of their lives and experiences within the wider social world.

## Overview

Individuals often seek to make sense of their lived experiences through personal narrations and storytelling. A narrative is an account of connected or interrelated events derived in written or spoken formats. Narrative analysis concerns the assessment of participants' life stories and narratives on specific events and situations in ways that make sense of their narrations and provide the necessary context for interpretation and analysis. The analysts focus on the stories told by different participants and seek to retell these stories from their own perspective but in keeping with the true essence of the original story. The aim is to listen and understand a narration or story from the participant's perspective and seek to make sense of this story by drawing relationships between the experiences of the individual and the overall social and cultural context of the participant. Narratives can be expressed in different ways, formats, and structures including:

- Written stories or personal accounts of experiences.
- Documented events and the meanings attached to those events.
- Oral accounts through recordings and interviews with key participants.

## Types of Narratives

Various types of narratives suitable for narrative analysis include:
- Oral narratives
- Written narratives
- Life-story narratives
- Historical or personal narratives
- Isolated events narratives

Within qualitative research in general, the interview method is the most popular way of collecting narrative data. Two types of interview methods are the life-history interview and the episodic interview. The life-history interview captures data related to broad, extensive biographical assessment of the participants' life story, whereas the episodic interview focuses extensively on specific topics or key events in a life history.

## Phases in Narrative Analysis

Several procedural models exist for conducting narrative analysis. However, the most influential model is the Crossley's (2007) analytic method. In order to initiate this approach, it is important that qualitative interview transcripts are developed. The key phases of this narrative analysis approach are as follows:

**Phase 1 – Reading and Familiarization:** Reading repeatedly, carefully and thoroughly the interview transcripts or other narrative materials to attain a high degree of familiarity with the data. This phase is a good starting point for searching for key narrative themes.

**Phase 2 – Identifying Main Elements/Concepts:** This phase involves a careful understanding of the key concepts from the narrative(s) with respect to its tone, imagery, and themes. This leads directly to the activities in phase 3.

**Phase 3 – Identifying Narrative Tone, Themes and Images:** This phase involves an active extraction and assessment of the narrative tone (the core contents of the narrative and the manner and style of reporting the experiences), themes (overarching patterns in the narrative), and images (personal symbols/metaphors captured in experiences).

**Phase 4 – Building a Coherent Story and Write-up:** This phase involves pulling together all of the various themes and images into a coherent and meaningful story format. The write-up flows logically to address the key research questions, highlighting the process and outcomes of the analysis.

Narrative analysis is generally based on semi-structured interviewing.
It therefore requires the researcher to have a good understanding of the appropriate conduct and protocols involved in such interviewing exercises.
Narrative analysis is the least structured of all qualitative analytical techniques.

# CONVERSATION ANALYSIS

 Conversation Analysis is a form of qualitative analysis which focuses on the assessment of naturalistic conversations used for qualitative research.

## Overview

A conversation is a structured and coherent form of talk which communicates key aspects of meaning for qualitative researchers. Conversation analysis represents a key qualitative analytical method for assessing and studying natural conversation. It focuses particularly on how participants utilize different conversational methods and tactics as well as how the general conversation operates within and across different contexts.

## Types of Conversational Pieces

Conversational analysis involves an assessment of a number of key units of various conversational pieces which represent key focal areas of study for the analysis including the following:

*Turns and Turn-taking*: A turn refers to an individual's turn to speak before different persons take over the conversation. A turn may involve a large set of words or a shorter phrase or 'word' within a conversational piece. Turns are major units of analysis for conversational analysis. Understanding the process of turn-taking (movements and transitions towards turns) generally involves assessing the coherence and adjacency of various conversational turns with a piece of conversational communication.

*Adjacency Pairs:* Turns normally occur in pairs, that is, two turns are attached to different speakers in a piece. The focus of conversation analysis is to ascertain how the second turn is designed to fit with the prior turn. These are also referred to as adjacency pairs. Examples may include question and answer, greeting-to-greeting, and request and response scenarios in which a given speaker's turn ignites a natural reaction (return) from another.

*Repairs:* When errors or gaps occur in natural conversation, participants within conversational pieces often attempt to correct or 'repair' these issues. Without repairs, the intended message or meaning within the conversation is likely to be affected, which essentially impacts the natural flow of returning conversation from other speakers within the same general conversation. Hence, the repair is usually conducted by the speaker who made the initial error or created the gap. For example, a mother may ask for help from her two children; however, she may quickly repair the 'lack of clarity' by specifically indicating which child should provide the assistance.

*Opening and Closing Conversations:* The concept of 'opening conversation' refers to the forms of words or phrases that are sequenced to open different classes of conversations (e.g., 'Hi, I am Gregg, do you like ice-skating?'), whereas the notion of 'closing conversations' speaks to the closing sequences of words that point to conversational closure (e.g., 'Ok, I will see you then...').

*Gaps and Overlaps:* Gaps are places in conversation in which there are transition spaces (i.e., spaces in which any participant/speaker may take over a conversation at a given point). However, some gaps create uncertainty (e.g., a long silence) to acknowledge which speaker should take over. Gaps are usually elements in conversations in need of repair by speakers. Overlaps occur where a 'returning' speaker enters the conversation (engages in the turn) too early or when the first speaker may have signalled the end of a turn but continues the conversation. An example could be where a child asks a parent a question and the parent begins answering the question before the question is fully formulated.

***Membership Categorization Device:*** This is where the conversational analyst assigns particular membership categories to different processes, actions, and participants (speakers) in conversations to provide some meaningful context to the nature of the conversation. A collection of membership categories in a given conversation is a membership categorization device (e.g., teacher versus student).

## Phases in Conversation Analysis

Conversation analysis involves three comprehensive steps which are described below:

**Step 1 – Recording of Conversation:** Conversations under study can be sourced through audio and/or video material. The researcher may be responsible for the recording of the primary conversation or may rely on existing sources of recorded conversations such as recorded telephone conversations or interviews. In cases where the researcher is seeking to record conversations, consent must be obtained from the parties involved. Online talk or conversations are becoming increasingly popular sources for conversation analysis.

**Step 2 – Transcription:** Conversation analysis requires that all conversations are essentially and properly transcribed to initiate the analysis. Detailed transcripts of conversations allow the researcher to become strongly intimate and familiar with the various forms of words and building units in conversation within a textual context. It is important for the researcher (usually based on underlying research interests or questions) to focus on specific features of the conversation within the transcript. It is also important that researchers conduct a detailed, intensive, and repeated reading of the textual transcript.

**Step 3 – Analysis and Interpretation:** A detailed assessment of the conversational episode becomes a critical part of the analysis taking into account the various elements of conversations previously discussed (turns, gaps, repairs, membership categories etc.). Another goal for the analyst is to develop a comprehensive understanding of the key rules used by people in the conversation and their interpretations of the given interaction.

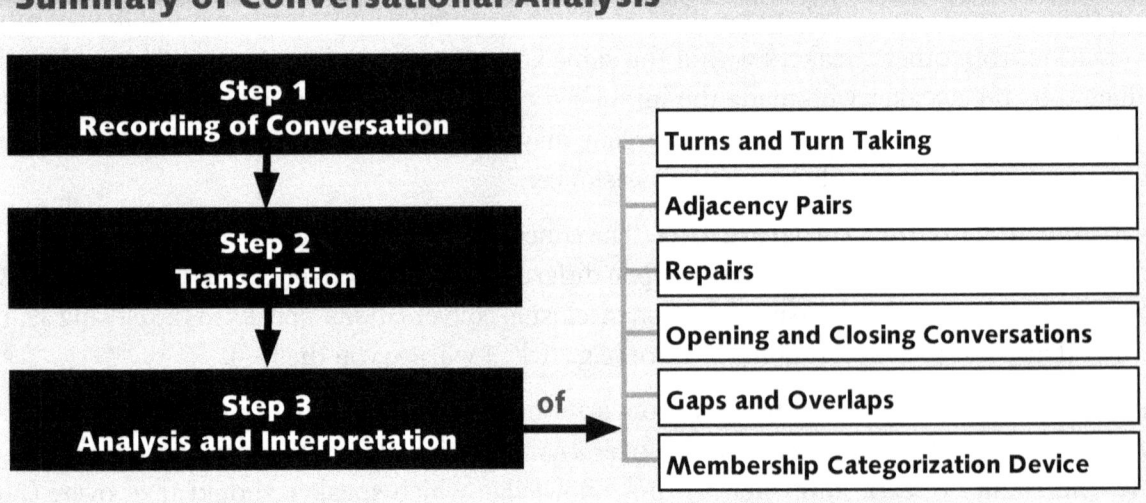

# Qualitative Data Analysis

**TIP:** Conversation analysis is not a general approach to analysing qualitative data like thematic analysis.

It is designed specifically to assess how participants form meaning through natural conversation.

# GROUNDED THEORY ANALYSIS

Grounded Theory Analysis is an advanced form of qualitative data analysis which involves a systematic analysis of data which inform the development of theory.

## Overview

Grounded theory analysis opposes traditional hypothesis testing quantitative research principles in which a deductive approach is taken to statistically examine the propositions and tenets of some conceptual framework or theory against observed data. This popular analytical method allows an analyst to uncover latent and emergent theoretical constructs and frameworks through an intensive investigation of data gathered in the field. Grounded theory adopts an inductive but comprehensive methodological and analytical approach to gathering and assessing data with the aim of building theoretical models and concepts from the ground or from the experiences and data derived from the various sources of evidence.

## Characteristics of Grounded Theory Analysis

There are a number of noteworthy features and characteristics of grounded theory analysis that distinguishes it from other qualitative analytical techniques. These features are discussed below.

### Generating Theory from Under Theorized Contexts

Grounded theory is the only formal qualitative analytical technique that aims to generate a theoretical framework at the end of the process using a systematic approach to gathering data. Naturally, grounded theory analysis is applied to contexts in which little or no theoretical bodies of knowledge have developed and hence provides a perfect opportunity for exploratory research on research topics that require further theoretical exploration and understanding.

### Emphasizes the Notions of Fit, Generality, Understanding, and Control

Four features relevant to grounded theory are fit, generality, understanding, and control. Grounded theory is linked to *fit*, that is, the extent to which the theory corresponds to (or fits) the real world or extent to which the derived theory fits the facts/evidence?

Grounded theory is also linked to *generality* which involves the degree to which the derived theory can speak to situations outside of the primary one that generated the theory in the first place (within the original study). Generality points to the application of theory outside of the specifics of the actual study to other similar realms of experience. For example, a particular grounded theory speaking about a revised approach detailing the appropriate ways of handling persons suffering from schizophrenia in the workplace might also have potentially useful applications for dealing with persons suffering from other types of mental disorders in the workplace.

Finally, the notion of *understanding* suggests the extent to which the derived theory is clearly interpretable and understandable, while the notion of *control* speaks to the practical nature of the derived theory in terms of its ability to cater to real world results and problems outside of its abstract nature.

### Ongoing Data Collection and Analysis Throughout the Research

Grounded theory does not operate in distinct phases but through overlapping and interconnected stages of data gathering and analysis. Oftentimes, both activities are done in tandem from start to finish.

## Phases in Grounded Theory Analysis

Essentially, the steps involved in grounded theory analysis bring the researcher into deep familiarity with the data as well as allow for systematic coding and synthesis of data and comparisons of the data with developmental categories of theory. Grounded theory analysis can rely on interviews, biographical data, observations, and conversational data. It is also critical that grounded theory analysis assesses multiple and diverse sources of data. In light of the nature of grounded theory, the process of the analysis begins at the level of the research question. The phases are as follows:

**Phase 1 – Formulating the Research Question**: The overall research question in grounded theory should be concerned with the need to address some core study objective that is directly answerable by some theoretical process, system or classification. The research question does not need to have any basis in existing theory or a body of knowledge – it can be a 'new' research objective.

**Phase 2 – Theoretical Sampling**: In grounded theory, theoretical sampling involves the sampling of participants for data until the researcher decides that any additional data is unnecessary for arriving at the theoretical insights needed to address the grounded theory research questions. All data from sampled units are documented in research memos to allow the researcher to determine whether additional sample units and data are needed in their interpretations and analyses.

**Phase 3 – Descriptive Coding/Naming**: Once the various forms of data are gathered and transcribed/collated, the grounded theory researcher conducts a thorough and complex assessment of the various sources of data. Textual data are read and inspected using a line-by-line approach where lines are numbered in sequence for referencing purposes and descriptive codes established at each line. A descriptive code is an explicit abstraction of a textual line of data. In light of the need to graduate from codes to higher levels of theoretical abstractions, it is normal for initial codes to be closely related and explicit to the data. The overall final stage of coding creates a textual transcript populated with codes on every line. This provides the researcher with broader ideas and perspectives of the general text as well as how codes relate to each other. Several types of coding in grounded theory exist:

- **Open Coding**: This type of coding is the same as explicit, descriptive coding (mentioned earlier) which results in smaller chunks of categories that are closely related to original text.
- **Axial Coding:** This coding process involves a continual and systematic process of linking the earlier derived codings with each other to inspect any underlying patterns and relationships across the text. This process concerns the relationships between codes and extracting core concepts and themes rather than going through the actual text itself. Similar to thematic

analysis, codes with commonalities or shared features are grouped to arrive at these broad concepts or thematic categories. Researchers may need to move back and forth between open coding and axial coding.

- **Selective Coding:** This coding process involves the selection of a core thematic category as the principal theme to which other revealed thematic categories/concepts are related. This central theme governs the overall narrative of the storyline and analysis.

It is important to note here that axial and selective coding processes are instrumental in the next phase; whereas open or descriptive coding is popular in the current phase.

**Phase 3 – Development of Thematic Categories/Concepts:** This phase builds from the open-coding phase (mentioned earlier) and takes into account the organization and categorization of derived codes into broader and more meaningful categorizations. A synthesis that conceptually extracts underlying latent themes ensues allowing analysts to arrive at better and more comprehensive analytical perspectives of the actual data. However, these higher-level categories should still remain consistent with their lower-level codings. In order to cement category development, it is essential that constant comparisons be done of the following:

a. Differently coded lines versus similarly coded lines.

b. Different samples of interviewees in similar roles/positions or contexts in the same dataset.

c. Actual derived categories versus original codings.

**Phase 4 – Theoretical Saturation and Further Sampling:** Once no new data is emerging or provides no further theoretical insights to the analysis, the analyst has reached a saturation point. This is called theoretical saturation. Saturation then suggests that, following on from phase 3, doing further comparisons and assessment will fail to create any further revisions, refinements, and new insights into the theoretical development process. However, it is possible that researchers may re-engage in theoretical sampling processes to gather new data to examine against established categories and relations between them.

**Phase 5 – Theory Generation:** Once the necessary relationships and processes have been established, the researcher may move on to theory development. A theory is derived as a verbal statement of conceptually related categories, a visual model, and/or a series of hypotheses. The theoretical depiction should sufficiently explain the phenomena under study as it is relevant to the overall research question or purpose. It would be important to examine the adequacy and applicability of theory in future research.

## Summary of the Grounded Theory Approach

**Grounded Theory**

- Phase 1 – Formulation of Research Question
- Phase 2 – Theoretical Sampling
- Phase 3 – Development of Thematic Categories/Concepts
- Phase 4 – Theoretical Saturation and Further Sampling
- Phase 5 – Theory Generation

**TIP:** Grounded theory is not restricted to a particular type of qualitative content (e.g., like discourse and narrative techniques).

It is thus a highly flexible and accommodating technique that can be used across a range of qualitative studies and data sources.

# 9 The Research Paper

- Planning Tips for the Research Paper
- Writing Tips for the Research Paper
- Structure of the Research Paper
- Presenting the Research Paper

## PLANNING TIPS FOR THE RESEARCH PAPER

 **Planning Tips for the Research Paper embody important guidelines which novice and experienced researchers can use to plan their research projects and papers.**

### Overview

As previously alluded to in this book, the research process involves a considerable degree of planning which normally involves a number of critical decisions and actions towards moving a chosen topic to a final paper or document. Irrespective of whether you are a student or a seasoned researcher/academic, planning is critical to the success of all research endeavours.

Think of a plan as a roadmap. If you are in unknown territory, you would use a road map to travel from Point A to Point B. Similarly, a properly crafted detailed research plan will successfully move you from *start* to *finish* of the research process. Specifically, a well designed plan will enable you to move from conceptualization of an idea – to execution – and finally write-up. Planning takes time and effort. However, the payback from planning is quite rewarding. Therefore, invest sufficient time upfront to develop a proper plan to guide your research efforts.

### Planning Guidelines and Considerations for Novice Researchers

Planning considerations and guidelines will differ between students and academics. For novice researchers/students, planning is particularly critical. As you conduct more and more research, you will start to get a good understanding of the research process and this will make planning easier. However, your first planning effort may prove to be a relatively tedious process. Do not despair. The following guidelines are intended to help you – the novice researcher – to develop a proper workable research plan.

- Document all key decisions and actions throughout the research process. These include topic selection, review of the literature, development of your sampling procedure/plan and instruments, and the adoption of the data collection and administrative procedures. Proper documentation is important in any research endeavour. For example:
    - Note the names and contact information of important contact persons with whom you have spoken so that if you need to follow up you can do so quickly.
    - When you write your literature review, create your reference list at the same time so that you do have to go back and hunt for the citations that you used in your literature review at the end of the process.
    - When you enter survey data into SPSS, number your surveys prior to data entry so that if an error is discovered, you can quickly locate the survey form.
- Obtain the necessary guidelines for the structure and content requirements for your research paper from your university, faculty, or department and follow these guidelines closely.
- Ensure that once your research proposal is approved that you do not make any changes without consultation with your supervisor(s).
- Check to see if IRB approval is necessary. Most scholarly work requires IRB approval. Keep in mind that this can take several weeks so submit your documentation early. Also note that once approval is given you cannot make any substantive changes without IRB re-approval.
- Work with your supervisor to schedule and honour appropriate meeting times throughout the lifetime of the research process.
- For every stage in the research process, start early or on time to execute. Remember that all steps in the process are interdependent and interrelated. What happens in an earlier step affects what happens in the later steps.
- Seek as much feedback as possible on every decision or action that you plan to take within the process, even if this input comes primarily from your rigorous review of methodological or research best practices within the existing literature.
- Examine completed research projects in your area or similar areas to obtain ideas, guidance, and a fuller understanding of what is required in the paper and its preparation.
- Consult with prior students to secure realistic expectations regarding the research process, its challenges, and opportunities.
- Ensure that you meet with your supervisor(s) and set up a proper communication channel. Many students disappear once they start their research project, make no effort to contact their supervisor(s), and then just expect magic to occur when a problem surfaces.
- Note that the role of your supervisor is not to come up with the ideas for your research project or to act as an editor for your drafts. Rather, the primary role of the supervisor is to help you to develop and improve your ideas, help you to think through the issues that you need to address, challenges that you might encounter and what you should do and so on. This means that you must have some preliminary ideas to start the discussion. If the supervisor has to constantly give you ideas and tell you exactly what to do, the research project cannot be truly considered as your own work.

- If you experience problems or get bewildered and cannot move forward, quickly get in touch with your supervisor for advice. This means that you should have contact information such as email addresses and phone numbers. If you send an email and do not receive a response, try calling since the email may end up in the recipient's junk mail. Do not leave things to chance and get frustrated. Leave multiple messages with the secretary in the departmental office if necessary.

## The Research Plan

The aforementioned discussion focused on a number of key considerations that you need to keep in mind when planning your research endeavour. This section will now focus on the actual research plan. A research plan essentially represents a brief outline or proposal documenting relevant proposed decisions and actions occurring in various aspects and stages of the research process. Both novice and experienced researchers find research plans useful in providing them and others with the needed support and direction in completing their research and preparing and drafting the paper. A research plan normally has the following components:

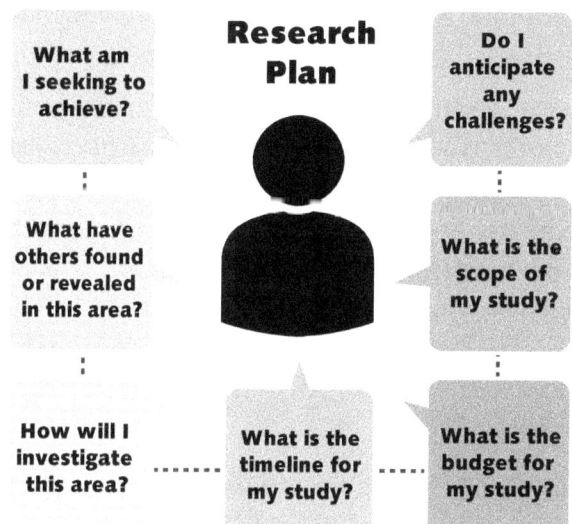

### What are you Seeking to Achieve?
The research plan would normally begin with a broad overview of your topic areas and a guiding purpose statement, a set of research questions, or a list of objectives or hypotheses that you are seeking to address at the end of the research process.

### What Have Others Found or Revealed in this Area?
The research plan should present a brief review of existing literature (i.e., existing empirical work and other readings) within the chosen topic area to help understand what is known or has been learnt about this area to date.

### How do you Plan to Investigate this Area?
The plan should document how you plan to approach your research paper in terms of the methodology and methods, sampling and data collection procedures, instrumentation and measures, as well as analytical tools and reporting standards you are seeking to employ.

### What is the Timeline and Budget for your Research?
This is a critical aspect of the research plan that is often overlooked by many novice researchers. It is important for researchers to document appropriate timelines and scheduling for different individual activities inherent in the process from topic selection and literature review to data analysis and report/paper preparation and drafting. It is also realistic for most research projects or papers to identify and estimate a suitable budget that is needed to finance various aspects or phases of the research prior to its commencement.

Many novice researchers tend to grossly underestimate both their timelines and budget for their research. Be realistic when estimating both time and cost, and provide some cushion or contingency to cater for the unexpected. The best way to ensure that both your timelines and budget are reasonably accurate is to list each activity that will be done and then assign a time duration and cost to each activity.

To begin the process of estimation of activity durations, think about when your paper/project/thesis/dissertation is due. Once you know your completion date, it will be easy to estimate your start date. Next, brainstorm activities that you need to do. Order does not matter at this point. Try to be very precise in terms of your activities. For example, if one activity is survey development, think about all the sub-activities that are essential to get this primary activity done. This will help you to get a more accurate estimate for the overall duration for survey development.

Next, arrange your activities in sequential order of how things must be done. Keep in mind that it may be possible to execute several activities concurrently, while others may be dependent on getting a predecessor activity completed first. After you arrange your activities, enter estimated durations and cost for each activity. Ensure that you provide a contingency cushion to cater for delays and other unforeseen events which could happen. Sum the duration of all activities keeping in mind those that will be done concurrently. Finally, use your completion date and work backwards to determine when you need to start your research project. For instance, if your paper/project/thesis/dissertation is due on October 13, 2018 and your total duration in working days is 50 days, you should be starting your project around the first week of August 2018.

If you are a full-time student and can work on weekends, your start date can take this into account. However, do not procrastinate and start too late or you may end up running into real problems and miss your submission deadline which will often carry penalties for late submission. Note also that if you do not spend sufficient time on your research paper, you may also end up producing a poorly conceptualized paper which will not earn you a good grade.

If this is your first research plan, once you have prepared the draft of your activities, timeline, and budget, consult with your supervisor to ensure that these are realistic. Note that your initial activity plan (with durations and cost) is referred to as your baseline plan. Note also that your actual plan will often deviate slightly from your baseline plan. That is to say, you may exceed the time on one or more activities, as well as the cost for a particular activity. If you have a set budget and timeline, this may mean that you will have to reduce the time and cost on other activities so that you can keep within your original estimates. Table 9.1 shows a baseline master plan for a typical research project.

### What is the Scope of your Study?

When developing your plan, keep in mind that the scope of your work will impact your duration and budget. For example, although a research paper in a class assignment and a thesis may have very similar activities, the scope will be quite different since your class assignment may be worth .5 of a credit while your thesis may be worth six credits. Many inexperienced researchers either have a very narrow scope or too broad a scope for their study. If you are unsure, speak with your supervisor or lecturer to get proper guidance or you may submit a paper that is either inadequate in scope or have a scope that is so broad that your research project becomes unmanageable.

### Do you Anticipate any Challenges?

It is important to brainstorm and document any anticipated challenges that you are likely to encounter in the research process and any worthwhile strategies for overcoming them.

## Table 9.1: Baseline Master Plan for a Typical Research Project

| Activities | Duration | Start | Finish |
|---|---|---|---|
| **Phase 1: Conceptualization of Research Topic** | | | |
| Brainstorm to get some potential research ideas | | | |
| Conduct a preliminary literature review on generated ideas to see what has already been done and think about how you can improve, refine, or add a new dimension | | | |
| Focus/narrow topic | | | |
| Review literature again, zooming in on your refined topic | | | |
| Finalize research topic and develop some research questions/hypotheses | | | |
| Meet with your supervisor to discuss | | | |
| Revise or modify topic/questions in light of discussion | | | |
| Conduct a detailed literature review (focus in on the research methodology and design used in similar research) | | | |
| **Phase 2: The Research Plan** | | | |
| Determine research methodology | | | |
| Determine research design | | | |
| Determine sample size and sample demographics | | | |
| Identify a suitable sampling frame or modify or create a sampling frame | | | |
| Develop instrument for data collection | | | |
|     Prepare draft instrument | | | |
|     Discuss draft instrument with supervisor | | | |
|     Pilot test instrument | | | |
|     Modify instrument based on feedback from pilot test | | | |
| Write research plan | | | |
| **Phase 3: Seek IRB Approval** | | | |
| Use research plan to fill in IRB form | | | |
| Get relevant signatures | | | |
| Take ethics test | | | |
| Submit IRB form, data collection instrument, ethics test results | | | |
| Await IRB approval (estimated time three to six weeks) | | | |
| If approved, commence data collection. If revisions are required, revise, and resubmit and await approval. | | | |
| **Phase 4: Data Collection** | | | |
| Collect data | | | |
| Follow up on non-responses | | | |

| Activities | Duration | Start | Finish |
|---|---|---|---|
| **Phase 5: Data Cleaning, Coding, and Entry** | | | |
| Create code book | | | |
| Number surveys prior to data entry | | | |
| Enter data into SPSS | | | |
| **Phase 6: Data Analysis and Interpretation** | | | |
| Run descriptives and statistical tests | | | |
| Analyse and interpret results | | | |
| **Phase 7: Writing the Research Paper** | | | |
| Abstract (usually written last) | | | |
| Introduction | | | |
| Literature review (can be done in advance) | | | |
| Methodology (can be written in advance, challenges can be added at this phase) | | | |
| Results | | | |
| Discussion | | | |
| Conclusion | | | |

## Helpful Guidelines when Publications are Being Considered

In academia, publication is a normal activity. However, getting your research published can be a frustrating process for many, even for seasoned academics who already have several published works. If you plan to publish empirical or research papers in scholarly journals, the following guidelines will prove useful:

- Identify the most appropriate journals for your research topic and paper. Journals can be assessed in terms of scope, content domain or area, and intended market and audiences.
- Locate credible journals. There are as many authentic journals as there are questionable ones. Check for established sites and institutions which provide lists of the highly credible and reputable journals in your discipline.
- Remember that journals differ in quality. High quality journals tend to have the highest rejection rates. Choose wisely and ensure that the journal is appropriate to the nature and context of your research paper.
- If you are an inexperienced academic/student, seek to be mentored by more senior or experienced academics at your institution. Always be ready to listen and learn from their experiences.
- Try to conduct research and publish with other colleagues to gain a greater foothold in the research process as a growing academic. Once you have had sufficient experience publishing in a collaborative unit, you may branch out to engage in single authored publications.
- Assess your strengths and weaknesses within the research process. For example: Are you afraid of statistics? Are you intimately familiar with your methodology and its associated pros and cons? Do you know how to address reviewer comments competently? Always find ways to address your weaknesses and/or capitalize on your strengths in the research process.
- Be prepared to get some harsh criticism from reviewers, and many possible publication rejections. This can severely impact your motivation and you may often feel like giving up. Do not lose heart.

Let your paper rest for a few weeks and then review the reviewers' comments and try to address all comments. Even when your paper is rejected, you are still provided with reviewers comments. Use these comments to improve your paper and then resubmit to another journal.

Always seek to develop a research plan before initiating any research project.

Sometimes research plans or proposals can be used to secure funding or other resource support for researchers attempting major academic or applied projects.

Note also that your research plan will essentially contain all the information needed to fill out your IRB application form.

# WRITING TIPS FOR THE RESEARCH PAPER

Writing Tips for the Research Paper are important guidelines for novice and experienced researchers writing research papers.

## Introduction

For many, the writing phase in the research process is considered to be tedious, daunting, and arduous. Less experienced writers and researchers express great challenges and stress in this phase. In contrast, individuals with great passion and skill argue that writing represents a perfect time to bring to life critical ideas and thoughts on paper.

If you fall into the former category, you are by no means alone. Writing is an art which becomes easier with practice. Although you may never have to write another research paper in your lifetime, you will most likely have to write many memos/letters later in life. More importantly, however, you need to get a good grade on your research paper so you must put aside negative thoughts and demonstrate your professionalism by doing what is necessary to secure a good grade.

## Key Challenges in Writing Research Papers

Whether you are a student researcher or a novice scholarly academic researcher, the challenges to writing seem to be generally similar:

*Insufficient Experience*: Writing is as much a skill as developing a research instrument, running and interpreting an appropriate statistical test, or conducting an engaging and rewarding focus group interview. Hence, students and academics with little experience or history in scholarly or academic writing find it quite difficult to master the art and science of research writing.

*Insufficient Reading*: Students and academics who do not sufficiently expose themselves to a variety of academic and scholarly readings and papers in the literature normally would lack the appetite and competency to write in powerful academic language.

***Insufficient Passion***: Students and academics who do not find enjoyment or passion in academic writing normally do not emerge as strong academic writers. Passionate and involved writers ensure they have a greater grasp on scholarly terms, concepts, and language as well as develop greater scientific arguments for their claims and hypotheses. They are actively engaged in their reading and their writing and are always willing to improve their style and nature of writing to fit different contexts.

***Insufficient Time:*** A common challenge confronting both novice and experienced researchers is insufficient time. If researchers do not dedicate sufficient time to gather data, read, and of course write, it is almost impossible to achieve a proper scholarly or academic paper with a strong narrative. Time is the researcher's greatest resource, but it can also be his or her most formidable enemy when it is not properly managed throughout the process.

## Strategies for Improving Scholarly Writing

If you are one of those persons who experience stress because you have to write a research paper, there are number of useful and practical strategies that you can use to gain greater control over writing in academic and research arenas:

***Attend Writing Workshops or Clinics***: Writing workshops/clinics provide training support for inexperienced writers by giving them exposure to critical learning experiences and approaches that instill the necessary competencies and foster effective transfer of learning outside of the training environment.

***Have a Buddy (Mentorship) System***: A buddy system in academic writing involves pairing up with someone who is a more experienced or seasoned writer. This system would allow you to receive regular and useful feedback on the quality of your writing as well as provide similar guidance (once you improve your profile) to your peers or those that you will then mentor.

***Get Familiar with Scholarly Work:*** If your writing is to reach a standard that is acceptable in academia, you need to make the time to locate and read other scholarly writings from reputable journals and other sources. The more intimate you are with these materials and sources, the more confident you will become when you write and/or speak about your research paper.

***Practice, Practice, Practice:*** Nothing beats practice. The best solution to overcoming writing barriers is to start writing more often.

A critical barrier to writing is finding a suitable time to write. Many researchers and writers claim that certain times of the day are most conducive to writing. Hence, you have to find what works best for you (e.g., morning, afternoon, late night).

# STRUCTURE OF THE RESEARCH PAPER

Structure of the Research Paper refers to the key segments of an academic research paper.

## Overview

The structure of the research paper varies according to the context or outlet (e.g., journal, magazine) to which the paper is being submitted. However, both students and academics tend to favour a popular structural outline for their research paper which is functional for communicating the purpose of their research, design and methodological approach, key findings, and conclusions and implications.

## Structure of the Research Paper

Whether you are a student researcher or a scholarly academic researcher, the following is a conventional structure for a typical research paper.

## Abstract

The abstract represents a complete but brief summary (between 150 and 200 words) of the entire research paper. It provides the reader with a succinct overview of the research objective(s), methodological approach and sample, and key findings and conclusions (see example 9.1). The abstract is normally written when the paper is complete.

**Example 9.1:** Abstract (Sample)

The purpose of this study was to examine the effects of work stress on physical and mental health among primary schoolteachers in Barbados. Using a randomly selected sample of 300 teachers across 22 schools, a self-administered survey was conducted. The key findings revealed that work-related stress significantly and negatively affected mental health but did not affect the physical health of teachers. The findings suggest the need for both primary and secondary interventions for stress alleviation and management within the primary school setting for the teaching population.

## Introduction

The introduction of the research paper is reserved for providing the broad overview and background to the research topic and paper, explicitly emphasizing the key research questions, objectives or hypotheses, and overall justification and rationale for the research (see example 9.2).

> **Example 9.2: Introduction (Sample)**
>
> The present study seeks to examine work-related stress and its consequences for primary schoolteachers' physical and mental well-being. Work-related stress has gradually emerged as a critical concern for organizational psychologists, academics, and practitioners alike. Within the teaching community, calls have been made to empirically investigate the causes and consequences of work-related stress within the school setting and ways in which this phenomenon can by addressed by appropriate interventions.
>
> Against this background, this study seeks to address the following research questions: (1) What is the relationship between work-related stress and health outcomes among primary school teachers? and (2) What strategies can primary schoolteachers utilize to combat work related stress?

**Literature Review**

This section presents a discussion of the existing literature and sources (e.g., books, journal papers, online material) on the area being researched (see chapter 2). It should provide a cohesive and coherent review of existing works and the key conclusions emanating out of these works, to communicate to the reader what has transpired within the given subject area. Typically, the literature review section follows the introduction section of the research paper, although it is also possible for some outlets (e.g., professional and academic journals) to require that the literature review section be integrated into the introduction section. Example 9.3 provides a brief synopsis of how a literature review is written. Note that the actual literature review will be considered longer and can range from 1,000 words to more than 25,000 words.

> **Example 9.3: Literature Review (Sample)**
>
> Work-stress is defined as core demands and pressures arising out of a work context with potential to affect the quality of work produced (Gerry, 2010). Patton (2011) noted that the psychosocial work environment has the potential to produce different forms of work stressors for workers with different kinds of reactions. However, Jones (2015) suggested that these reactions normally depended on diverse individual and contextual factors...

## Methods

This section presents information on the approach of the research including:

***Chosen Research Design and Methodology and its Justification*** (e.g., whether quantitative versus qualitative; survey design versus case study is being used – see example 9.4).

> **Example 9.4:** Methods – Research Design (Sample)
>
> The study adopted a longitudinal quantitative survey research design to examine the causal relations between Time 1 stressors and Time 2 health factors of teachers. This type of design is adequate for assessing the temporal nature of causal relationships.

***Sampling Methods and Key Sample Characteristics*** (e.g., discussion of key sampling procedures, methods and sample characteristics – see example 9.5).

> **Example 9.5:** Methods – Sampling Methods (Sample)
>
> Using a proportionate stratified random sample according to size of school student population, the study sampled 300 teachers across small, medium, and large-sized primary schools across Barbados.

***Research Instrument or Measures*** (e.g., discussion of the key research tools and data gathering instruments – see example 9.6).

> **Example 9.6:** Methods – Research Instruments or Measures (Sample)
>
> Using a standardized survey instrument, work stress was captured by the Life Stress Inventory II (Gregg, 2001) which comprised 20 Likert items (based on a five-point scale ranging from 1 to 5), and physical and mental health were captured by the Jill Hendy's (2005) 10-item Burnout Inventory where the first five items captured physical health and the latter five items captured mental health based on a four-point scale ranging from one to four.

***Data-Collection and Administrative Procedures*** (e.g., discussion of the data-collection, ethical, and administration procedures and protocols carried out in the research – see example 9.7).

**Example 9.7:** Methods – Data-Collection Procedures (Sample)

Principals of selected schools were approached to obtain permission to conduct the research survey. Once permission was granted, teachers were selected and given the survey to complete at the start of the day and these questionnaires were collected by the enumerators by the end of the day. All international best practice ethical protocols were followed.

***Data Analysis Procedures*** (e.g., discussion of the chosen data analysis procedures for the analysis of the data according to method such as quantitative or qualitative – see example 9.8).

**Example 9.8:** Methods – Data Analysis Procedures (Sample)

Descriptive statistics followed by linear correlation and multiple linear regression statistics were chosen to examine the main research questions in the study.

### Results/Findings

This section presents key findings from the applied quantitative and qualitative analytical techniques aimed at addressing the central research questions, objectives or hypotheses (see example 9.9).

**Example 9.9:** Findings (Sample)

Descriptive statistics and correlations among variables are presented in Table 1. Correlation results revealed that there are statistically significant relationships between stressors and health variables. Linear regression was employed to examine the main research questions. The results are presented in Table 2. Work-related stress was negatively and significantly related to mental health (B = -2.21, p < .001) but not related to physical health.

### Discussion and Conclusion

This final narrative section of the paper summarizes the key findings and the answers to the central research questions, objectives or hypotheses. It compares and contrasts these findings with those of prior works, acknowledges key limitations and implications for practice, theory and future research, and concludes the research paper (see example 9.10).

**Example 9.10:** Discussion and Conclusion (Sample)

The purpose of the study was to examine the effects of work stress on mental and physical health in a sample of primary schoolteachers in Barbadian schools. The results revealed that work stress had a negative effect on mental health but not on physical health. The findings suggested that the mental wellness of teachers is at a higher risk in high-stress settings than their physical wellness. These findings conflict with Holder (2013) who acknowledged that work stress should equally impact physical and mental health in all settings...

## Summary of Structure of the Research Paper

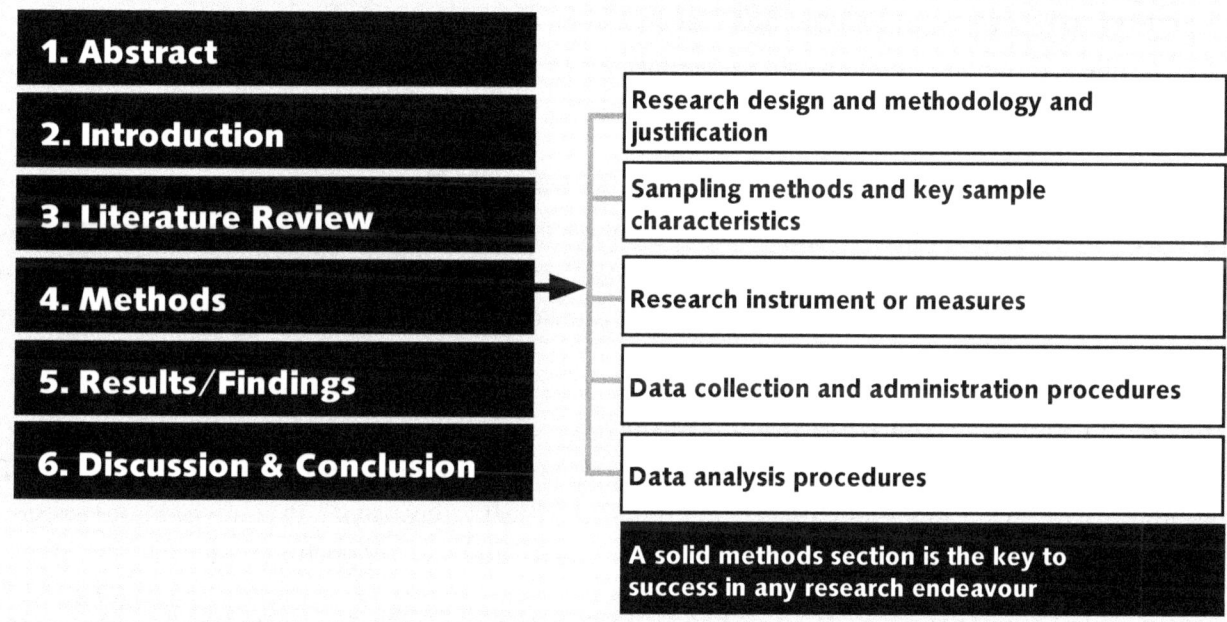

1. Abstract
2. Introduction
3. Literature Review
4. Methods
   - Research design and methodology and justification
   - Sampling methods and key sample characteristics
   - Research instrument or measures
   - Data collection and administration procedures
   - Data analysis procedures

   A solid methods section is the key to success in any research endeavour
5. Results/Findings
6. Discussion & Conclusion

Remember at the end of all academic papers, a reference list is necessary. This is a list of all cited work in the research paper.

Always determine the appropriate referencing system for your paper, as different reference systems have different requirements and guidelines for in-text citations and end of paper references.

# PRESENTING THE RESEARCH PAPER

 Presenting the Research Paper is important for disseminating information and sharing knowledge and is also a mandatory requirement for doctoral theses.

## Overview

Oftentimes, researchers are expected to present the results of their research to various audiences. Some common scenarios include:

- Students making oral presentations on their final research project within a classroom setting at the end of the semester.
- Doctoral students/candidates making a formal oral presentation as part of their defence for their doctoral thesis.
- Doctoral students presenting their research at an academic conference.
- Professors making regular oral presentations to their students in classroom settings or to their colleagues in an academic conference setting.

## Preparing for Oral Presentations of Research Papers

Organizations and disciplines have different guidelines and tips for oral presentations. Notwithstanding, there are some general guidelines and tips that can benefit all researchers (students and academics) which can assist in helping individuals effectively prepare their research for contexts in which oral presentations are required.

### What is the Key Message from the Research?

What is the key message that you want to communicate to your audience? What is the purpose of your presentation and what main lessons learnt would be critical 'takeaways'? It is advisable to spend some substantial time preparing your oral presentation narrative and any supporting materials long in advance.

### What Equipment/Materials/Technology are Needed for your Presentation?

It is common for presenters to utilize supporting devices such as laptops, projectors, PowerPoint slides, flip charts, and other visual aids to deliver attractive and engaging presentations. Get familiar with the resources that will assist you to deliver effective and high quality presentations. A well organized presentation will usually give you confidence and can also serve to distract the audience from looking directly at you which may be helpful if you are nervous.

### How Long is your Presentation?

The expected length of your oral presentation will dictate the amount of material and narrative you are planning to deliver at the particular forum. Longer presentations provide greater flexibility to the presenter whereas shorter presentations place greater burden on presenters to be succinct. Most organizations have strict guidelines pertaining to presentations. For example, doctoral students generally have 15–30 minutes maximum to present their work. The rest of the time is reserved for discussion, questions, and answers. Conference settings also generally only allow 15–20 minutes for a paper.

Such strict time frames require that a presenter is properly prepared to ensure that s/he stays within the allocated time frame. This may necessitate running your presentation several times in advance to see how long it takes. A good rule of thumb when preparing PowerPoint presentations is one slide per minute. Keep in mind that if you have not done an oral presentation before, you may get nervous and take more time. Therefore, if your pre-run took 18 minutes, you need to cut some slides and re-run until you come in at exactly 15 minutes if that is your allocated time for the presentation.

Use a watch or timer and keep track of the time. The worst thing that can happen is for you to spend most of your time on just the background and methodology and then rush through the results which are the most important part of your research. Also, keep in mind that when multiple presenters are presenting in the same time slot, those ahead of you may use more than their allocated time if the Chair is not very vigilant. This means that you will get less time because if four presenters are scheduled from 9:00 a.m. to 10:00 a.m. and you are the fourth presenter, you must clear the room at 10:00 a.m. sharp so that the next session can commence on time. In such cases, you may need to cut some of your slides to get to more important issues.

### What is the Format for your Presentation?

There are different kinds of oral presentations. For example, some presentations require interactive contexts in which the presenter should master the ability of handling questions, comments, and other interactions from the audience while delivering his or her message. Effective time management is critical here. In another kind of presentation, presenters are allowed to deliver their presentation free of interaction and accept questions and comments at the end. The type of presentation format chosen will influence how you prepare and plan for oral presentations in terms of style, content, and approach to delivery.

### Have you Rehearsed Sufficiently?

Rehearsing your presentation in advance of a formal presentation event is always advisable. It helps you to strategize time management and your delivery approach. It also helps to reduce anxiety (especially if you are nervous) because you generally become more confident as you become more familiar and proficient with your materials.

### Is your Font Size and PowerPoint Background Suitable?

PowerPoint has many great presentation templates that can enhance your presentation. However, often a particular template may look perfect on your computer screen but look totally different when projected. If possible, you should run your presentation in the actual room to gauge the light conditions and so on in advance to see if you need to choose another template. This is possible if you are presenting at your university or institution. However, if you are presenting in a totally unknown venue, your best strategy is to use a template that is mostly white with crisp black font which usually shows well regardless of the light conditions.

Font size is also important. About 80 per cent of all presentations that we have witnessed are hardly visible to the audience in the back of the room. Moreover, we have noted that many presenters have poorly formulated diagrams and graphs which are virtually useless because even those in the front of the room cannot read them. The purpose of a PowerPoint is to share information. Therefore, if no one can read the information, it is a waste of time.

## Key Tips for your Actual Oral Presentation

Irrespective of whether you are novice or a seasoned presenter, we have a number of useful tips which can help to enhance the overall impact and delivery of your actual presentation:

### Dress Appropriately

Formal presentations generally require professional attire. However, professional attire does not always require wearing a suit. If you are not sure about the dress code, ask a question beforehand so that you can dress suitably. When thinking about shoes, keep in mind that you may have to walk long distances to get to your venue. Therefore, you need comfortable walking shoes.

### Arrive Early

Being early at the venue/site is critical to ensuring that you have adequate time to inspect the room, set up your devices and materials, and gradually attain a sense of comfort before the start. If you arrive late, you will probably be quite flustered, and you may get nervous since your audience will already be waiting.

### Start in an Engaging Way

Presenters have quite different styles of presenting and there is no golden best practice rule for presentations. Some presenters like to introduce some clean humour prior to the start of their presentation. If you are comfortable with this, you can use this strategy. For example, you can ask some engaging questions to the audience or open with an interesting story leading up to the presentation.

### Note your Body Language and Voice

Be cognizant of your body language since body language speaks louder than words. Make sure your body language is not misleading and conflicting with what you are orally delivering. Ensure also that you are reading your audience's body language to determine if you have them engaged. Speak in an audible and clear voice or your audience will quickly lose interest if they cannot understand what you are saying.

### Maintain Eye Contact with the Audience

Many new presenters are so nervous that they read from their notes or visual aids and do not have any eye contact with the audience. It is important that you maintain periodic eye contact with your audience. For example, as lecturers, when we see frowns on students' faces, this is usually an indication that students do not understand what was said and provides an opportunity for us to use a different example or illustration. Similarly, you need to see how your audience is reacting. Is the audience paying attention or are they looking bored? Are people walking out? It also important to ask for feedback from your audience to ensure that they understand the material you are presenting.

### Present at an Appropriate Pace

Sometimes anxiety or excitement results in presentations that seem rushed. Be self-aware and vigilant of your anxiety or excitement and how fast you may be speaking to your audience.

### Manage your Visual Aids

Your visual aids are critical to your presentation. However, do not let them lead the discussion. Avoid reading the presentation and allow the audience sufficient time to take in each PowerPoint slide.

## Dealing with Audience Interaction and Questions

Remain patient and tolerant to all forms of interaction with your audience. Listen carefully before responding. Ensure you have addressed the questions posed before moving on. Be diplomatic at all times. If you are unable to complete or answer a question, it is fine to acknowledge that you do not have the information to answer the question at this time. For example, you could diplomatically say *'You have raised a really interesting point which I have not considered. Could we discuss it further during the break?'*

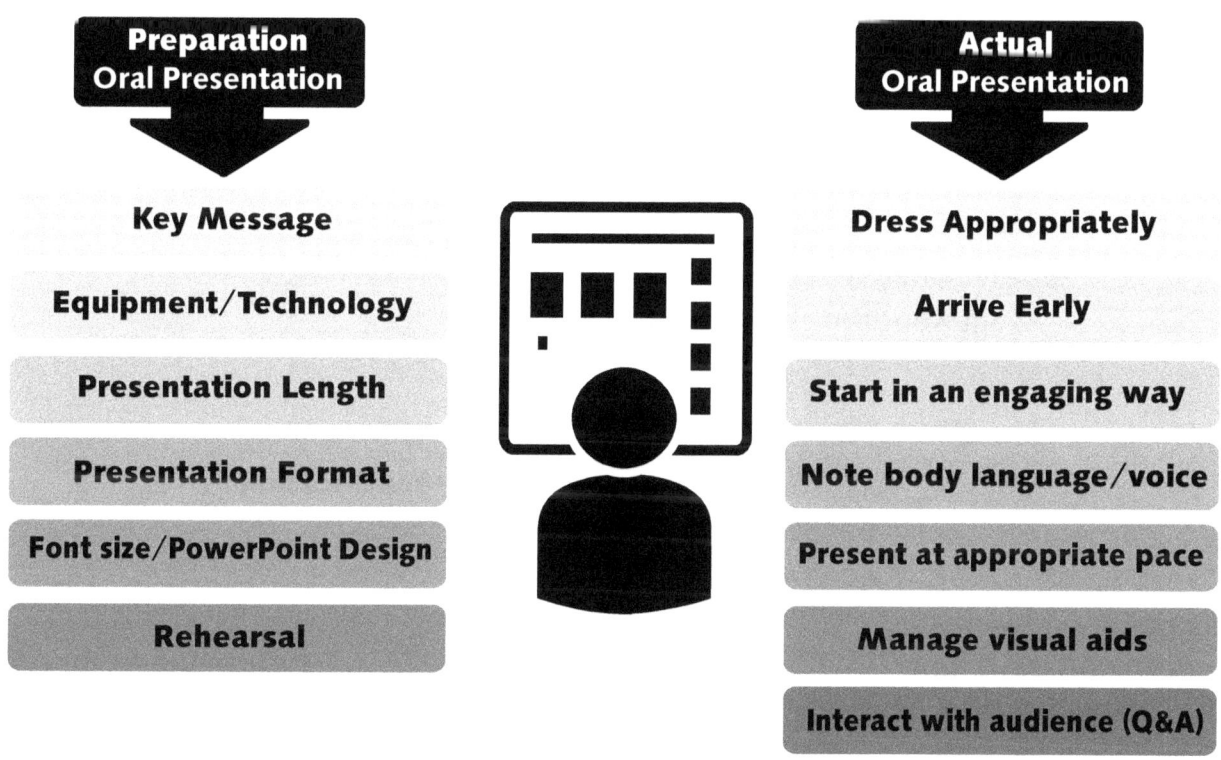

Preparing for an oral research presentation requires a lot of time and commitment. Practice in front of friends, family, and peers so that they can challenge your skills/comfort levels. This will help you to prepare well for the actual presentation and boost your confidence.

# 10 Putting it All Together: The Research Process Checklist

- Topic Identification
- Determine Research Methodology
- Determine Research Design
- Determine Sample Design and Demographics
- Develop Data Collection Instrument
- Determine if IRB Approval is Required
- Data Collection and Security
- Data Sorting, Coding, and Entry
- Data Analysis and Interpretation
- Data Reporting and Write-up

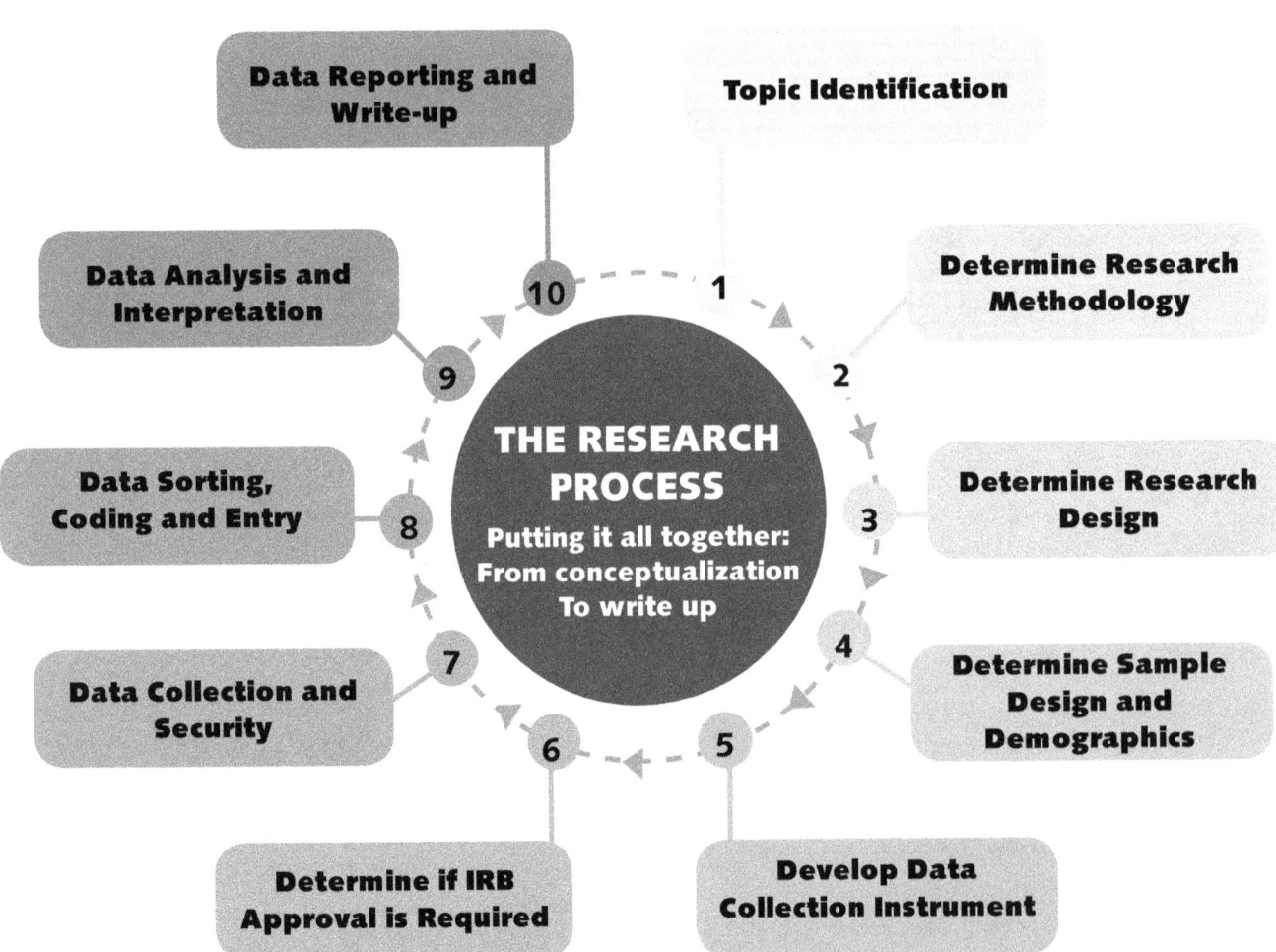

# Planning the Research Paper

**STEP 1**

**Strategies for Topic Selection**
- Brainstorming.
- Review of the literature.
- Conversations on topic of interest.

**The Literature Review – CRITICAL**
Review literature to see what has already been done on topic of interest.

**Focus/Narrow Topic**
Refine your topic to see how you can make a useful contribution by adding new knowledge and/or adding to the existing body of knowledge. Can you contribute by:
- Examining a new culture, group, or country perspective.
- Examining a different dimension related to the topic.
- Replicating a study to support an existing theory.
- Exploring something entirely new.

**WHAT IS THE VALUE ADDED?**

**Topic Identification**

**ROUGH TOPIC**

**CLEAR TOPIC**

- **Attractiveness of Topic**
  (Is the topic generating current discussion and attention?)
- **Significance of Topic**
  (How impactful is the topic within academic literature and practice?)
  - Academic Significance
  - Practical Significance
- **Realism of Topic**
  (Is the topic feasible, manageable, logical?)

**Develop specific**
- Research questions
- Hypotheses

**Review literature again:**
- Synthesize information on various sources to provide perspective for your research questions or hypotheses.
- Pay attention to the methodology used since a similar approach will be needed especially if you are replicating or adding a new perspective.

**STEP 2**

**STEP 2**

## Determine Research Methodology

### QUANTITATIVE

Questions reflect quantifiable numerical data from close-ended questions.

- **Descriptive Research Questions**

  (Provide a statistical/mathematical account/description of a single variable under study)

- **Associational Research Questions**

  (Examine relationships between two or more variables)

- **Comparative Research Questions**

  (Examine statistical differences between two or more groups)

### QUALITATIVE

Questions reflect textual non-numerical data from open-ended questions or documentary sources.

### MIXED METHODS

- Do your research questions allow for a mixed methods approach?
- What are the advantages of using a mixed methods approach?
- Do you have the skills to conduct a mixed methods study?

**STEP 3**

Planning the Research Paper

**STEP 3**

**Determine Research Design**

**QUANTITATIVE STUDY**

**QUALITATIVE STUDY**

**MIXED METHODS STUDY**

**Types Of Research Designs**
- **Experimental Design**
  - Independent Measures Design
  - Repeated Measures Design
- **Observation**
  - Naturalistic (overt or covert)
  - Ethnology (overt or covert)
  - Laboratory Setting
  - Field Studies
- **Surveys**
  - Paper-based
  - Web-based
  - Telephone
- **Interviews**
  - Formal (structured)
  - Informal (unstructured)
- **Focus Groups**
- **Case Studies**

**STEP 4**

# STEP 4

**Determine Sample Design and Demographics**

**Does study require a target population to be identified?**

**Do you want to generalize from your sample to the population?**

### Yes → Probability Sampling (allows generalizations)
- Simple Random Sample
- Systematic Random Sample
- Stratified Random Sample
- Cluster Sample

**Sample Frame**
- Are you going to be using an existing sampling frame? If so, ensure that it is current, complete, accurate.
- Do you need to update an existing sampling frame?
- Will you have to create a sampling frame?

### No → Non-Probability Sampling (does not allow generalizations)
- Convenience Sample
- Purposive Sample
- Snowball Sample
- Quota Sample

**Determine Sample Size**
- Sample size will depend on the following:
    - The nature of your research.
    - Research methodology and design.
    - Cost and time constraints.
- Use a sample size calculator to calculate the sample required for probability samples.

**STEP 5 →**

Planning the Research Paper

# STEP 5

## Develop Data Collection Instrument

In Step 3 you determined your Research Design

In this step you need to determine if you will develop your own instrument or if you will use an established instrument.

### Yes

**Instrument Development**

Issues to keep in mind:
- Types of questions.
  - Open-ended
  - Close-ended
  - Mixed
- Number of questions.
- Sequencing of questions.
- Attractiveness and layout (font size etc.).
- How will you ensure that the instrument is both reliable and valid?

### No

**Using an Existing Instrument**

Issues to keep in mind:
- Is the adopted instrument going to be used in its entirety? If so, perform checks to determine who developed the instrument, how it was used, reliability and validity issues, etc.
- Does the instrument require modification to make it more relevant to your culture, sample, and environment? If you modify it, how will this affect reliability and validity?
- Is permission needed to use the instrument?

### Pilot Test

- Use similar participants to your actual sample.
- Use at least ten participants.
- Check clarity of instructions and questions, if time provided for completion is sufficient, potential logistical problems such as distribution process, etc.
- Evaluate carefully and revise your instrument if necessary.
- Note that even if you are adopting an instrument in its entirety, it is still a good idea to pilot test it, especially if it is being used in a different culture or context.

**STEP 6**

# STEP 6

## Determine if IRB Approval is Required

### Not Sure

**How To Know if IRB Approval Is Required?**
- Research conducted in most educational and research institutions require IRB approval. Check your institution's guidelines.
- Even if your institution does not require IRB approval, it may be required if you plan to publish your work. Therefore, check your discipline or journal to ascertain the requirements.

**Note also:**
- If you collect data and complete your research without IRB approval and it is an institutional requirement, your work will be discredited and you will not be awarded your degree.
- IRB approval is never retroactive.

### BEFORE DATA COLLECTION

**IRB APPROVAL GRANTED**
Proceed with Research

Once IRB approval is granted, no changes (even minor ones) can be made without IRB re-approval.

### Yes

**IRB Approval Required**

Note the following:
- A mandatory ethics test is required prior to submission of your IRB form and data collection instruments. A link to this test will usually be available on your institution's website.
- Note that this test has to be retaken every five years. If you submit your documents and you need to retake the test, this will delay approval.
- Approval may take several weeks.
- May not be approved on first submission since REVISIONS may be necessary which will increase the timeline for the research.

**IRB Approval Pending Minor/Major Revisions**
- Do not proceed with research.
- Revise and resubmit.

**STEP 7** →

# Planning the Research Paper

## STEP 7

### Data Collection and Security

#### Data Collection
Issues to keep in mind:

**Field Work**
- Conduct training if several interviewers will be used.
- In some types of research, it may be advantageous to match interviewers with interviewees on demographic characteristics.
- Develop an interview protocol guide.
- Dress appropriately.
- Be punctual.
- Choose venue carefully.
- Maintain professionalism.

**Use of Incentives**
- Determine if incentives will be used.
- Choose an incentive that will be appealing to the entire sample.

**Follow-Up**
- Follow-up may be required for surveys which may increase the timeline and cost.

**Time Frame**
- Choose a time that is suitable to the respondent.
- Note calendar events such as holidays, etc.

#### Data Security
Issues to keep in mind:
- Time period for data retention.
- Who is responsible for data storage?
- How will data be protected?
- How will data be secured?
- Costs involved with data security and protection.
- How will the data be disposed?

### Must comply with international best practices

**Which includes:**
- **Participant's right to autonomy.**
- **Participants right to anonymity and confidentiality.**

This means that participants can decline to participate altogether, or start and then discontinue, or skip questions that might be too intrusive without any penalties.

**STEP 8**

## STEP 8

### Data Sorting, Coding and Entry

Will depend on the Research Questions and Research Methodology used.

**Quantitative Study**

Issues to keep in mind:
- Which software package will you be using to analyse your data?
- Who is going to prepare the initial codebook and how is it going to be checked to ensure that it is properly set up?
- Will several research assistants be involved in data entry? If so, training may be necessary to ensure that everyone understands how to enter the data?
- Is there going to be some sort of validation process to ensure that the data was correctly entered?
- Is reverse coding required for some questions?

**Qualitative Study**

Issues to keep in mind:
- Coding qualitative data is much more complex compared to coding quantitative data.
- Training is *critical* for all research assistants involved in data entry so that everyone enters similar data under the same themes.
- What process will be used to identify initial themes?
- What criteria will be used to collapse themes?
- Is there going to be some sort of validation process to ensure that data in each theme belongs to that theme?

### Mixed Methods

STEP 9

# Planning the Research Paper

**STEP 9**

## Data Analysis and Interpretation

Will depend on the Research Questions and Research Methodology

### Quantitative Study

**Issues to keep in mind:**
- What types of data analyses will you be conducting and why?
- What type of descriptive statistics will you be reporting?
  - Univariate
  - Bivariate
  - Multivariate
- Which inferential statistical tests will you be using and why?

**Associational Inferential Statistics**
- Pearson Chi-Square Test
- Pearson Correlation
- Linear Regression

**Comparative Inferential Statistics**
- Independent Samples T-test
- Paired Samples T-test
- ANOVA

- Do you understand the assumptions for the test(s)?
- Are you sufficiently skilled to interpret the results generated by the test?

### Qualitative Study

**Issues to keep in mind:**
- What types of data analyses will you be conducting and why?
- Types of Qualitative Data Analysis
  - Thematic Analysis
  - Discourse Analysis
  - Interpretative Phenomenological Analysis
  - Narrative Analysis
  - Conversational Analysis
  - Grounded Theory Analysis
- Are you sufficiently skilled to perform the data analysis proposed?
- Are you familiar with any special qualitative software or will you be doing your analysis manually?

**Results are Statistically Significant when $p \leq .05$**

**STEP 10**

## STEP 10

### Data Reporting and Write-up

**Quantitative Study**

Issues to keep in mind:
- Descriptive statistics are presented before your statistical test results.
- Different statistical tests have a uniformed format for the presentation of results which may differ by discipline.
- All statistically significant results (p-value ≤ .05) must always be reported with an interpretation of the results.
- Note if your results have practical significance. Recall that practical significance examines whether significant differences are large enough to be important (e.g., effect sizes).
- Results that are not statistically significant (i.e., p-value > .05) are mentioned. However, limited write-up is provided.

**Qualitative Study**

Issues to keep in mind:
- Verbatim quotes can provide rich insight and provide powerful impact in certain types of research. Notwithstanding, if the quote can be traced to the respondent then you should not include it.
- Are all thematic categories emerging from the analysis clearly presented and correctly interpreted?
- Are all analyses supported by relevant quotations?

**Mixed Methods**

**Format for Scholarly Write Up**

# Planning the Research Paper

### ABSTRACT
- A single paragraph (100–150 words).
- Explain purpose of study.
- State research questions/hypotheses.
- Explain briefly how study was done.
- State major findings.

### INTRODUCTION
- Summarizes similar research on topic.
- Discusses your contribution to the topic (how your research will add to the body of knowledge and improve that knowledge).
- Lists your research questions/hypotheses.

### LITERATURE REVIEW
- Provides a succinct review of scholarly work on the topic and what was found.
- Do not interject any personal opinion in this section – it is a review of the literature.
- Ensure that each paragraph flows from the previous paragraph and that the review is not simply cut, paste, and rearrange with no logical sequence.
- Use subheads to group like topics.
- Remember to use quotes sparingly.
- Cite correctly using the citation style of your discipline/university.
- Quotes must be in quotation marks with a page number. Block quotes do not require quotation marks.

### CONCLUSION
- Reintroduce the purpose of the study.
- State major results and findings.
- Indicate how research has made a contribution.
- State major limitations of study.
- Indicate future research directions/implications.

### DISCUSSION
- Provide arguments to support your findings, but use careful language (e.g., *'this may suggest', 'a possible reason for this finding may be because'*).
- Remember to link your findings back to the literature.
- Note that non-significant results also need to be linked back to the literature or be adequately explained.

### JOURNALS, THESES, AND DISSERTATIONS HAVE DIFFERENT WORD LENGTH REQUIREMENTS

### METHODS
Discusses process for study including:
- Research methodology used.
- Research design used.
- Sample design, size, etc.
- Discussion of type of instrument.
- Reliability and validity issues.
- Data collection procedures.
- Research ethics protocol (IRB, etc.).
- Statistical tests conducted.
- Software used for data analysis.

### REFERENCES
- Use correct citation style for your discipline/organization/journal.
- Ensure that all citations in your paper are on the reference list. Ensure that your reference list does not include references which are not cited in your paper.

### RESULTS
- Provide demographic results.
- Present and narrate your statistical test results.
- Use tables and figures to present results.
- Use separate paragraphs for addressing different research questions or hypotheses.
- Check your discipline to see the correct way to present your test results.
- Note that some journals allow results and discussion to be merged.

**FINISH**

# Congratulations!

We hope that our book *Nuts and Bolts of Research Methodology* has simplified the research process for you and that it has helped you to complete your research paper successfully.

*Nadini Persaud*
*Dwayne Devonish*
*Indeira Persaud*

# Bibliography

Adam, T.C., and E.S. Epel. 'Stress, Eating and the Reward System.' *Physiology & Behavior* 91, no. 4 (2007): 449–58.

Agresti, A. *An Introduction to Categorical Data*. 2nd ed. Hoboken, NJ: John Wiley & Sons Inc., 2007.

Ahrberg, K., M. Dresler, S. Niedermaier, A. Steiger, and L. Genzel. 'The Interaction between Sleep Quality and Academic Performance.' *Journal of Psychiatric Research* 46, no. 12 (2012): 1,618–622.

Allion, P.D. *Multiple Regression: A Primer*. Thousand Oaks, CA: Pine Forge Crest, 1999.

American Psychological Association. *Publication Manual of the American Psychological Association*. Washington, DC: American Psychological Association, 2001.

American Psychological Association. 'The Basics of APA Style.' *APA Style*, 2018. http://www.apastyle.org/learn/tutorials/basics-tutorial.aspx.

American University. 'Citations and References.' *American University Library*, 2018. http://subjectguides.library.american.edu/c.php?g=175008&p=1154150.

Babbie, E. *The Practice of Social Research*. 10th ed. Belmont, CA: Wadsworth/ Thomson Learning, 2004.

Bandura, A., D. Ross, and S.A. Ross. 'Transmission of Aggression through Imitation of Aggressive Models.' *Journal of Abnormal and Social Psychology* 63, no. 3 (1961): 575–82.

BibMe (2018). *The Online Writing Center*. BibMe, 2018. http://www.bibme.org.

Bland, H.W., B.F. Melton, P.D. Welle, and L.E. Bigham. 'Stress Tolerance: New Challenges for the Millennial College Students.' *College Student Journal* 46, no. 2 (2012): 362–75.

Busari, A.O. 'Identifying Difference in Perceptions of Academic Stress and Reaction to Stressors Based on Gender among First Year University Students.' *International Journal of Humanities and Social Science* 2, no. 14 (2012): 138–46.

Caldwell, S. *Statistics Unplugged*. 3rd ed. Belmont, CA: Wadsworth Cengage Learning, 2010.

Campbell, D.T., and J.C. Stanley. 'Experimental and Quasi-experimental Designs for Research.' In *Handbook of Research on Teaching*. Boston: Houghton Mifflin Company, 1963. https://www.sfu.ca/~palys/Campbell&Stanley-1959-Exptl&QuasiExptlDesignsForResearch.pdf.

Chatterjee, S., and A.S. Hadi. *Regression Analysis by Example*. 4th ed. Hoboken, NJ: John Wiley & Sons, Inc, 2006.

Cite This for Me. 'Citation Generator.' *Cite This for Me*. http://www.citethisforme.com/citation-generator/apa.

Crossley, M. 'Narrative Analysis.' In *Analysing Qualitative Data in Psychology*, ed. E. Lyons and A. Coyle, 131–44. London: SAGE Publications Ltd, 2007.

Devonish, D. 'Job Demands, Health, and Absenteeism: Does Bullying Make Things Worse?' *Employee Relations* 36, no. 2 (2013): 165–81. doi: 10.1108/ER-01-2013-0011.

Dillman, D.A., J.D. Smyth, and L.M. Christian. *Internet, Mail, and Mixed-mode Surveys: The Tailored Design Method*. Hoboken, NJ: John Wiley & Sons, Inc., 2009.

DkIT Library Guides. 'Quick Guide to Harvard Referencing: Sample Assignment.' *DkIT Library Guides*, 2018. http://dkit.ie.libguides.com/harvard/sample.

Donatelle, R.J. *My Health: An Outcomes Approach*. San Francisco, CA: Benjamin Cummings, 2012.

Dyson, R., and K. Renk. 'Freshmen Adaptation to University Life: Depressive Symptoms, Stress, and Coping.' *Journal of Clinical Psychology* 62, no. 10 (2006): 1,231–244.

EBSCO Industries Inc. 'Research Databases.' *EBSCO*, 2018. https://www.ebsco.com/products/research-databases.

Edmonds, E., and M. Gonzalez. *Caribbean Religious History: An Introduction*. New York, NY: NYU Press, 2010.

Gravetter, F.J., and L.B. Wallnau. *Essentials of Statistics for the Behavioural Sciences*. 5th ed. Belmont, CA: Thomson & Walworth, 2005.

Fox, K. 'The Keenex for Men Crying Game Report: A Study of Men and Crying.' *The Social Issues Research Centre*, 2004. https:// www.sirc.org/publik/Crying_Game.pdf.

Freud, S. 'Analysis of a Phobia of a Five Year Old Boy.' In *The Pelican Freud Library*. Vol. 8. Harmondsworth: Penguin, 1977. First published 1909.

Grammarly. 'Better Writing, Better Grades.' https://www.grammarly.com.

Gudrun G., B. Covarrubias Venegas, P. Simbrunner, and G. Janous. 'Impact of Stress Factors on Part-time College Students.' *International Journal for Cross-Disciplinary Subjects in Education (IJCDSE)* 3, no. 2 (2012): 692–98.

Jacobsen, W.C., and R. Forste. 'The Wired Generation: Academic and Social Outcomes of Electronic Media Use among University Students.' *Cyberpsychology, Behavior, and Social Networking* 14, no. 5 (2011): 275–80.

Levin, J., and J.A. Fox. *Elementary Statistics in Social Research*. 9th ed. Boston, MA: Pearson Education Group, Inc., 2003.

Lorenz, K. 'The Establishment of the Instinct Concept.' In *Studies in Animal and Human Behaviour*. Vol. 1. Trans. Robert Martin. Cambridge, MA: Harvard University Press, 1970.

Mayo Clinic. 'Social Support: Tap This Tool to Beat Stress.' *Mayo Clinic*, 2018. http://www.mayoclinic.org/healthy-lifestyle/stress-management/in-depth/social-support/art-20044445.

Nohria, N., T.R. Piper, and B. Gurtler. *Malden Mills*. Boston, MA: Harvard Business School Publishing, 2006.

Obsessive Compulsive Cognitions Working Group. 'Cognitive Assessment of Obsessive-compulsive Disorder.' *Behaviour Research and Therapy* 35, no. 7 (1997): 667–81.

OWL Purdue. 'Chicago Manual of Style 17th Edition.' *OWL Perdue*, 2018. https://www.cavehill.uwi.edu/cermes/getdoc/4115ae89-95554b41-ae32-b28739335d34/cite_chicago_style_dec2013.asp.

———. 'CMOS NB Sample Paper.' *OWL Purdue*, 2018. https://owl.english.purdue.edu/owl/resource/717/11.

———. 'Online Writing Lab.' *OWL Purdue*, 2018. https://owl.english.purdue.edu/owl/ resource/560/02.

———. 'Transitional Devices.' *OWL Purdue*, 2018. https://owl.english.purdue.edu/owl/resource/574/02/

PaperRater. 'Grammar and Spelling Check.' *PaperRater*, 2018. https://www.paperrater.com.

Persaud, N. 'Interviewing.' In *Encyclopedia of Research Design*, vol. 2, ed. N.J. Salkind, 632–36. Thousand Oaks, CA: Sage Publications, 2010.

———. 'Pilot Study.' In *Encyclopedia of Research Design*, vol. 2, ed. N. J. Salkind, 1,032–33. Thousand Oaks, CA: Sage Publications, 2010.

———. 'Primary Data Source.' In *Encyclopedia of Research Design*, vol. 2, ed. N.J. Salkind, 1,095–97. Thousand Oaks, CA: Sage Publications, 2010.

———. 'Random Selection.' In *Encyclopedia of Research Design*, vol. 3, ed. N. J. Salkind, 1,213–216. Thousand Oaks, CA: Sage Publications, 2010.

Persaud, N., and I. Persaud. 'The Relationship between Socio-demographics and Stress Levels, Stressors, and Coping Mechanisms among Undergraduate Students at a University in Barbados.' *International Journal of Higher Education* 5, no. 1 (2016): 11–27.

Persaud, I. 'A Mixed-methods Design in Educational Institutions: Gender, Teacher Praise and Criticism, and Student Motivation in St Vincent and the Grenadines'. *SAGE Research Methods Cases*. Sage Publications, 2017. http://methods.sagepub.com/case/mixed-methods-gender-praise-criticism-motivation-st-vincent-grenadines.

Potter, J. 'Discourse Analysis and Discursive Psychology.' In *Qualitative Research in Psychology: Expanding Perspectives in Methodology and Design*, ed. P.M. Camic, J.E. Rhodes and L. Yardley, 73–94. Washington, DC: American Psychological Association, 2003.

Ragsdale, J.M., T.A. Beehr, S. Grebner, and K. Han. 'An Integrated Model of Weekday Stress and Weekend Recovery of Students.' *International Journal of Stress Management* 18, no. 2 (2011): 153–80.

Rajasekar, D. 'Impact of Academic Stress among the Management Students of AMET University – An Analysis.' *AMET Journal of Management* (2013): 32–39. http://www.ametjournal.com/attachment/Ametjournal5/5%20Rajasekar%2016-8-13.pdf.

Roasoft. 'Sample Size Calculator.' *Roasoft*, 2018. http://www.raosoft.com/samplesize.html.

Random.org. 'Random Sequence Generator.' *Random*, 2018. https://www.random.org/sequences.

Salant, P., and D.A. Dillman. *How to Conduct Your Own Survey*. New York: John Wiley & Sons Inc., 1994.

Schneiderman, N., G. Ironson, and S.D. Siegel. 'Stress and Health: Psychological, Behavioral, and Biological Determinants.' *Annual Review of Clinical Psychology* 1 (2005): 607–28.

Search Engine Reports. 'Free Online Plagiarism Checker.' *Search Engine Reports*, 2018. https://searchenginereports.net/plagiarism-checker.

Small SEO Tools. 'Plagiarism Checker.' *Small SEO Tools*, 2018. http://smallseotools.com/plagiarism-checker.

Smart Words. 'Transition Words.' *Smart Words*, 2018. http://www.smart-words.org/linking-words/transition-words.html.

Sulaiman, T., A. Hassan, V.M. Sapian, and S.K. Abdullah. 'The Level of Stress among Students in Urban and Rural Secondary Schools in Malaysia.' *European Journal of Social Sciences* 10, no. 2 (2009): 179–84.

Szuchman, L.T. *Writing with Style: APA Made Easy*. Pacific Grove, CA: Brooks/Cole Publishing Company, 1999.

Thawabieh, A.M., and L.M. Qaisy. 'Assessing Stress among University Students.' *American International Journal of Contemporary Research* 2, no. 2 (2012): 110–16.

The Chicago Manual of Style Online. 'Find it. Write it. Cite it.' *Chicago Manual of Style*, 2017. http://www.chicagomanualofstyle.org/home.html.

———. 'Chicago-style Citation Quick Style.' *Chicago Manual of Style*, 2017. http://www.chicagomanualofstyle.org/tools_citationguide.html.

Thigpen, C. H., and H. Cleckley. 'A Case of Multiple Personality.' *The Journal of Abnormal and Social Psychology* 49, no. 1 (1954): 135–51.

Trockel, M.T., M.D. Barnes, and D.L. Egget. 'Health-related Variables and Academic Performance among First-year College Students: Implications for Sleep and Other Behaviors.' *Journal of American College Health* 49, no. 3 (2000): 125–32.

Turnitin. *Number One Solution for Evaluating Written Work*. Turnitin, 2012. https://turnitin.com/gateway/index.html.

United Nations Educational, Scientific and Cultural Organization-UNESCO. *Definition of Bullying*. UNESCO, 2017. http://www.unesco.org/new/en/education/themes/strengthening-education-systems/quality-framework/technical-notes/definition-of-bullying.

University of Birmingham. 'Harvard (author-date).' *University of Birmingham*, 2018. https://intranet.birmingham.ac.uk/as/libraryservices/library/referencing/icite/referencing/harvard/index.aspx.

University of Leicester. 'Author-date (Harvard).' *University of Leicester*, 2018. https://www2.le.ac.uk/library/help/referencing/author-date.

Waqas, A., S. Khan, W. Sharif, U. Khalid, and A. Ali. 'Association of Academic Stress with Sleeping Difficulties in Medical Students of a Pakistani medical School: A Cross Sectional Survey.' *Peer Journal*, no. 3 (2015): 1–11.

Whitman, N. A., D.C. Spendlove, and C.H. Clark. 'Students: Effects and Solutions.' *ERIC Digest (1985)*. Retrieved from ERIC database (ED284514).

Zafar, S.N., R. Syed, S. Waqar, A.J. Zubairi, T. Vaqar, M. Shaikh, W. Yousaf, S. Shahid, and S. Saleem. Self-medication amongst University Students of Karachi: Prevalence, Knowledge and Attitudes. *Journal of Pakistan Medical Association* 58, no. 4 (2008): 214–17.

Zotero. *Your Personal Research Assistant. Zotero*, 2018. http://www.zotero.org.

# Index

Abstract: of the research paper, 205, 225
Academic significance: of the research topic, 3
Active listening: in research, 130
Active observation: in research, 130
Adjacency pairs: in conversation analysis, 191
Adjusted R-Square statistic, 161
Align property: in the SPSS worksheet, 13
Alternative hypothesis, 14
American Sociological Association: 'Ethical Principles of Psychologists and Code of Conduct', 118
Analysis (qualitative research): discourse, 183–85, 186; IPA, 188; thematic, 182–83;
Anonymity, 60; right to, 121
ANOVA results, 161. *See also* One-way ANOVA.
APA publication manual: citation guide, 29–36
Applied research, 19, 20
Associational hypothesis, 12
Associational inferential statistics, 155
Associational research questions, 10
Assumptions: in statistical tests, 165
Audience interaction: in the oral presentation, 213
Australian Code for Responsible Conduct of Research: and the period for data retention, 123
Autonomy: right to, 120–21
Axial coding: in grounded theory, 194

Background information: in conducting an interview, 95
Baseline master plan for a typical research project, 201–202
Basic research, 19–20
Belmont Report (1979): global research protocol, 117–18
Best practice: in research, 119, 122
Bivariate statistics, 142
Block quotes, 33–34
Body language: in the oral presentation, 212
Brainstorming: as a research strategy, 4
Brown-Forsythe Test, 170

Case studies: overview of, 66–67; pros and cons of, 52
Categorical responses: in survey design, 78
Causal research methods, 53
Central research question, 18
Central tendency: measures of, 143
Checklist: research process, 214–25
Chicago: citation styles, 35–36
Chi-Square: tests: interpretative write-up of results of, 157–58; Pearson, 155–57
Citations: in the literature review, 29–37
Classroom observations (qualitative), 71
Close-ended questions: construction of, 80–81; vs open-ended questions, 78
Close-ended responses: vs open-ended responses, 79
Cluster sampling, 104, 106
Code book: preparation of the, 133; for qualitative data, 138–39
Codes: generating, 181
Coding: in grounded theory, 194–95; IPA, 188; process, 184, 186; qualitative data, 138–39, 181–87; quantitative data, 132–37
Coefficient of determination, 161
Cohen's $f^2$, 174
Columns: in the SPSS worksheet 137
Comparative hypothesis, 13
Comparative inferential statistics: defining, 163–64
Comparative research question, 10
Comparative tests: effect sizes for, 174–75
Comprehensive statistical package (SAS): and data coding, 132
Computerized storage: cost of, 124
Conceptualization: in research, 72; linking operationalization and, 73
Conclusion: of the research paper, 208–209, 225
Confidence level, 101
Confidentiality: right to 121
Construct validity, 88
Content validity, 88

Control: in grounded theory, 194; of interview, 131–32
Convenience, 60
Convenience sampling, 110
Conversation analysis, 191–92
Core research questions: in qualitative research, 17–18
Correlation coefficient, 158
Costs: associated with interviews, 60
Coverage, 60
Cramer's V, 173–74
Criterion related validity, 88
Cross referencing: in qualitative research, 139
Crosstabulation: definition of 151, 152

Data: analysis for the research paper, 208; disposal of, 124; familiarization, 181
Databases: cost of storage in, 124; popular, 48; for the research paper, 207–208. *See also* Computerized storage. *See also* Data storage
Data collection: best practices in, 120; ethics and, 117–22; methods, 6, 179, 185, 222
Data entry training, 137
Data Protection Act, 1998 (United Kingdom), 123
Data retention: and data security, 122; time period for, 122–23
Data saturation, 100
Data security: cost of, 124; data retention and, 122; and protection, 123, 222
Data sources: IPA, 188; qualitative, 178–80, 188; reviewing, 4
Data storage: responsibility for, 123
Decimals: in the variable type menu, 135
Declaration of Helsinki (1964): global research protocol, 118
Demand characteristics, 55
Demographics: and population size, 101
Dependent variables, 7–8
Descriptive research methods, 53
Descriptive research questions, 9
Descriptive statistics: definition of, 141–42; employing, 142types of, 141
Design and methodology: research paper, 207
Directional associational hypothesis, 12
Directional comparative hypothesis, 13

Discipline specific: citation styles, 36
Discussion and conclusion: of the research paper, 208–209, 225
Distribution mode: and questionnaire response rate, 112
Document review and analysis: conducting, 68–69; pros and cons of, 53; in qualitative research, 16
Dress: appropriate interview, 127

Effect sizes: for comparative tests, 174–77; definition of, 173
Electronic data: disposal of, 124
Electronic survey, 62
Empirical sources, 24
Employee performance: as a prospective topic, 3
Eta-squared calculations, 174–75; and paired samples t-test, 176
Ethics: and data collection, 117–22
Ethics review board (ERB), 118
Ethnographic research, 179
Ethology, 58, 179
Etiquette: fieldwork, 128
European Union General Data Protection Regulation 2016, 123
Experiments: pros and cons of, 51; in quantitative research, 6
Exploratory research methods, 53
External validity, 88
Extraneous variables, 57
Eye contact: in fieldwork, 128; in oral presentation, 212

Face-to-face interviews: social skills for, 129
Face validity, 88
Field studies technique, 59
Fieldwork: conduct, 127–32; etiquette, 128; strategic planning for successful, 124;
Final interview question, 96
Findings: presenting the research, 208, 225
Fit: in grounded theory, 193
Focus group interviews: pros and cons of, 52; purpose of, 64–65; in qualitative research, 16
Formal interviews: vs informal interviews, 63
Free narrative: advantages of, 126
F-test results, 161

# Index

Games-Howell Test, 171
Gaps and overlaps, 191–92
General Data Protection Regulation 2016 (European Union), 123
Generality: in grounded theory, 193–94
Graduate record examination (GRE), 89
Grounded theory analysis, 193–96

Harvard: citation styles, 35–36
Historical research methods: in qualitative research, 16
Human Subjects Institutional Review Board (HSIRB), 118
Hypotheses: developing, 14; generating, 185

Impartiality: in interviews, 130
Incentives: cost of, 115; definition of, 115; types of, 15
In-depth interviews, 278–80
Independent ethics committee (IEC), 118
Independent measures design, 54
Independent samples t-test: definition of, 164, 168; interpretative write-up of, 166; reliance on eta-squared effect size or Cohen's d, 174; effect size, 174
Independent variables, 7–8; manipulation of, 56
Inferential statistics: comparative, 163; definition of, 153–54
Informal interviews: vs formal interviews, 63
Institutional Review Board (IRB): approval, 220; definition, 117, 118
Instruments: development of data collection, 219; survey, 77
Instrumentation: and measurement, 72–81
Intellectual property: respect for, 121
Internal consistency reliability, 85
Internal validity, 87
International Research Protocol: definition of, 117
International standards: in research, 117
Inter-observer reliability, 85
Interpretive phenomenological analysis (IPA), 187
Inter-rater reliability, 85
Interval: measurement, 75
Interview: analysis and interpretation of the, 192; body, 96; control of the, 131–32; costs associated with the, 63; design, 94–97; length of, 131; modes, 63; pros and cons of, 52, 63–69; recording the, 192; schedule, 125; training, 124–25; transcribing the, 192
Interview fieldwork: preparing for, 124. *See also* Fieldwork
Interview location: choosing an appropriate, 125
Interviewing skills: in research, 96, 129–32
Introduction: of the research paper, 205–206, 225; script for the interview, 95

Key work motivators, 181

Label: in data coding, 134; in the variable type menu, 135
Laboratory setting, 59
Language: for fieldwork, 128
Levene's test for Equality of Variances results, 165, 169
Likert scales, 91
Linear regression: definition of, 160; and Pearson correlation, 174
Linear regression results: interpretative write-up of, 162; SPSS generated analysis of, 161
Listening: interviews and effective, 130
Literature review, 21–25; process, 26–28; research paper, 206, 225
Location: choosing an appropriate interview, 125

Macro-textual discourse analysis, 186
Manipulation of independent variables, 56
Mannerisms: fieldwork, 128
Margin of error: and sample size, 101
Mean: defining the, 143–44
Measure property: in the SPSS worksheet, 137
Measurement: definition of, 74; levels of, 74–75; and statistical tests, 76
Measures of central tendency: defining, 143–45
Measures of dispersion: defining: 148–49
Median: definition of, 145
Membership categorization device, 192
Methodology: research paper, 207, 225
Micro-textual discourse analysis: in qualitative research, 185
Missing values, 136–37

Mixed methods: challenges, 69; pros and cons of, 53
Mode: definition of, 146
Multivariate statistics, 142

Narrative analysis, 189–90
National Research Act (1974): global research protocol, 118
Naturalistic observation, 58
Nominal: measurement, 76
Non-directional associational hypothesis, 12
Non-parametric tests, 76
Non-participant observations: in qualitative research, 16
Non-probability sampling: definition of, 110; function of, 110; methodologies, 110; selection process, 111
Non-response: reasons for, 112
Normal distribution, 147
Note-taking: in qualitative research, 181
Null hypothesis, 14
Numeric data, 134
Nuremberg Code (1948): autonomy and the, 120; global research protocol, 118

Observational research: active, 130, 179; ethical concerns with, 59; pros and cons of, 51; when to use, 58
Observer or inter-rater reliability, 85
One way ANOVA: definition of the, 168; interpretative write-up of results of the, 172; reliance on the eta-square effect size measure, 176; SPSS generated analysis of the, 168
Open coding: in grounded theory, 194
Open-ended free response question, 83
Open-ended questions: construction of, 82–83; vs close-ended questions, 78
Open-ended responses: vs close-ended responses, 79
Opening and closing conversations: in conversational analysis, 191
Operationalizing: of variables, 55; ways to, 73–74
Oral presentation: of the research paper, 210–13
Ordinal: measurement, 76
Organizational policy: on research, 118–19

Other: in survey design, 78
Outlier: definition of, 14
Ownership: and use of data, 121–22

Paired samples T-test: definition of the, 166–67; eta-squared effect size measure, 176; interpretative write-up of the, 167; SPSS generated analysis of the, 167
Paper-based mail survey, 62
Paper records: disposal of, 124
Parallel form reliability, 86
Parametric tests, 76
Participant observations: in qualitative research, 16
Participant: in pilot studies, 114
Pearson Chi-Square tests, 155–57, 173
Pearson's correlation coefficient, 86
Pearson correlation results: interpretative write-up of, 159; SPSS generated analysis of, 159
Pearson correlation tests, 158–60; and linear regression, 174
Pearson product moment correlation. See Pearson correlation tests
Personal space: in fieldwork, 128
Phi coefficient, 173
Pilot study: definition of, 113; participants, 114; evaluating the, 114
Placebo, 55
Plagiarism: avoiding, 45–46; definition of, 46
Pooled standard deviation, 175
Population size, 101
Post-Hoc test, 170–71
Posttest only control group design, 56
Practical significance: of the research topic, 3; vs statistical significance, 154
Presenting the research paper, 210–13
Pretest-Posttest group design, 57
Primary sources, 24
Probability sampling, 103–106; costs associated with, 105; methodologies, 103, 106; selection process, 105
Properly worded questions: and data collection, 121
Professionalism: in interviews, 130
Publication: guidelines for research, 202–03

Punctuality: in fieldwork, 127
Purposive sampling, 111
P-Value, 153–54

Qualitative coding, 138–40, 224
Qualitative data analysis, 178–96, 223
Qualitative purpose statements, 18
Qualitative research, 15–18; developing a storyline for, 138, 139; sample size for, 100; strengths and limitations of, 180
Qualitative study: reporting on, 224
Quantitative coding, 132–37, 223
Quantitative data analysis, 141–77, 223
Quantitative descriptor, 9
Quantitative research: attributes of, 6, 132; data collection in, 6; definition of, 5; hypotheses in, 12; research questions in, 9; sample size for, 100; variables in, 7
Quantitative study: reporting on the, 224
Questions: and data collection, 121; proper wording for, 121; sensitive, 131; sequence of, 126, 131; types of, 126
Questionnaire: design, 77; length, 78; response rate, 112; scales, 6
Quota sampling, 111
Quotations: in the literature review, 32–34

Random interviews, 71
Random sampling, 103
Range, 148
Rapport: building, 131; pre-interview, 128
Ratio: measurement, 75
Realism: topic, 3
Recording: the interview, 129, 181, 185, 192
References: vs bibliography, 37–42; research paper, 225
Reliability: defining, 84
Repairs: in conversational analysis, 191
Repeated measures design, 54
Research: definition, 1; good, 1; international best practice in, 119; misconduct, 19; organizational policy on, 118–19
Research design, 217; qualitative, 179
Research ethics board (REB), 118
Research hypotheses: in quantitative research, 12

Research instrument or measures: used in the research paper, 207, 219
Research methodology: definition of, 50–53; description of, 207; determine, 216
Research paper: the, 197–213
Research process, 1–2; checklist, 214–25
Research questions: in grounded theory, 194; qualitative, 179; in quantitative research, 9
Research topic: focusing the, 4; identifying the, 2, 215; significance, 3
Respect: in interviews, 130
Response distribution, 101
Response rate: defining, 112; improving, 112; incentives and, 115
Results *see* Findings.
Review of final grades (quantitative), 71
Role property: in the SPSS worksheet, 137
R-Square statistic, 161

Sample: demographics, 55, 101, 218; size, 100, 101
Sample size calculator: for quantitative samples, 101
Sampling bias: causes of, 108–109; defining, 108; determining, 109; reducing, 109–10
Sampling error: defining, 107; reducing, 107; rule, 107–108
Sampling frames: creating, 99, 218; examples of, 99; function of the, 98–99
Sampling methods: used in research paper, 207
Scale construction, 91
Scheduling: interview, 125
Scheffe Test, 171, 172
Scholarly writing: strategies for improving, 204
Scientific research: process, 2
Secondary data analysis: in quantitative research, 6
Secondary sources, 24–25
Selective coding: in grounded theory, 195
Semantic differential scales, 93
Sensitive questions, 131
Short quotes, 33
Simple random sampling, 103, 106
Single blind: vs double blind procedure, 57
Snowball sampling, 111
Social skills: in research, 129

Sources: of Literature, 23
Specific responses: in survey design, 78
Standard deviation, 150
Standardized observations: in quantitative research, 6
Standardized surveys: in quantitative research, 6
Stata: and data coding, 132
Statistical package for social sciences (SPSS): and data coding, 132, 133; variable view worksheet, 133–37
Statistical significance, 153; vs practical significance, 154
Statistical tests: assumptions in, 163; measurement and, 76
Stimuli control, 60
Storyline development: in qualitative research, 138, 139
Stratified random sampling, 103–104, 106
String data, 134–35
Structure: of the research paper, 205–209
Student survey (quantitative), 71
Survey design: vocabulary and audience in, 78
Surveys: characteristics of, 60; issues, 60; pros and cons of, 52, 62
Sub-research questions: in qualitative research, 17
System-missing values, 136
Systematic random sampling, 103, 106

Telephone survey, 62
Tertiary sources, 25
Test-retest reliability, 84–85
Thematic analysis: phases in, 181–83, 184
Themes: defining and naming, 182–83; development of, 195; in qualitative research, 139–40, 181–83; reviewing, 182; searching for, 182, 188
Theoretical sampling: in grounded theory, 194
Theoretical saturation: in grounded theory, 195
Theory: generation, 193, 195
Thurstone scales, 92–93
Topic: attractiveness of, 3
Training: in data entry, 137
Transcribing the interview, 192
Turns and turn-taking: in conversational analysis, 191

Understanding: in grounded theory, 194
Unique identification number: in data coding, 133–34
United Kingdom: Data Protection Act, 1998, 123
Univariate statistics, 142
User-missing values, 136

Validated instruments/scales, 89
Validity, 86
Values: missing, 136; in the variable type menu, 135–36
Variable names: in data coding, 134
Variable type menu: and data coding, 135
Variable View Worksheet: navigating the SPSS, 133
Variables: in quantitative research, 7
Variance, 149
Versatility, 60

Welch Test, 170
Width: in the variable type menu, 135
Writing: the research paper, 203–205, 224

CPSIA information can be obtained
at www.ICGtesting.com
Printed in the USA
FSHW020606141020
74678FS